D0108566

LETTERS OF FATHER PAGE, C.S.C.

LETTERS OF FATHER PAGE, C.S.C.

WITH A LETTER OF INTRODUCTION BY
THE MOST REVEREND FRANCIS J. SPELLMAN

Before Life's throne he stands a page,
holding with reverence
his tiny flame of light
to mark with joy
the Presence
of The King.

LONGMANS, GREEN AND CO.
LONDON · NEW YORK · TORONTO
1940

LONGMANS, GREEN AND CO.
55 FIFTH AVENUE, NEW YORK
221 EAST 20TH STREET, CHICAGO
88 TREMONT STREET, BOSTON

LONGMANS, GREEN AND CO. LTD.
39 PATERNOSTER ROW, LONDON, E.C. 4
17 CHITTARANJAN AVENUE, CALCUTTA
NICOL ROAD, BOMBAY
36A MOUNT ROAD, MADRAS

LONGMANS, GREEN AND CO.
215 VICTORIA STREET, TORONTO

FIRST EDITION

PRINTED IN THE UNITED STATES OF AMERICA

TO

MARY

MINDFUL OF HER

MOTHERHOOD

Imprimi Potest

Thomas A. Steiner, C.S.C.

October 29, 1939

Nihil Obstat

Arthur J. Scanlan, S.T.D.

Censor Librorum

Imprimatur

✠ Francis J. Spellman, D.D.

Archbishop, New York

New York, January 11, 1939

Acknowledgments are due to John Donahue and *Columbia*, and to Father Patrick O'Connor and *The Far East*, for the permission to republish; and to Brassil, Mildred and Marge, for editorial assistance no less valued because fraternal; and to Francis J. Gyra, Jr., for his drawings.

ARCHBISHOP SPELLMAN'S LETTER OF INTRODUCTION

Rev. Gerald M. C. Fitzgerald, C.S.C.,
Rector of Our Lady of the Holy Cross Seminary
North Easton, Mass.

Dear Father Fitzgerald,—

I am pleased to learn that your writings known as the letters of Father Page are soon to appear in book form. I hope that many will read them and enjoy them and profit from them as I have done.

Devotedly in Christ
+ Francis J. Spellman.

New York, N.Y.
October 21, 1939

A NOTE OF EXPLANATION

Dear Reader:

Now that Archbishop Spellman's gracious note has served to introduce and at the same time identify "Father Page," a word of explanation as to the origin and meaning of the Father Page Letters may not be amiss.

Myles Connolly, the former editor of *Columbia*, bears a large part of the responsibility for the inception of these letters, even as John Donahue, the present editor, does for their continuance. It was under the former's inspiration that the idea of the Letters was conceived; it is by reason of the latter's friendship and patience that they have been continued.

The letter-form furnished a natural medium for a priest whose friends and spiritual children were being carried far afield by the exactions of time and vocation. *Columbia*, and more lately *The Far East* as well, have served to give a valued extension to this medium.

A letter is, indeed, a most personal thing, but the needs and problems of individual souls have ordinarily a universal aspect which gives more than individual value to their solution. Father Page is far from presuming to furnish a happy solution for all problems, yet he is convinced that such a solution is possible along the following lines:

> God's beauty, God's holiness, God's goodness, are to be found in all things, great and small, save only in that departure from God's Will—itself a negation—which Christians at least still term sin. Catholicism is essentially a joyous thing by reason

of its source in God's Love, and is God's answer to the spiritual needs of men.

There is not only no gap between true piety and sanity, but on the contrary, true piety is but common sense, illumined and motivated by faith and grace, and carried to a logical conclusion.

Here then is the viewpoint of these Letters; and if they do not emphasize the shadows of the Cross, it is because these shadows prove the existence of the sunshine; and in deeper reality because it is assuredly God's plan that His Son's Cross should cast not shadows but lengthening pathways of light. In these pathways it is Father Page's desire to walk humbly, with friendliness for all, and love for all in God and God's Most Holy Mother.

GERALD M.C. FITZGERALD, C.S.C.

Feast of
Christ, the King
1939

CONTENTS

JANUARY

January's cold hands have conquered lawn
and woods; but not the sparrows
chirping in the midday sun.

THE OPEN HEARTH

DEAR FRIEND:

Now that the Christmas rush is over I must let you know how much I appreciate your thoughtful invitation to spend a few days at "The Cedars." Nothing could please me more and it would do me a world of good, but the sheep must come before the shepherd and I cannot leave my work at the present time.

In spirit, however, I shall be with you. I shall walk with you over the frozen roads, talk with you of the old days and rest before the wonderful open fire in your living room.

An open fire—how I love it. Perhaps I am a bit old-fashioned, but then, what sane human would not prefer the cheerful, singing, radiant heat of a fire on an open hearth to gas logs or a radiator?

The open hearth—how it seems to draw to its burning focus the hearts of a home and hold them there within the magic circle of its light. The hiss of the burning logs soothes tired nerves and in the glowing embers one can picture again the scenes of one's childhood. So you can see how much I would have enjoyed the little vacation your thoughtful charity offered.

However, not for all is given the blessing of a home like "The Cedars." Some of us must wait for our Eternal Home and the welcoming arms of the Master. This is at once a priest's greatest sacrifice and his greatest consolation. He must learn to be at home with God and rekindle his strength and courage at the Open Hearth of God—the Heart of Jesus in the Blessed Sacrament. And so, do you thank God for the hearthstone He has given you and do you help me to thank God for the Hearthstone He has given me. I know I am always welcome at yours and you should know that you are always welcome at mine, for both are the dwelling places of God.

With best wishes for every blessing upon the New Year.

"IN THE BEGINNING"

Dear ——:

You know that I wish you every happiness in your new life. You know well enough too I would have preferred—had such been God's designs for you—the life of one who rides alone for God. But you know too, that it is for Jesus to call to this riding whom He will, and not the least of His graciousness is His manner of making each of His creatures, when they are conformed to His Holy Will, content and happy in their own particular sphere of action—the workman at his bench, the mother at the cradle, the priest about His Father's business, the nun alone with God. Every creature conformed to God's Holy Will has here on earth its own little heaven, each is most happy and wonderingly grateful to the Divine Beneficence which has given them their status.

Begin then your new life in Nomine Domini et Mariae, let your home be their home, your heart their heart—wherein the Holy Family shall find sweet memories of Nazareth—its labor and its peace. God bless you for your ideals. God keep you and the partner He has given you to share them and make them fruitful. God bind you both together by the magic of little arms and faces, and guide you along the home-road, helping you over the hard places, carrying you both in His tireless arms out of the night into the radiant warmth and peace of His own Fireside—where you shall find Mother Mary, and I hope—Father Page.

HIS GIFT MOST PRECIOUS

Dear ——:

How I wish I could give you a share in that gift most precious which God has given unto me, my Faith. Yes, truly can I say most precious for it is my Faith which makes my life truly precious and joyous, and without Faith I would not care to live. Cling to life, I suppose I would, but certainly not joyously but only because of natural instinct and because to do otherwise would mean to act cowardly, and cowardly I do not wish to be.

My Faith, the Faith, how I love it. Thanks be to God, it has always been robust, but as I grow older — come to know God more deeply and His creatures better — so does my Faith grow stronger and deeper, my Faith in Him, in His Love for us and in His Holy Church.

To many without, like you, and even to many within the True Fold, the intermittent breakdown of the human elements in Christ's Mystical Body — I mean especially the failures of His servants to be truly such, — has constituted the great objective barrier to Faith. This will always be so, and Christ Himself foretold it when He said that scandal needs must come. Yet ——, this very failure of the human elements in His Church serves but to reveal more clearly to discerning eyes the Soul Divine within! Christ is there and hence the Church goes on, on, on, in her proud albeit persecuted march adown the centuries. Human nature fails Him and fails His spotless Bride today, even as it failed Him and His Sinless Mother in the beginning, but Christ goes on and His Church goes on, rising as He rose once, nay thrice, above the weakness of humanity by reason of a strength that was and is Divine.

Consider then, I beg you, dear ——, that Beautiful Figure which dominates the centuries, consider Him in that Church which alone can authenticate its claim historically of reaching back to Him. What if some of His have denied Him, have we never done the same? What if some of His have put self first, shall we blame Christ for this? What if some of His do not follow in His footsteps, does this excuse us from the trail? The story of the True Church simply reiterates the life story of the True Redeemer—it is a story that unfolds the surpassing mystery of our existence—the mystery of the greatness of God's love for us and the littleness of our love for God!

Pray above all for light, that light that I too shall pray for for you—that the Light of the World may shine upon you through the cold damp mists of these materialistic days, may shine upon you and guide you safely into the Harbor of Faith where may you anchor and find peace in His Heart and Mother Mary's.

THE PILGRIMS

My Dear ——:

This is the Month of the Magi, and of their arduous yet joyous questing of a Baby King. I wonder have you ever reflected how like to their journey is our life-purpose? By our very calling we have declared openly to all men that we seek Him who is born King of mankind. To this end we have torn asunder the ties of home and blood, and at least in spirit the ties of country as well. To this purpose we have dedicated our lives and push as pilgrims along Life's Highway, pausing in the tents of strangers, asking like the Magi only one question of all—"Where shall we find Him who is born King of our hearts?"

Now we seek Him under the burning sun of the desert; now in the traffic of city streets; here in the silence of four gray walls; there in the souls of little children. But wherever we search for Jesus, it is always the star of Faith that guides us, and we find Him always in the arms of Mother Church.

As little ones of His Kingdom we found Him in joyous wonderment amid the straw of the Christmas manger. As we grew older, the monstrance became more vivid than the manger, the Tabernacle the Goal of our questing. If we live long enough and become little enough, we shall find Him before we die hidden away in our own very souls and come to realize that for this was Manger and Tabernacle planned, that God's creatures might find their Saviour-King, and a creature's Creator find a lasting resting place in the souls He created to cradle His Love, His Will, His Heart.

This quest is of course, Sister, as you well know, the work of a lifetime, not the achievement of a day. There is much to discourage us, even as there was much to discourage the Magi. Desolate deserts where the parched soul seeks in vain for refreshment; human hearts that bid us tarry, hidden, powerful enemies who would keep us from our Goal. All would be dark were it not for the light of Faith shining over us, and the trust that He whom we seek wills our seeking with a will all powerful and Divine. And thus, if we but persevere, we shall come in the eventide at least to the realization of how close Our Jesus was to us all the time. For Jesus is already with the soul that humbly seeks Him, even as with the disciples on the road to Emmaus. Having sought Him in life, we shall find Him at least in death, and having found Him in death we shall possess Him, shall we not, forever!—and thus come to understand how precious a thing it was to be pilgrims of the Lord. May the Mother of the Little Pilgrim guide our steps.

BLACK INGRATITUDE

Dear ——:

I am going to say to you now, privately, what I

wanted to say to you last week, but the right opportunity did not present itself. I may lose your friendship, but I prefer that to you losing God, and so here is the story.

Dear ——, do you realize—you do not—the black ingratitude your frequent use of God's Holy Name involves! Surely you are not one of those moderns whose own intelligence is so centered flylike on the crumb of self that they cannot take in the possibility of another intelligence beyond and above their own. You believe in God; how dare you insult Him? And insult Him you certainly do, for I myself have heard you.

Were you a poor stevedore or a little factory worker, who heard little else but a litany of blasphemy all day, I might try to find excuse for you. Were you loaded down with the crushing weight of trials, physical, mental or economic, these might lessen the malice, though never justify the offense. But you are surrounded with most of the earthly blessings that a Good God can give. You have a splendid position, a beautiful, faithful wife in the setting of an exquisite home, bright with the sparkling laughter and eyes of little children who love you and call you Father, and you outrage the name of Your Father, Who has given you all this. This is what I call ingratitude, black ingratitude, and the fact that there are thousands of others guilty of the same ingratitude only intensifies your own.

You will say that I am angry. Yes, I admit it; I am. The ingratitude of man grows upon me as I grow older, perhaps because as I grow older I recognize more and more the gracious, providential love of Our Father Who Is in Heaven. I love Him, it is true, and because I love Him, I hate to hear and to know how frequently He is insulted by those upon whom He has lavished so much, even His Son's Life Blood. I want His Name to be exalted, to be hallowed in every heart and by every tongue, and every intelligence to bow in intelligent reverence to the constant and countless manifestations of Supreme Intelligence and Power and Goodness that our daily lives involve.

Dear ——, the abuse of God's Holy Name is one of the blackest forms of ingratitude that I know of. I beg you to put this ingratitude and all ingratitude, both to God and to His creatures, out of your life. Carelessness is no excuse, for carelessness has no reasonable place in the lives of those of whom God has been so careful. God has always been careful of you and yours. He is always careful of His children, even though His child be but a beggar; after all, a beggar who honors His Father's Name is richer in God's sight than the wealthy man or woman who dishonors that same Name, for the beggar is rich with paid-up shares in the Bank of Heaven, while you, who are rich in the things of this world, live on margin in the things that pertain to your Eternal interests. Many rebuke the faults of the poor, few the sins of the rich; I rebuke you, dear ——, for dishonoring your Father's Name, and I beg you to put this ingratitude forever from your life. Ever in Mary.

EVERYBODY'S VOCATION

Dear ——:

In your last letter you wrote me of your conviction that you had no vocation. Very well; but please remember this: much as I love to see a soul give itself to God in the oblation of the religious life, yet never have I failed to recognize that though everyone has a vocation, not everyone's vocation is to the religious life. Besides, I love my own vocation too deeply to desire any recruits save volunteers; volunteers who come of their own free will because of love to serve the God of Love. Our Lord, Himself, has made His consecrated service a matter of invitation. "If you will be perfect," He says to those who stand at the crossroads. If you do not feel drawn thereto by love, then by all means do not go forward. We need priests, yes, but only real priests who will be concerned about the interests of Jesus, first, last and always.

However, please do not say you have no vocation. Everybody has a vocation, every soul that comes into this world has a vocation, and all vocations are essentially one—to know, to love, and to serve God. Everybody's vocation is the loving service of God.

It seems to me this great truth which lends such dignity to human life is too little reflected upon by men. Perhaps we should preach more upon this subject. The husband, the wife, the father, the mother, older brothers and sacrificing sisters, all of us share in one vast beautiful plan of the Almighty. All, if we be governed by His laws, speaking to us through the voice of conscience and the lips of Mother Church, all of us are carrying on for God, one Plan for His external glory which involves, by reason of His essential and infinite Goodness, the eternal happiness of our immortal souls.

O, let us hasten to fulfill to the fullest our little part of this great Plan. Let us strive each in our own God-given sphere, be it at the Altar of God, or in the Chapel—which a truly Christian home really is—to carry out our vocation in its fullest measure of perfection. Then, truly will all the world be one vast Cathedral of the Living God, resounding with His praises, manifesting His Glory, receiving His Benedictions and blessed by His abiding presence, which brings with it Peace to the restless souls of men. May Our Lady bless our strivings.

WITHOUT AMENDMENT

Dear Sister:

Your letter gave me happiness in the realization of

your genuine sympathy for God's poor. Rest assured there is no surer way to winning the love of Our God, than the practice of charity toward our fellow creatures. This is a truth that, at least in the individual practice, has been too often lost sight of in these days when things are so often organized and carried out in a big way by civic and other groupings. Yet it is just as vital today as when Our Blessed Lord first enunciated it. "Thou shalt love thy neighbor as thyself!"

If we to whom God has given the light of Faith would only carry out this Second Commandment of Our Lord without amendment or compromise, we would allow His Faith not only to illumine our minds but to warm our hearts as well—and how swiftly would the souls of good will, the millions of sincere Americans who really want the Truth, be led by our example to find it where their forbears found it and where they themselves would even now possess it had not the love of gold and the evils that are its camp followers dried up the wells of Charity in too many of the leaders and children of the Faith in the sixteenth century.

Well, let us profit by the lessons of the past, let us make our own the sentiments of that modern apostle of the poor, Mother Catherine McAuley, who could write from her heart: "I had rather be cold and hungry myself than that the poor should suffer!" Then, indeed, dear Sister, will we be most truly preaching Christ, for we shall be living Christ, yea, we shall be living Christs and, as such, worthy of the Eternal Love of the Master and His Blessed Mother.

TENANTS-AT-WILL

Dear Sister in Christ:

I had tentative plans of paying a visit to my Dominican children this week but Our Blessed Mother had other plans for me. These notes are to say just what I would say were I to appear in person.

Firstly, thanks for the remembrance of our Birthday. I am so glad the Good God gave me life and only hope that His Most Beautiful Mother will see to it that despite all the abiding flaws therein, in the end, by His Most Merciful Grace, it shall be made perfect according to His Eternal Will.

When we reflect on the hurrying feet of time that are carrying us onward to a goal which at most is not far distant, then surely of how little consequence become the passing pleasures and vanities for which the crowd reach and to which our foolish hearts are oft-times attracted. Only one life, and then an Eternity with or without Our God! Oh, why do intelligent beings do anything except prepare for that inevitable conclusion of this earthly existence!

Your hospital course will teach you many things but it can teach you nothing so profitable to your soul's eternal peace than:

The swift flight of youth and earthly beauty.

The coming of the evening when no man can work.

That God gives no leases to these human dwellings of ours—we are but tenants at will—and that

All is vanity, save to love God and serve Him only.

They live in vain in palace or in hut,
Alike shall lie forgotten 'neath the sod,
Unless they turn from out the common rut
And build within their souls a Home for God!

Never, amid the busy hours, forget Him to Whom your fingers, your eyes, your mind, your body, your soul, your will, your heart belong. That He may dominate your whole being more and more in Our Blessed Lady's Service is the abiding desire and prayer of FATHER PAGE

NEAR TO GOD'S HEART

My Dear Sister in Christ:

I am very happy, as you know, in my particular branch of God's Service, but as you also must realize, I have never made the mistake of thinking it was the only branch, or that it alone called for the highest sacrifice and completest consecration.

Never forget for an instant, as you busy yourself with the endless duties of wifehood and motherhood, that you share in that vocation that God gave to the noblest of His creatures, and that a real Christian Mother is very, very dear, and near to the Heart of God's Eternal Son.

It is true there is no vocation worthy of such designation that does not involve sacrifice, no Christian vocation that does not translate itself ultimately into the carrying of a cross. Nevertheless, a cross carried for love, and beyond all, and above all, borne for the love of God and His Incarnate Son, will always be in the end, as it shall be for that same Saviour, a throne of glory, a symbol of victory, the pledge and the proof of eternal love.

Be of good heart, therefore, dear Sister; from the holy tabernacles of our Christian Mothers come forth the priest-hosts of tomorrow and the lily-chalices of God's spouses-to-be. Pray for me, as I for you, as we work together for the selfsame Cause, God's Glory and the salvation of His children's immortal souls. Ever in Mary.

CHRISTIAN FATHERHOOD

My Dear ——:

This is a rare autumnal afternoon here at —— with all Nature waiting tranquilly for the white blanket of winter, like a tired child waiting for her mother to tuck her away under the white coverlets for the night.

I, too, am waiting, if not so tranquilly at least with good courage, for the black shoulder cape and cord which, please God, will soon be mine, mine forever! But this is a Birthday letter for you, so you must be the subject of my thoughts.

You know without my telling you how dear you and ——— and the little ones are to my heart; you have together a little niche (perhaps a pew would be more comfortable for the five of you) in the little church of my soul, and there I pray for you all and present you to God's Most Holy Mother and beg her to draw you as most dear children each day closer to her Heart and the Heart of her Divine Son, Jesus, Source of All Consolation, Strength and Light and Truth.

Please give my love to everyone, Joe and Ed and Julia and Bertha—to all. Tell Ed not to think of making the trip for my Big Day. It is too long a journey and, please Our Lady, at Christmastide or soon after I shall be able to see you all, and what a joy that will be for us!

The great moments of joy in this life must be rare, otherwise we would forget to search for Heaven! Find your joy, my Brother, look for your consolation, in the faithful accomplishment of your high vocation as a Christian father and husband. What is a true father on earth in the truest sense of the word but the earthly reflection, the bright shadow of Our Father who is in Heaven! Seek, then, your happiness in the faithful fulfillment of your God-given and God-blessed duties, and if at times these duties seem weighty, be grateful that the Heavenly Father has deemed you worthy to shoulder a heavier portion of that mystical cross that all His children share with His Son Divine!

Pray for me that I may advance daily more deeply in the knowledge and love of my Divine Master, and rest assured that the further I advance in the knowledge of God and the depths of the Sacred Heart, the more I shall love you because the better shall I realize how much God loves you and the precious souls whom He has committed to your care.

Ever your brother — Jesus, Mary and Joseph.

AS YOU GO FORWARD

My Dear ——:

By now the rush of events will have subsided somewhat and time permits of quieter reflections. In their light, I think we can discover a profound lesson that doubtless you have already made your own. It is not by any means a new lesson, yet it is one that the world does not like to have intruded on its moments of triumph and it is, as well, quite obvious — too obvious to furnish excuse to those Catholics in high places who are unmindful of the conclusions to be drawn therefrom.

Kneeling beside your dear father-in-law as the last chapter of his noble life was being finished, was it not apparent that here was a nobler consummation than any political eminence? Here was a career which God could crown with an eternal and everlasting election.

As you go forward, ——, and there is no reason you should not go forward if you maintain those high principles upon which your present success is primarily founded, do not forget the lessons of ——'s life; be true to your family, be mindful of God's poor, remember that in a democracy the soundest of party policies is the defense of the commonweal. Remember, also, that a Catholic in public life cannot fail in the exemplification of the moral virtues without bringing undeserved shame on the Holy Mother who gave him spiritual birth.

Go forward, therefore, dear ——, and do not fail us who in this hour are so happy and so proud of you. Asking Our Lady to bless you and guide you.

MERRY NEW YEAR

My Dear ——:

Now that the Christmas tide has begun to ebb a little, I have found a moment to devote to a New Year's letter for you. Have you ever reflected how gracious it was of Our Blessed Saviour to have placed His Birthday celebration at the most trying time of the year (at least in these climes of ours)! Christmas sweeps in with its floodtide of joyfulness, both spiritual and material, just when otherwise we would be most unavoidably confronted with the sterner realities of earthly existence. Surely the Little Christ has proved Himself "the burning Babe" of Whom the gentle Southwell sang, and surely He has not ceased to warm with the memory of His smile a world which otherwise would have but little cause for merriment.

Yet because the Christ-Child has smiled upon this little world of ours and because His smile has brought and still brings to the cold and sin-bound hearts of men the tidings of a gracious and eternal spring that awaits men of good will beyond the horizons of time, because of this and the ramifications thereof, we have a just foundation for our cheerfulness, a right to be fundamentally optimistic, a duty to be cheerful. And that is why I write you, dear ——, at this hour to wish you not merry Christmas, but a merry and blessed New Year.

Our Christian optimism has been the sustaining force of millions of our fellow beings who have gone before. It should be the source of unlimited power and energy for us and our fellow beings of today. But, alas! how often our fellow citizens fail to recognize the reality of God's love for them, hesitate to answer the smile of the Christ-Child, because they find so little a reflection of that love and that smile in the lives of those whose heritage it was to be born within the radiant circle of the Faith. One New Year's resolution, therefore, of every thoughtful Catholic (and you are such, dear ——) should be to let the smile of the Christ-Child find a fairer imaging in their life and activity during the pilgrimage that lies before them than could be found along the road of their past.

Asking Our Lady to bless you each day of this Merry New Year.

WHEN WINTER DIES

Dear Father in Christ:

I am so glad that you are going South. These months are very trying here and I am pleased to have you escape by way of Holy Obedience (and let us add by Divine Providence which is another way of saying God's over-shadowing love) from the rigors of a New England winter. One needs to be young and vigorous to enjoy at least the outdoor life of New England in winter, and you know, dear Father, you are no longer young and the duties of the past few years have taken their toll upon your vigor and strength. Assuredly, these years were well-spent and were they to be still yours, how better could they be expended?

God keeps us from any smug complacency, for complacency is too closely allied to spiritual insanity—or had I better say, spiritual suicide—to be indulged; yet surely it is reasonable to recognize what has been done in God's grace. Certainly we are permitted to rejoice in the good accomplished so long as we are mindful "that it is God Who worketh in us both to will and to accomplish." After all, God has done some little good, indeed, great good, through you, and so I pray that, as you speed southward, your heart may rest in the arms of God and hymn with Mother Mary a fervent "Magnificat."

Then, when Winter dies and Spring promises anew her gracious wayfaring, follow her northward and bring us the inspiration and blessing of your presence.

Asking Our Lady to bless you.

"THEY ALSO SERVE"

DEAR SISTER:

I am writing to you to enlist the prayers and sufferings of your little community in a cause that I know is very dear to your heart. God has told us that His mercies are above all His works, and therefore those who claim the service of the Queen of Mercy as their very own, will not hesitate to listen to the plea of others who are starving in soul as well as in body.

We read in the papers of famine and flood in China, of the marching and counter-marching of undisciplined hordes, or the ever-spreading flame of communism that threatens to burn away the fruits of hundreds of years of apostolic zeal. We read, I say, of all this, and yet how few are the hearts that are deeply touched by the knowledge of these things. Sufferings and sorrows must needs be close to home in order to touch the heart of the average man or woman. Only such as have a love like unto the heart of God which encompasses all His creatures, only such as love with the Heart of Jesus are capable of feeling with the Heart of Jesus the sorrows of all mankind.

Now, Sister, I feel that your little band of souls dedicated to suffering and prayer are capable of being atuned to the heart of Jesus, are brave enough to sip of His Chalice as well as rest at His Banquet-board; and therefore I write to you to beg from them an alms of prayer and sacrifice for China and her enslaved and impoverished millions. Never before in her long history has there been need of more gallant soldiering in her behalf than now. Others have sought there material advantages; our soldiers — our missionaries — seek there only the extension of the Kingdom of God. Enlist your little band in this noble cause so dear to the Hearts of Jesus and Mary, the work of prayer and sacrifice for missionary perseverance in prayer and sacrifice in the no-man's land of the East.

FORWARD

My Dear Child:

I do, I am afraid, find myself drawing apart from souls that lag on the path of sanctity, from souls that refuse to be generous with God. But I have no reason to believe you are not pressing forward courageously, generously, in the Service of Our Blessed Lord and Master, and therefore, you are wrong in thinking that there is a "big gap between us." On the contrary, the deeper you advance into the Sacred Heart of Jesus, so much nearer and dearer you will be to your spiritual father.

It is true my time is not my own (I am writing this letter after midnight). It is true also that most of my letters are answers to letters, and ——, you must confess, write very, very seldom, and I think it is reasonable to presume that Communities that do not write, do not desire correspondence. But this being said, let me assure you, dear daughter, that your courageous perseverance in your arduous missionary vocation is a source of great consolation to me.

When I directed you, I knew Christ wished you to be one of His truly heroic lovers, i.e., one of His saints, and remember God does not change His Holy Will. Forward, therefore, my dear, dear child, follow the Master in cheerful courage and with the abiding conviction that His Love is all sufficient for you and all your needs. In spirit, I am always with you, and bless you daily in His Heart and Mary's Service.

OVERSEAS

Dear Brother in Christ:

When this letter catches up to you, you will be already "overseas" actively campaigning for Our Eucharistic King. Blessed are they who for the love of Jesus have put the leagues of sea and land between themselves and their dear ones. Has not the Master promised them a hundredfold reward?

I am pleased to see how promptly you have acquiesced to the wish of your Superiors.

Prompt obedience is the first essential of a real soldier, and you, by your vocation, are called upon to be a soldier of Jesus Eucharisticus. As such, Jesus in the White Host must ever be your Supreme Model and Exemplar, and where more perfectly than in His Eucharistic Presence does Jesus illustrate the beautiful virtue of Obedience?

Nay more—when we obey our Superiors we are in reality obeying God through them. When Jesus places Himself beneath the Eucharistic Species, is it not rather God obeying His creatures? Still, therefore, may He say to us, "Learn of Me, for I am meek and humble of Heart!"

Dear Brother, I will pray for you, and you, I know, will pray for me, and since we both have opportunity for so much intimacy with God, surely in His Heart we shall meet each morn and walk with Him the selfsame path of Sacrifice and Immolation.

THE ROADS IN EGYPT

My Dear ——:

If you have not heard from me it is not because I have not thought of you, but because of my various duties and obediences which this year especially make it difficult for me to attend to the needs of my spiritual family, except by prayer.

One month from tomorrow, please God and Our Lady, I shall be professed; and then I hope to have more time to give to the care of the souls that are so dear to me. So be patient, little Mother, and all your desires will be fulfilled, for what you seek, after all, is but the Will of God, His glory in the sanctification of your own soul and that of the souls His Love has committed to your care.

Be patient and watch in prayer and sacrifices, especially the little daily ones. That was the program of the Little Flower — that must be our plan of campaign. As little children let us cling, 'mid the darkness of this life, to Mother Mary. Let us rest in her arms, sleep there, live there; and thus we shall be imitating the Incarnate Son of God, our Captain and Model Supreme.

You remember, perhaps, how I liked to compare this life to the Flight into Egypt. I have never found a better comparison. Tomorrow! Is it not always a strange land into which we are hastening? Who of us knows what tomorrow holds! But this we do know, that if we wish we may have the sweet company of Jesus, Mary and Joseph, and after all, that should suffice for us!

Jesus, Mary, Joseph, may they be ever with you, little Mother, their Holy Names on your lips, their love in your heart, their Will in your will, and your soul in their keeping till our roads in Egypt cross once more!

THE SHORTEST WAY HOME

Dear Brother in Christ:

Among my papers not so long ago, I came across a number of photographs from Madagascar. As a consequence I am looking backward across the now misty spaces of the years that were, to the evening a newly ordained priest came to —— and found there friends to encourage him in the generous resolution that was soon to take him half-way 'round the world.

It does not seem so long ago, our meeting in ——, and yet already you are a veteran of Christ's foreign legions, while I am growing old, a private in the home guards. Another decade or two, perhaps much less, for we really do not know whether or not we shall be permitted to finish the rosary of our priestly years— another little while and you and I, dear Brother, will be seeking the shortest way home. Now the purpose of this letter is to propose this, to my mind, consoling truth: "that the longest way round is the shortest way home," when the longest way round happens to be the apostolic path of the foreign missions. The life of a missionary, if he but hold fast to his grace-bound course, cannot but prove a shortcut to Heaven. This then is what I want to say to you, dear Brother, as my New Year's greeting.

Today is the feast of one of the greatest missionaries of all time, if indeed he be not the greatest: St. Francis Xavier. For this humble son of St. Ignatius, this intrepid corsair of souls, I have a special and grateful veneration. He held to his course, he literally ran along it, and can we doubt that the exhausted athlete of Christ, dying on lonely Sancian, found Heaven nearer than China?

Forward then, dear Brother, to the work that lies at hand. It is the deep folly of human hearts to seek to tarry on this earth which is itself speeding to its allotted end. Life is a steamer ploughing its way across the ocean. From her dark holds and stifling engine-rooms, as well as from wind-swept decks, luxurious saloons and cabins, both passengers and crew must some day disembark. It is not the place we occupy on the steamer that really counts; what matters is the port whereat we shall be landed, the reception that awaits us when we shall step ashore.

You, dear Brother, are sailing by the shortest of routes to the port of happy souls. Your course God Himself has charted. His grace turns with divine energy the shaft of your turbines. You have but to hold the wheel aright.

May He bless you and all missionaries, our brothers, and bring you all by the light of the Morning Star to safe anchorage in that harbor where all human desires like the wavelets fall asleep and wake not, because God is now all in all.

THE BACK TRAIL

My Dear ——:

As the cry of the newly born babe gives assurance of physical life, so the voice of the little Child of Bethlehem announced the spiritual rebirth of Humanity: and thus it has come to pass, in a most profound sense, that at Christmastide we celebrate the birthday of all Christians as well as that of Christ. And, since missionaries are dedicated to interpreting the meaning of that First Christmas to the hearts of men, it is fitting that at this season they should greet those who have heard the precious Evangel from their lips and who in turn have pledged themselves to give both extension and intensification to the joyous message of Faith. Such is the purpose of these lines.

There is a deep significance in the choice of God, Our Father, of a manger as the first visible throne of His Incarnate Son. This little Child, through whose clear eyes Eternal Truth looks out upon the world, had come both to do and to teach. Having begun His Sacred Mission in the silence of His Mother's virgin womb, He continued it from the lowly pulpit of the manger—He who would conclude it presently from the loftier platform of the Cross. How eloquently the fundamental lessons of Christianity were preached from the crib of Bethlehem! Here He who is supreme in Power and Wisdom, in Glory and Goodness, taught the necessity of humility to men. Here One who was and is supremely rich, became, for the love of men, abjectly poor. Here He who had the inalienable right to command, committed Himself to the swaddling bands of infancy and the care—albeit the loving care—of His creatures.

Dear ——, the Babe of Bethlehem has a message

of ageless validity for America and for all the world. In vain shall we seek lasting prosperity, in vain shall we strive for abiding peace, till the children of men take the back-trail, and like the shepherds of old hasten up the hillside till they find the Child and His most holy Mother.

Today, as then, God's Son must be sought in the arms of a Mother, then Mary, now Holy Mother Church; and we who by God's merciful grace have found Him there, we who know of His abiding Presence therein, shall we not share in the joyous mission of the angelic hosts of the first Christmas midnight?

Such is the vocation of missionaries, and such, too, by the grace of God and the understanding of your Christian heritage, is your mission in the truth-seeking America of today. In the fulfillment of this mission we ask the Christ Child and His Mother to bless you at New Year's beginning and always.

THE GREATER LINK

Dear Brother in Christ:

Here is a letter to greet you for the ending of one year and the beginning of another, may it serve as a happy reminder of that divine link which fraternal charity has forged for our souls.

You write me of your inactivity, or rather of the difficulty of finding something to do at the present moment. Since this is unusual for one qualified as you are, I feel that in this circumstance there is contained a quiet invitation from the Master to avail yourself of this temporary situation in order to deepen your spiritual life and weld your heart and will more firmly to a Will and Heart Divine. After all this is what most matters for us. This is what God has destined us for, union with Him in Christ Jesus. This is that seeking first the Kingdom of Heaven that Jesus recommended to His disciples; this is that better part which He commended Mary for having chosen; this is the greater link which is essential for our souls if they are to have peace in their journeying and God at the end of the road.

I do not mean, Brother, that it is impossible to accomplish this union while engaged in the active life. Far from it, many of the greatest contemplatives have been souls immersed in a sea of apostolic activity. But what I do mean is that your present solitude and freedom offer a most favorable occasion for the advancement of your spiritual interests. And as you advance do not forget to breathe a wee prayer for the writer who like the rest of mankind has many things to do but only one thing to accomplish.

Asking Our Lady to bless you.

THE PRICE OF VICTORY

Dear Brother in Christ:

I think it will be abundantly clear upon reflection that we will never make the proper adjustments of our own lives to the necessities of our state, without first lifting our eyes above creatures to the Creator and more specifically to the Creator in the Person of the Divine Son enthroned upon His Cross. Only in the light that streams therefrom can we hope to read aright the trials that come to us from the limitations of creatures. Only by God's grace can we interpret these limitations as offering us precious opportunities for advancing God's glory and our own eternal happiness.

It is in this manner that I would beg you to react to the decision of your superiors in giving you this trying obedience under such unusual circumstances. If you do so, I promise you an ever-deepening peace and a fruitful apostolate; if you fail to do so, the prospect is one of turmoil in your own soul, and souls in turmoil can hardly hope to be efficient preachers of the Gospel of Peace.

There are always two fundamental reactions possible to every trying situation, the reaction of nature and the reaction of grace. There are times, doubtlessly, when these reactions synchronize with facility, but there are other occasions, and you now face one such, when nature and grace are more or less in conflict. A Divine Commander is watching your reaction. I am confident He will not be disappointed. Remember, following through on the lead of grace means even now souls for Jesus and your own soul triumphant in the peace of God that is purchased by self-conquest.

FEBRUARY

February lights a candle against the death
of winter, but the candle will burn
to its socket ere its purpose is fulfilled.

CANDLES

Dear Mother in Christ:

This note is to wish you joy on your Profession Anniversary. The joy of the angels—yes, I wish you that—but besides I wish you a share in the joy of the Virgin Mother herself—on this the Feast of her Purification.

How fitting for a Profession Day is this Feast of Our Blessed Mother. For the Purification is the day for blessing candles, and you by your Profession have become a blessed candle for the Altar of God and the Heart of His Beloved Son.

Reverend Mother, you know that the Church wants the candles destined for the altar to be of the purest beeswax. So too, Jesus wants the candle of your life to be molded with greatest care of the purest of materials. Cease not, therefore, to the end in the work of refining the sentiments of your heart and soul, that the flame of divine love may not waver in the drafts of this life, but burn ever steadier, ever more brightly in the sight of God and men. Cease not to beg the Holy Spirit to carry on this work of sanctification which so far exceeds our own unaided efforts. Ask Him to trim the wick of your intention lest there collect thereon the black carbon of self-love and the flame of your candle give off smoke.

All lives are burning candles, yet all do not burn unto the Glory of God. Some burn with a sickly glow before the shrine of wealth, some burn with a lurid light before the shrine of Passion. How blessed are those candles that burn serene before the speaking silence of God's Altar where rests His Son's Sweet Heart.

Thank God, then, dear Mother, for all the graces

He has bestowed upon you, and may your life so gleam as to console Jesus and guide others through the darkness into the Cloister of His Heart.

For this I shall pray, and do you pray for

FATHER PAGE

HIGH FINANCE

DEAR SISTER IN CHRIST:

Although we have never met, yet I feel that I know you through our friend, and besides are we not most intimately related, we who labor for and in the Heart of Jesus Christ. And so I write to congratulate you on your bank account—the fruit of twenty-five long years in the Service of the Master and His poor—yes indeed this is just reason for joy, for the Master pays well, one hundred per cent. interest for the service of His poor, and you have served His poor. And so being poor you have become rich in Him who became poor for us that we might become rich in Him. "Silver and gold" indeed, you may say with St. Peter—"I have not, but what I have I give thee." Give, then, dear Sister, give without faltering, without tiring, pour out on your aged poor, on their gray heads and bent shoulders, the benediction of your Faith and Hope and Love. Give till the twenty-five shall have become fifty, and your life like a Rosary well said shall be kissed by Mother Mary and tucked away forever in His Heart.

FAITH MEANS FAITH

DEAR ——:

You tell me your difficulty is "not with us but with some of our beliefs." Very well, you have touched a vital spot, indeed you have remarked the wide chasm between our Faith and yours. You take the words of Christ, weigh them, accept them or dismiss them to suit your individual judgment, does this really mean Faith in Christ, is it not rather faith in self? Christ spoke and every word He spoke had a definite meaning — one meaning. He commissioned His Apostles to teach that meaning to the world — Go teach all nations. This authoritative interpretation is necessary as the present widespread confusion without the Church amply proves. We Catholics accept the truths of Faith not because they seem plausible, not because they appeal to our heart and emotions, but simply because we believe God has revealed them as the truth, God who is Truth, God who can neither deceive or be deceived.

But our Faith does not stop there. By Faith we accept the Truth, we enter the Household of God and having entered we find ourselves very much at Home — somehow everything fits into its proper place. Our Host has gone upstairs to prepare our night's lodgings. There is the Table gleaming white — always set and awaiting the famished, a cool pump in the courtyard where we may wash up first. Plenty of pictures are on the wall to inspire us with the thought that God's friends are His and ours still, even that silent form over the doorway which seemed so awesome becomes very human, for there is a little Child in its arms and after all a Mother has a right to hold her child. So, we settle down to rest at the Hearth where God's Love waits to thaw our chilled and sluggished hearts.

O child, Faith means faith. It is a gift of God — but ours for the asking — ask Him to give it to you, ask Him as did Newman and many, many another, to lead you amid the gathering gloom — across the threshold into the Home which began in an upper room in Jerusalem many centuries ago — and now extends around the world — Catholic in time, in place, in spirit, one fold and One Shepherd, as the Master wished it to be.

I shall ask His Blessed Mother, who is yours, to pray for you.

CANDLELIGHT

DEAR ——:

There is no doubt about the march of progress, materialistic progress at least, in this little old world of ours. But I sometimes find a wee little tug at my heart when I glimpse some of the old comforts that this busy age has discarded, the old woodstoves for example, or candlelight.

Candlelight, the very word has an appeal to me, soft and mellow, flickering or smoking at times—just like our spirits, but ever like a valiant soul rallying once more, striving upward and whispering to those in darkness, "I will stand by you, I will help you."

I will admit that candlelight had no place in the modern business world—but in our world, dear Sister, candlelight will always have a place. In the dim light of a cave rested the Light of the World, and by the candlelight of faith we walk bravely through the dark and the fogs of life. Were it not so, there would be no merit in our lives. Did we gaze on the brightness of the glorified Christ as did His Apostles on Mt. Tabor; did we see the glorified wounds as did Magdalen on the first Easter Morn; did we live in the brightness of His unveiled presence as do the Saints in Heaven, then we would not be members of the Church militant as we know ourselves very well to be.

But, that being so, is it not comforting that we have the candlelight of faith to guide our steps aright? Should we not be thankful to the good God Who has not left us alone and in the dark? Think of the teeming millions in distant lands, and indeed today, even in our own country, who have not recognized the star of Bethlehem, who do not know there is a Light in the world other than the light of their own intelligence. And would that they would follow the light of their own natural intelligence till they found *The Intelligence* which gave them theirs that they might seek and find Him, and Jesus Christ, Whom He has sent to claim the reasonable allegiance of every reasonable creature.

As for me, I must admit the candlelight of my faith has always burned brightly as far back as I can remember, unaffected by the passing winds of current thought and the breezes of human opinion. I thank my God from the depths of my heart that this be so, and I pray Him that it may be so until the brightness of eternal day. Through the dark places of life, through the mists of mystery, into the shadows of the valley of death, though by candlelight, I know I shall walk securely. I have no fear, no dread, that my light shall go out, or that I shall lose the way, for my hand rests firmly in the hand of Mother Church and God's love guards my candle and God's Mother my heart.

SNOWDROPS

DEAR ——:

On this sweet Feast Day of Our Blessed Lady's Purification, I am writing to you, that you, now a rather wee lady—shall I say?—just a snowdrop of the Spring, may grow always fairer in the sight of God's Angels until you are a stately white lily in the Gardens of Paradise.

Just put on your jacket and slip out to Auntie's flower-bed and you will find, I feel sure, as I found years ago, the tiny snowdrops bravely pushing upward out of the damp gray mold. Now the snowdrops have a lesson for all little children, and we are all little children in the sight of God. Even Grandmother and Grandfather are but children in God's sight you know. And the lesson of the snowdrops is this: Listen, for I am going to let them speak to you.

"Dear little one, you love us, do you not? And why do you love us? Because you see that we are sweet and white and fair; and we are sweet and white and fair because we have lifted our white heads up and hold them up bravely above the damp clay of Mother Earth's dark breast. Do you want to be loved, too? Do you want God and His Blessed Mother and His Angels and Saints to look on your soul and smile with pleasure upon it? You do; of course you do. Then you have only to imitate us. Lift your soul off the earth; lift it up, bravely, calmly. Do not let its fragrant petals drag in the soil; do not let selfish hands pluck you. Be not afraid that you will be crushed under foot. A Divine Gardener watches with jealous love over your growth, refreshing you with the gentle dew of His Heart's Blood, while He warms you with the Golden Mantle of His grace. It is true that we are on earth, but our souls are made to be lifted up, up from the earth to God. If you lift your soul up to God, He will use your life even as He has used ours; only yours in a nobler manner, to bring happiness to other lives and the fragrance of God's Love and the sweetness of God's beauty into the cloistered garden of a Christian home."

Thus, dear ——, the snowdrops are whispering this bright morning. We, too, are God's; we, too, are made to show forth His wisdom, His beauty, His power and His goodness. Do we do so, we find therein the greatest measure of earthly happiness and we make sure of our transplanting in God's good time to the gardens that clothe the Eternal hills with beauty. Only one thing can spoil God's plan. Only one thing can mar the image of God's Beauty in our souls. You know well what that one thing is, and I trust and pray that that one thing will never touch the petals of your soul, for I wish you to be ever a snowdrop, a little snowdrop, a virgin flower for a Virgin Queen.

THE CROSS OF GOLD

DEAR FATHER:

This little note is to bring you my greetings for the Golden Jubilee of your Priesthood. How happy I am over this great happiness, this great grace, that Jesus Christ has given unto you.

Whenever I think of the Priesthood, a wonderment comes over my soul, and the deeper I think, the deeper grows the wonderment, that God Almighty should have given such gifts and such a Gift to men.

Yet wonderful as the Gift of His Priesthood is—nevertheless it is a logical sequence of the Infinity of a Loving God, loving His creatures in and through the Heart of His Son Divine.

We, ourselves, when our hearts stir with noble, generous impulses, would like to multiply ourselves that we might do everything for everyone we love. The Heart of Jesus stirred with a like impulse, only infinite in Love and backed by infinite Wisdom and Power, and the result is His twofold multiplication of Himself—the Holy Eucharist and the Priesthood.

To a true Priest, his Priesthood is the supremest of God's Gifts. He holds It as a cross of gold to be kissed daily, kept without tarnish, and in death placed reverently, together with the soul upon which It was laid, like an accolade in the hands of the Virgin Mother to be presented to her Virgin Son.

Father, let us cherish with ever deepening gratitude our Cross of Gold. By Its powers it is our high destiny to exalt Jesus, the Son of God among the children of men, and if we strive to do so honestly and perseveringly, then by It shall we, too, be exalted, and this is the exaltation we should seek—that Jesus Christ may ever find consolation in our hearts, as in Mother Mary's.

THE PURIFICATION

MY DEAR ——:

It takes faith to see it, of course, but it is true that with earnest souls who are seeking God, every event of their lives is part of the journey to Him, part of the process of purification which is necessary for the creature who desires to be one with the Creator.

In this light I think you should see the present difficulties that beset you; they are meant for your purification. The closer God desires that we be to Him, the more necessary is it that He make us like unto Himself, and to be like to God is a difficult program for the children of men. Nevertheless, He can do all things, and we can do all things in Him Who strengthens us. Therefore, dear ——, have courage; do not flinch beneath the flails of tribulation and suffering. When God's winnowing is over, the pure wheat shall make a White Host for the honor of the living God.

I know that you will say, or at least think, it is easy to write advising others to have courage and patience to bear with suffering and injustice but it is a different matter to follow one's own advice when we ourselves are subject to the same. Very well; this is true, and so I pray you to pray for me, for this I know: that though my love for Jesus is very imperfect, His love for me is very great, and because He loves me, He will perfect me. And, therefore, you must pray that having advised others, I myself may not flinch when I find my soul amid the fires of tribulation.

The Spring is coming and after the Spring, Summer, and after Summer the Fall and the Harvest, and the grain falling in the ground must die if it would bear harvest to the Master. We are the wheat of Christ, as Ignatius of Antioch declared long ago, and the wheat of Christ must be purified by Jesus' Blood and Mary's tears to make a Host for God.

THE WHARF

DEAR BROTHER IN CHRIST:

This note, I trust, will reach you in the month when Nature begins to dream of the Springtime, and will remind you of your spiritual brother whom you loved in the springtime of your life.

Time has laid her gentle but firm hands upon him, but, like the old wharf, he is still solid and useful, ready to serve both new craft, putting out with the buoyancy of Youth upon the uncharted Sea of the Future, and old, storm-hammered vessels like unto yourself who must now be nearing their port and final anchorage in God.

And when you come, Brother of mine, whether it be trimly and under your own sail, or battered and water-logged, and in tow, always the old wharf will be there waiting, waiting patiently for your coming. As I conceive it, that is the part a true brother should play. He should not delay his brothers and sisters on the business of life. Rather should he assist them to outfit for the open sea. If he be true he will not delay their sailings, but will await with prayerful patience the hour of their return, and when those soul-ships come sailing back to port, he, like the faithful old wharf, should be waiting there to be of use, to facilitate their safe landing, aid in the making of necessary repairs, furnish wide spaces for the precious freight, and firm footing for sea-weary feet.

Dear Brother, it is rather a strange analogy, but I like it, and so, when you think of me, think of the old wharf at the waterfront still holding out against tide and wave—always ready for service, always waiting for your return from your sailings upon the ocean of God's Love, beneath the blue skies of Mary's mantle.

HOLY MOTHER

My Dear Child in Christ:

I am so glad you are moving slowly, at least externally. I want you to know Christ's true Spouse, Holy Mother Church, well, before you give yourself to her keeping. The better you know her the deeper will be your love for her, just as will always be the case with a wonderful mother—the better her children know her the deeper they penetrate her soul's depths, the deeper grows their reverence and gratitude to and for her.

Holy Mother, the Church, has nothing to fear from unbiased investigation; on the contrary, she has everything to gain, for to prayerful, which means humble, and honest investigation she will reveal herself in all her exquisite beauty as the Bride of the Canticle of Canticles, the Heavenly Jerusalem, Virgin Spouse of the Incarnate Word of God.

As you study the Church, however, always keep in mind the clear distinction between that which is Divine and that which is human in her. That which is divine in the Catholic Church is her Founder and Head—Christ and His Authority, His Sacrifice and Sacraments, His Grace and His Truth, which He has given her as her wedding gifts; that which is human in the Church is ourselves—her children—who can and indeed have failed Him and her so often and, at least historically speaking, so sadly and with such terrible consequences.

It is manifestly—and justly so—God's plan to require man's cooperation in his own and his fellow man's salvation. Every good Christian father or mother is a living illustration of this truth. Now, what is human can fail, and from time to time does fail, to do its part; but it is illogical to blame the Mother when her counsels and commands have been set at naught. Mother Church has always been a good Mother, the Good Mother Christ planned that she should be, even though from the beginning she has had sons and daughters unworthy of her.

I am so pleased over what you write me of your mother's attitude; the only thing more beautiful than one soul finding the Truth is two souls discovering it! Besides, it is especially sweet when two hearts that are by nature so united may add a supernatural bond to their union. Of course I am anticipating quite a bit, I know, but my priestly experience has taught me that almost always behind a generous soul — (be not proud but grateful to God who gave it) — will be a generous, noble mother and, therefore, I know she will follow if you pray God's sweet Holy Spirit to illumine and guide her steps.

He it is Who has given you the gift supernal of your new-found Faith. He is the Inner Source of your Vision. He, I know, will bring both you and your Mother to your Holy Mother here on earth and to that other Holy Mother of all Mothers, and her Son Divine, in Our Father's Home above.

WITH EYES UPLIFTED

My Dear Brother in Christ:

My heart is one with yours in the prayer that Our Blessed Lady will share her own beautiful Feast of the Purification with you for your Ordination, but my deeper heart-petition will be that you and our dear brothers will be ready, as Mary was ready for that momentous hour when her stainless soul, as a golden paten, lifted the tiny White Host of her Child — God's Eternal Son — for the first time in His Father's temple. To be sure, it was a priest of the Old Law who received the little Hostage, but Our Lady's being was ever and is ever so closely knit to her Son's as to make but one oblation in the sight of God and His Most Holy Angels.

See, therefore, dear brother, the most important of all the details of your preparation — the purification, the refining of the metal of your being till it be fit, by God's grace and Our Lady's prayers, for blending with the souls of Jesus and Mary in the priestly oblation.

I would not set this ideal before you did I not know your desires. There are those even among God's chosen servants who never lift their eyes, at least in sustained vision, to the hills of God. They are contented to walk in the valleys of men and find their consolation in the creature rather than in the Creator. By our religious profession we have professed our purpose of following the Master up the mount of the Beatitudes, and how shall we succeed unless we lift eyes of faith and hope and love, morning by morning, and let them follow the Host as we lift Him Who sustains us in the infinite resourcefulness of His Merciful Love.

Eyes of faith and of hope are not enough for a true priest; no, his eyes must be brilliant with love, so bright that he shall see clearly his own nothingness and His Master's greatness, so tender with devotion as to console One whose love still holds Him a Prisoner in the swaddling hands of Time.

So, dear Brother in Christ, may we hasten in love to the post God's mysterious designs have assigned us. The world is passing by, time's tide is running out; while there is yet light may we climb together the rocky path to the hill-top where gleams the White Beacon of Our Crucified Master. There we will find Mother Mary and there, I trust and pray, you will find — FATHER PAGE.

LOST BOUQUETS

DEAR SISTER IN CHRIST:

What a consoling thing it must be to have half a century of unstinted service safely to one's credit on the record books of Heaven. Today I am thanking God and Our Lady for this grace which is now yours. Actually, of course, whatever God wills for us is, in a relative sense, the greatest of graces, for it proceeds from Divine Wisdom moved by Divine Love, and that is why souls who truly know God's ways always sing one theme song, blessing in all things His Holy Will. You, of course, know this very well, dear Sister, for your little Mother, Blessed Julie, has left a most appealing illustration of this truth.

Nevertheless, only on earth can we suffer meritoriously and freely for Jesus; hereafter, we can suffer — most of us doubtlessly will — but only to make up for the sufferings we side-stepped here! So it is, indeed, a blessed thing to be permitted so long a time to gather flowers for the Master, and even though you may have dropped some — and who but Our Lady has not done likewise? — still you have had time to pick yours up again, and now have opportunity to arrange your spoil in massed fragrance and beauty.

You may feel, as you recross in memory the fields of yesterdays, that your bouquet is not at all what you would wish it to be. You may sense that many of its blossoms have long since lost their fragrance and no longer lift their painted heads to fill their appointed place in the design. You may even be convinced that you have lost your bouquet gathered so earnestly in Life's morning and hold now only a few humble perennials in your hands!

Thanks be to God, dear Sister, even as a loving father does not disdain the broken dandelion or tattered daisy proffered by the soiled fingers of his child, so, too, Our Heavenly Father does not refuse the simplest offering of His children, but rather welcomes them from the hands of His Divine Son wherein they are ever strangely freshened and restored. Besides, may we not always hope by reason of Christ's merits, to find again our lost bouquets in those same precious, pierced hands! You know we may believe that Our Father in the Infinitude of His Merciful Love restores the lost bouquets of merits when we return searching for them, humbly, at His mercy seat.

Now then, dear Sister, ere your golden sunset deepens into the darkening purples of the night, claim back, even as children are so wont to do, your lost flowers from your indulgent Father, bind them anew with the fair ribbon of a perfect abandonment (strange that abandonment should be able so to bind us), and then replace them with your own soul by the hands of Mary in the lap of God.

With love to all.

IF THERE BE LOVE

My Dear Child:

I am afraid my desire to help you has run ahead of my abilities and time. Often I am like one of those antiquated cars that runs gaily and with much rattling when it chooses but idles between times when not positively stalled. This morning I opened three letters that called for deliberation and response and yours is the first of these.

It seems to me a very necessary preliminary step in the building up of your spiritual life that you form a deep conviction, well meditated and thus engraven upon your consciousness, that it is God "Who worketh in us both to will and to accomplish." God is both the Architect and Master Builder, and it is essential from the first in the spiritual life that this truth be recognized in a very practical manner.

From this practical recognition of God's part in our sanctification there flow at once two truths of a paradoxical character: one the logicalness of profound humility, the other the reasonableness of high confidence. Since we can do nothing without God, we have no more reason for pride than a little child who negotiates the living room clinging grimly to father's hand. Since in God we can do all things, no difficulty except self (and self is a difficulty which grace can overcome) can bar successfully our spiritual progress if only we lean on God. Hence the logicalness of confidence.

These two virtues of humility and confidence I wish you, dear Child, to make the basis of your spiritual building; the one will assure you of a solid foundation upon the bed-rock of God's Holy Will, the other will keep you to your task, which will be life-long but worth while. After all what else is worth while in this crumbling existence of ours but to build in Christ Jesus "more stately mansions," as the keenest of our New England poets has expressed it. God's Presence once lent both character and dignity to a cave, so why need we despair! At least we have a cave to offer Jesus, and Jesus asks no more if there be love. In Mary.

HIGHER ALTITUDES

Dear Son in Christ:

This is the first letter of the New Year, i.e., after the Divine letter of the Mass said this morning, and like the last Mass of the old year carrying a message of deep gratitude to God for the many graces vouchsafed to me and those I love. Among these graces, not the least I hold to be those that have brought about the gradual resighting—revisioning—of your soul. This has been one of the dearest desires of my heart, and thus the past year closed for me with a mighty wave of consolation in the knowledge of the graces God was offering you. I have so wanted you to realize where rested the deeper values so often covered up beneath the cheaper offerings on the bargain counter of time.

You asked in your last letter two questions of considerable importance which I must answer. Paradoxically, the danger of lost grace rests for you, I feel, not so much in seeking recreations, as in permitting them to assume more than a recreational value. Recreations —so long as they contain no direct challenge to faith or virtue (some books do the former, some plays might the latter)—may be considered as God-given means of restoring and upbuilding our God-given powers of mind and body. As such I would say, at least while you feel their need, use them for their proper purposes, but not as a substitute for, or an escape from, Divine Love. There is a way which I think is possible and perhaps necessary—apart from the stages of sanctity which constitute an absorption of the soul's faculties in God—of taking recreation *with God and in God.* This can be done quite simply by gratitude (a grateful abiding remembrance of Him whose providence has provided the recreation) and by a quiet consciousness of Christ's presence in the soul.

This leads me to the second proposal, as to a positive means of strengthening the soul in Godliness. After the Sacraments and obedience to God's Laws, the most practical for you would be, I believe, the practice of mental prayer. I mean by this a quiet half hour spent alone thinking of and loving God in your own soul. If you find it helpful use a spiritual book as a basis, a flying field, as it were, from which to take-off. Then perpetuate the fruits of this thinking of God by the cultivation of an interior recollection by which, amid the surf of successive duties, you remain mindful of the undertow of Divine Love, moment by moment, to the end of another day:

Until amid the murmur of the violins,
The rise and fall of laughter's soft cascade,
The clipped speech of office, chatter on the street,
Another Voice shall speak within your deepest heart,
Another Hand be felt within your busy own,
And you be lonely in a crowd—yet not alone.

Dear boy, you see your spiritual father is asking of you higher altitudes, and these require courage and perseverance. But both of these graces He asks for you at Our Lady's feet today and always.

UNDER FIRE

DEAR BROTHER IN CHRIST:

It seems a long, long time since I have heard from you, and I know it is a long, long time since you have heard from me, at least directly. Our lives I sometimes think are so filled with daily duties that, like sailors in the storm, there is little time to think of aught else but the needs of the present moment. However, I pray for you and trust you do the same for me, that the Good God Who is not subject to the limitation of His creatures may care for us both and keep us unwounded under the shell-fire of the world.

To be safe under the myriad exactions of our daily lives, one thing above all else is necessary, that we never forget to keep the mainspring of all our actions firmly fixed in the love of Our Lord and Our God. I sometimes pause for a moment between duties before the Eucharistic Throne of Jesus and whisper to my unseen but not unseeing Master, "Dear God, I have many things to do but only one thing to accomplish, and that, the attainment of Thyself." The great danger, it seems to me, of the real earnest soldier of Jesus Christ, whether he be on the foreign missions or in the home-town parish, is this—that his zealous exterior occupations will cause him little by little to lose sight of the Alpha and Omega of his priestly life, that he will become so engrossed in working for Jesus that Jesus will be forgotten and his work come thereby to have little lasting value either for God or for himself.

Therefore, my dear comrade-in-arms, I beg you day by day as you hold the world's Creator in your hands, to beg of Him the grace to be always faithful, faithful in remembering that He Himself is the very purpose of your existence and that you will never draw souls to Him unless you yourself live in union with His Most Sacred Heart. Beg of Him that burning love which will give you courage, as it has so many other valiant missionaries of His, to do and dare, to persevere unflinchingly, unscathed under the drum fire of the world, the flesh and the devil at your lonely post, holding the lines for Christ, and His Most Blessed Mother.

BROTHER-IN-ARMS

Dear Brother in Christ:

This note is to thank you for your Christmas note and the accompanying gift. I cannot remember a volume of poems that has appealed to me so deeply. I love the singing hearts of poets who see in the drama of everyday life the divine Romance and magnificent Adventure of Christianity, and your little volume has revealed such a heart to me.

Therefore, I have presumed at once to adopt the author as a brother, a brother-in-arms in the Most Glorious of Causes, because it is the Cause of our First Cause and last and Happy Ending—Christ the Lord!

It needs must be that lovers should be poets, especially lovers whose love is God. When one begins to love God, one begins to grow in the appreciation of His Beauty as revealed in all creation, in all things great and small, and that is why—or so it would seem to me—so many of God's saints have been like Francis of Assisi or the Little Flower of our own age, Thérèse—singing poets of the Harmonies of God.

Well then, my brother of the singing heart, let us set out as comrades-in-arms traveling together on the King's Highway in the pursuit of His Enterprise which in the fulfillment will make all men blood-brothers of the Sacred Heart.

His Enterprise, His Crusade as you will term it, will

end only with the end of Time, and though we sit at desks rather than bestride restless chargers, and wield frail pens *in lieu* of gleaming blades and beflagged lances, yet we have the consolation of knowing that the stakes are ever the same, the battle as fierce, if not fiercer, the foe the same, and the fundamental difficulties the same now as ever, and what alone is of supreme importance to us, the Leader, Our Captain, is ever the Same—Jesus Christ, yesterday and today and the same for ever!

We shall, therefore, dear brother of mine—brother-in-arms—press forward together in spirit and in truth, and though we may never meet here below, yet shall we ride stirrup to stirrup to the charge and drink from the same Cup morn by morn, renewing in our Captain's Blood our Brotherhood in His and Mary's Blessed Service.

COMRADESHIP

Dear Brother in Christ:

I was so glad to hear from you even though time did not permit my seeing you before I left for ——.

I think it will be only in Heaven that we shall fully appreciate that mystic bond of which the Communion of Saints is the golden aureole. And why should it not be so? Men of the world—business men, professional men, soldiers, all have their friendships varying in their nobility upon the nobility of the characters and motives which have forged them. Now we are God's soldiers, and apart from the question of character, what nobler motive of friendship can be found in all the world than the mutual love and sacrificing service of Jesus Christ, Our Blessed Lord and Saviour?

Therefore, dear Brother in Christ, our friendship shall not be the less ardent, our comradeship less beautiful because of the lengthened distance between us at this moment. Indeed, are we really apart, we whose hearts meet each morning in the Eucharistic Heart of Christ, we whose lips are stained by the same Precious Blood, we who fight in the same Cause for the same Captain under the same Banner of the Holy Cross and have the same Mother and Queen to watch over us?

May she keep you till we meet again—and always.

HOMEWARD BOUND

My Dear ——:

I should have written you about a month ago, but since undoubtedly you have been forced to begin letters in this fashion I know you will understand and pardon me.

No wonder your past month has been rather a blurred one! Even though there be leagues of land and sea between us and our dear ones, their sorrows are our trials, their trials our keenest sorrows, and when the hand of Death rests upon the bowed head of one we love, it brushes our shoulder in passing. Eyes that we loved are closed forever upon this world and our eyes look out upon familiar scenes through a mist of tears. We walk as in a fog, yet therein lies our merit, for are we not following the Master and His Mother—Our Sorrowful Queen—and besides are we not also—homeward bound!

Homeward bound! What joy, what exultation these two words bring, and always must bring, to those who are far from home and dear ones! Who but God could sound the sentiments of the millions of earth's voyagers as their soul-craft are at last headed homeward?

Yet, my brother, do we not know well that our true home is not here? Our world once had an undiscovered hemisphere, lying to the west beyond the sunset. Our souls have still a mysterious Wonder-land, a Home-land Ineffable, beyond Life's sunset gates.

Courage then, dear brother, the passing of our dear ones must but serve to guide our course, the memory of their faith become our beacon, their prayers by God's grace a favoring breeze, while their love for us in God is part of the warmth of Our Father's Home that waits us in the Port of Eternal Peace, within the breakwater of Christ's protecting arms. My prayers I join to yours for your dear father's soul, my Mass I share with him each month of this new year.

OUR JOB

Dear Sisters in Christ:

I am answering your letter at once that you may know how I interpret the possibilities of your present situation.

In a mission where by the very necessity of things, Jesus in the Sacrament of His Love is often alone, He, Who is still our Teacher as well as our Divine Lover, has ample opportunity to manifest the abiding and universal character of His love for souls. Till now you have seen Him ministering to the multitudes of a great city; now you find Him reaching out patiently, untiringly, for the lone sheep of the countryside, and waiting amid the depressing cold and silences of a mission chapel to offer you the consolation of His divine comradeship.

Take advantage of this divine graciousness; give Him all you can but yet in an unobtrusive way. Be obedient to the expressed desires of your superior, and if this is done in a spirit of Faith, Jesus will be pleased whether you are with Him in His lowly chapel or He with you in the even lowlier chapel of your hearts. How wonderful a thing it is to have a lover who is always with us, and whose eyes hold even a smiling response to every glance of love!

To me, therefore, there is the evidence of the delicate Providence of Divine Love, in this that you are called apart from the busy highways of the city to the silences and dreariness of a country mission. Not only are you fulfilling the precept of fraternal charity but the first commandment as well; you are aiding not only your sisters but your Divine Brother as well.

The only recommendation I will add, beyond that of trusting Jesus blindly in all things, will be this: on lonely missions the great danger of Christ's servants is that of permitting the human loneliness to drive one to human consolations. I pray you, dear Sisters, be careful of this. Be sympathetic to all, but seek your own consolation only from Jesus, only in the silent eloquence of His Eucharistic Presence. Our job it is to lead souls as did the Holy Baptist—not to self but to Jesus, and to do that efficaciously we must ourselves seek in Jesus all our consolation, we must be sign-posts, not waiting stations, on the high road to Divine Love.

A DIVINE SUBSTITUTION

My Dear Sister:

When I saw you last, you asked me a question concerning the practice of the virtue of poverty that I promised to answer later. Here is the answer to the best of my ability.

The question, as I remember it, involved the difficulty in the practice of this essential virtue of the religious life. I readily grant the reality of the problem, for human nature finds in itself a well-nigh universal tendency to hold on, ivy-like, to material and spiritual objects. The natural, therefore, must be met by the supernatural, nature must be subdued by grace. And in the question of holy poverty, it seems to me that the only satisfactory thing to do is to substitute for our creature attachments that supremest attachment to which our affections can aspire. I mean the Heart of God.

Empty hearts, like empty hands, will always be

searching to possess, putting forth little tendrils of desire in a hundred directions and to a thousand objects. The problem of being truly poor in spirit reduces itself, therefore, to that of learning to attach our affections wholly and with finality to the divine realities, of making a divine substitution — if I may so speak with reverence.

Thus, in the matter of holy poverty once again the paradox of Christianity becomes evident. We are never successfully poor until we have become immeasurably rich, we are never completely stripped of the creature until we are fully clothed with the grace-woven robes of the Lamb.

This being so, there follows that there is a distinct advantage, if one utilizes it, in being — as so many of our missionaries are — close to actual poverty. The human heart is capable of great subtleties, and the actual proximity of the poverty in which Christ was born, lived and died, accentuates for heroic souls their progress towards divine affluence.

May the dear little Mother who had but two doves — the offering of the poor — to give in redeeming her Lamb, accept the offering of our poverty and share with us her Treasure.

IN THE PURSE OF POVERTY

My Dear Child:

At last I can write to you for at last you have found the great treasure that awaits the soul which, stripped of all earthly consolation, turns under the impulse of Faith — and the necessity God's loving providence has provided — and finds the most satisfying of all consolations, God Himself. This is the great grace Jesus for a long time has been intent upon giving you, and now that it is yours, I trust and pray you will appreciate and cling to it with all the might at your command.

Have you reflected that when you abandoned the

idea of claiming creature consolation and permitted grace to reveal the wealth of poverty, how soon like Anna and holy Simeon you discovered in the arms of Poverty the true and only abiding Treasure the world holds out to men?

How happy I am that you have found the vein of gold hidden beneath the surface of your hard and erstwhile lonely life. Now you have found the silver in the purse of the poor—of the poor, that is, who by faith and God's grace know that the measure of earthly possessions is not the measure of Divine Love.

You are no longer young, dear Child, and I beg you to make good use of the golden opportunities your present straitened circumstances offer you to die rich in the sight of God and His holy angels. I know I preach and have always pointed out a rather austere program for you, a pathway devoid of human consolations, a desert trail with few oases and with not a few mirages, which were more often than not the fruit of your own will as yet unwedded to the Will of God. Only when you come to know God's will in the full light of the Beatific Vision will you understand why He permitted you to be led by such a lonely road into the garden of His Heart. And yet when you do come to know and understand His dealings with your soul you will likewise understand why He permitted you to be treated so rigorously by one who willed to be always His servant and His Mother's faithful page.

THE RESOLVE TO SANCTITY

My Dear ——:

Please pardon my coming at once to the business at hand. As regards the trials of which you wrote, take this attitude: either I have or I have not offended my Divine Lover. If the latter is true, *all is well*; if the former, then I know His Love is quite sufficient to forgive, even were my guilt that of the most hardened of criminals, and because of the greatness of His Love, *He finds joy in forgiving.* Since this is so, it is foolish of me to spend vain regrets over the past; to do this will be but a means of nursing my injured self-esteem. Why should I be exempt from the universal weakness and limitations of my fellow beings? One thing, however, I will do; like Peter and Magdalen I will refuse to remain in my weakness, my desertion; I will arise and return to my Father's House where, even though my Elder Brother may seem not to regard my face, I will abide and partake humbly of the bread of compunction, until such time as His voice shall lift my eyes to see again the love-light in His own.

Besides, does not Our Lady as the Refuge of Sinners offer a sure meeting-place for us, faithless ones, with One who cannot be less than true?

MARCH

March winds are sweeping God's
fields for Easter.

BEING SICK

DEAR ——— :

I am at present enjoying the luxury of being sick. Tonsillitis tripped me up quite neatly Monday last, and left me, where I remain, in bed.

Being sick has some advantages over being well. It gives one food for reflection on the frailty of one's make-up, and from such reflection can come humility — the stuff of which saints are made. Most of the Saints have been physically afflicted, and perhaps more than we realize, these infirmities helped to make them saints. Sickness was the cradle of St. Ignatius' spirituality. Sickness was the treatment which gave Ignatius' compatriot in the work of Catholic education, little Mère Jule, such robustness of soul. Sickness was the hot-house whence sprang the fragrant lilies of St. Gabriel of Our Lady of Sorrows and St. Theresa of the Child Jesus. Let us hope and pray that what wrought so mightily in the saints, may at least work in us to the forgiveness of sins.

Then, too, being sick offers to those around one a chance to practice in a special manner that fraternal charity which was so dear to the Heart of Our Blessed Lord. And surely that state is blessed which is the occasion of special consolation to His Heart. Whenever a patient hand rests on a feverish brow, wherever a kindly ear listens to catch the faltering footsteps of a tired burdened heart, there Jesus is consoled, there the merciful love of God is glorified. It is more blessed to give than to receive, but when the blessedness of giving is denied one, let one claim the blessedness of receiving in His Name and for His Sake and Mother Mary's.

Now besides these manifest benefits of being sick, there is still another which appeals to me in particular, and that is this: If I were not sick, this half hour would not be at my disposal, and you would not hear that, sick or well, I pray for you that your soul may grow ever more sick of the world and its pomps, and ever closer to the Heart of the Divine Physician, In Whose Mother's Service I am.

"EVERYBODY'S MODEL"

DEAR ——:

You know that I have much to do and therefore you will understand why I cannot visit you at present. In this note I will try, however, to say just what I would say were I to visit you.

You, by your vocation, are dedicated in a special manner to the love and imitation of the Guardian of the Holy Family. Do you realize what this means? St. Francis of Assisi has been called and indeed well called "Everybody's Saint." St. Joseph deserves an even higher title—he is in very truth Everybody's Model—for he was above all others, save only Mary, the perfect servant of God, and as such the model for all God's servants no matter their state of life. The laborer, the husband, the priest, the Sister, both acting and contemplating, each can look to Joseph, and learn from the silent eloquence of his hidden life how to serve God, how to live for God and with God, how to die in God's and Mary's blessed arms. No one has ever been so dear to Jesus and Mary, no one has ever merited so deep a place in their affection as Joseph—Joseph whom God the Father was willing should be in the eyes of the world the father of His Son; Joseph, whom God the Son was willing to accept as His father and guardian on earth; Joseph, whom God the Holy Spirit was willing should be the spouse of His Virgin Bride, the pure heart to whose keeping was confided the Vessel of Election, that Chalice destined to enclose the living Body and Blood of God!

Let therefore these things be the subject of your

meditations, and growing in appreciation of his glories and his virtues, you will surely come to appreciate more and more deeply your privilege of being his daughters, of bearing his beautiful name, of being under his ceaseless, dauntless protection. In a word you will rejoice with Jesus and Mary in the company of the humble carpenter of Nazareth, you will learn the lessons of his life — purity, poverty, persevering toil and prayer and unwavering devotion to the Person of the Incarnate Word and to the Word's Sinless Mother.

You should be very happy in your life, and if you are not, ask your father Joseph for that happiness which he enjoyed so long. Ask him to give you Jesus, Mary and the Cross — therein you will find happiness, and I hope, say a prayer for FATHER PAGE.

SOLDIERS OF MARY

DEAR ——— :

How grateful we should be for the privilege of being the servants of the Immaculate Heart of God's Blessed Mother. Would that we might love that Heart as did Jesus and serve that Heart as did St. Joseph. But we have neither the depth of love of the One nor the purity of soul of the other, yet Joseph has interceded for us and Jesus has invited us who are sinners to take refuge close to His Blessed Mother's Heart — nay more, He has invited us to become the consecrated servants of that Heart, soldiers of Mary in the time-old battle with the forces of darkness and of sin.

Shall we not glory then, in our calling? In the morning of Creation when God's kingdom had been assailed, God Himself accepted the challenge and foretold the final victory of the children of Our Blessed Lady — "I will place enmities between thee and the woman, and thy seed and her seed; she shall crush thy head, and thou shalt lie in wait for her heel."

Do you realize all this means? It means God knew the ceaseless battle that would be waged for the possession of immortal souls and decreed this lifting aloft of a new standard. The first mother of men had betrayed them, His Son's Blessed Mother would reclaim them, protect them, lead them to victory, lead them to Paradise, to God. Consider the armies of the late war—what a mighty host in arms! But what is this host to the endless regiments of massed humanity of every land and clime and age who have battled 'neath the standard of the Cross and the colors of Our blessed Lady for the salvation of their own and other souls!

In the beautiful Canticle of Canticles, God's Holy Spirit has set down these words: "Put me as a seal upon thy heart." Dear Sister, let us take the Pure Heart of God's Blessed Mother and place It reverently as a seal upon our own. Where her Heart is, there will Her Son's Heart abide, there will be God's strength, God's holiness, God's love, God's victory. Then shall we be "terrible as an army in battle array" to His enemies, beautiful and comely in the sight of God and His friends. Jesus will look upon us and see Mary, His blessed Mother Mary will look upon us and see Jesus. Thus shall we come unscathed, unconquered through life's warfare and pass with souls uplifted in ecstatic bliss in review triumph before the throne of God.

"SURSUM CORDA"

Dear Brother in Christ:

This evening I opened and read your greetings of the Holy Season. I return them with all my heart. What a wonderful bond of union should exist between those who partake of the Priesthood of Jesus Christ. As that Priesthood is One, as their Master is One, as their Love is One, so should their hearts be one in the Heart of Jesus and the arms of Blessed Mother Mary.

I do not, I cannot, concede that you are correct as to my intimate union with Our Blessed Lord. It is necessary that one be honest with oneself or else there can be no real progress in holiness. And to be honest, I am very far from that much-to-be-desired goal of intimate union with Jesus. To be sure Jesus treats me, treats all of us, with the greatest graciousness and affection; He invites us to the most intimate and holiest of unions of heart and will, of soul and body; but let us never forget He did the same with Judas. Judas, too, was not refused the privileges of a trusted friend.

Now the truth is more like this: God has given me of His own free choosing a very strong and lively Faith. This Faith has kept the fires of Hope burning steadily, but Hope has not yet blazed into that flame of Love which consumes all that is earthly in man and leaves only the pure gold of a perfect love of God and Mary.

So much for my soul. As for yours, that you are concerned, that you are anxious to be "a man of God," is the very best earnest that you are already well on the way thereto. I think it was St. Thomas of Aquin's sister who once asked him how she should become a Saint. His answer has some value surely. His answer was, "*will it.*" That, dear Father, is all we need to do in order to become men of God; simply to will it, to will it steadily, hour by hour, day by day, year by year. Do this and you may rest assured of the result, for if there is one thing above all others that we may be sure of, it is this: God wants His Priests, God wills His Priests, to be men of God. It would be blasphemous to think otherwise, and, therefore, has His Spirit declared, "be ye holy, ye who carry the vessels of the Lord."

Besides, even among the enemies of Mother Church, an unworthy Priest is looked upon as a caricature of Christ, and surely Jesus does not want such mockery, even though He bears it patiently today as He bore it patiently long ago in His own Most Sacred Person.

So, dear brother, let us lift up our hearts and souls on high. God the Father loves us with a very special love, for He has identified us in a very special manner with the Person of His Son. God the Son loves us with a love of predilection and has identified us with His mission and His Heart. God the Holy Ghost loves us with a love of Union which holds Him a Prisoner of Love within the depths of our souls and gives us a pledge of His all-powerful assistance in the work of our sanctification. Let us go forward, therefore, with confidence, day by day, along the road of life, our wills one with God's, our hearts one with Mary's. Thus we will be one with God in this life, one with God forever. Let us beg this grace of graces for each other.

GOD WILLS IT

DEAR ——:

In centuries past the crusaders went forth to fight for the Holy Land with the cry "God Wills It" ringing in their ears. You, dear ——, should have the same cry thrilling your soul as you fight day by day, that God may possess the Holy Land of your soul.

I am never tired of telling the souls that I love that God wills their sanctification. O, if souls in general would only recognize that truth, how much nobler would their lives be, how much happier would be their careers, how much more inspiring the record of their lives. God is holy, God is Infinite Holiness, and how can Infinite Holiness will otherwise than that His creatures be holy?

The evil which confronts us in this world is the product of wills, human and angelic, that abuse and have abused their God-given and noble freedom. It is the plan and the will of God to lead free creatures by the gentle invitations of grace, secured by the Supreme Oblation of Divine Love in the Person of God's

Son, back to the possession of God, back to the Home of God, back to Paradise.

You, dear ——, have only to make use of the gifts of God, I may even say reverently you have only to make use of God, to attain to the heroic heights of sanctity. Every morning at the altar-rail God gives you Himself, and with Himself all His holiness, all His strength, all that you need to make you like unto Himself. Day by day His Blessed Mother, who is yours as well, prays for you and watches over the progress of your soul in virtue, begging of her Divine Son those graces that you stand the most in need of for the perfection of your soul. Saints and angels vie with one another to promote God's glory through your advance in virtue, and friends on earth add their mite of prayer and good example to aid you up the rugged path. Away then with any truce with mediocrity in your spiritual life. God has given generously, be generous with God; that is all a saint is — one who has been generous with God, generous not by fits and starts, but steadily generous through a life, long or short, as God may have willed, but generous — always generous.

Will you pray to Mother Mary that I may be generous too?

RESTING FOR GOD

Dear ——:

I am sorry in one way to hear that you have been sick, but God knows best what we need, and I think you needed the rest God has made you take.

Rest when one is tired, rest that comes after honest toil and taken with a good conscience, is one of the sweetest things I know in the human order. By the necessity of rest, God is constantly teaching us the lesson of our limitations. It ought to make us humble; it would if we would but reflect upon it. The greatest scientist, the greatest military genius, the learned theologian, the captain of industry, the fervent saint, all must yield sooner or later to the demands of their humanity and sink into that oblivion in which they are as helpless as newborn babes. Whether we will or no, a large portion of our life is passed in sleep and for us who have Christian Faith and Hope and Love, not only that portion of our lives, but the whole of our lives should be passed in the Arms of God and close to the Heart of Mary.

I have a special devotion to those three stations of the Way of the Cross that remind us that Our Lord willed to share in His Human Nature that depth of tiredness and fatigue that is one of the most trying things that I know of. If we could only remember when we are tired in His Service that He Who was God and is God was tired to the point of complete exhaustion in ours, how much strength we would draw from His weakness. However, it is well for us to examine whether our tiredness proceeds from labor for Him or from the seekings of self. I have been tired often, more often I am afraid from the pursuit of little earthly recreations than I have been from labors undertaken for the Biggest of causes.

Take, therefore, dear ——, a good rest, take it in gratitude to the God Who gives it to you, take it with the intention of strengthening those God-given powers of body and mind, that you may be the better able to use them in the service of Jesus Christ. One does not need to be a Priest in order to serve God; God has need of servants in every walk of life; God, indeed, wills that all men should be His faithful, loving servants, and by adoption His faithful, grateful sons. I know your soul is fervent in faith, buoyant in hope, and I want it to be perfect in love; then it matters not what road you walk, that road will be always a road that leadeth Home, that road will give always to you, as to the Disciples on the way to Emmaus, the companionship of Jesus Christ. Rest now with Christ, that you may go forward with Christ tomorrow, through the busy marts of men, signed with the Sign of the Cross, a champion of Christian living, a defender of Catholic Faith.

May our Blessed Lady bless your rest, your sleeping and your waking, bless you now and always.

THE SUPREME LESSON

My Dear ——:

This is a birthday note for you. In your Christmas note to me, if you remember, you were trying to make up your mind as to whether or not you liked the weather you were then having in ——. Now, that little mental debate of yours offers your uncle an opportunity to point out to you the supreme lesson that life teaches all of us sooner or later, and, because it is the supreme lesson of life, the sooner we learn it the better for ourselves and for all others.

Now the lesson, dear ——, is this: to love and accept always and under all circumstances that which God wills, and God's will, you know, extends even to the weather.

This world of ours is the handiwork of a Master Craftsman Who loves and guides both directly and indirectly by the forces which He has created and the laws which He has given this vast universe of ours. Now little boys and girls, whether they be still young or already grown-up, will find happiness on earth and in Heaven only when they have found out as children find out who have good and wise parents that things turn out best when they obey and accept with loving trust the plans of their parents.

No snowflake falls upon the bosom of Mother Earth save by God's will, no little heart beats its joyous rhythm save by His designing, and the same supreme Creative Will of God that made the snow and your heart wills that each should fulfill in its own way His beautiful design.

Of course, there is this difference between your heart and the snowflake; the snowflake will never know its own beauty, will never be able to thank God for having created it, has never been touched by the red Blood of God's Divine Son, will melt away and become only a little tear lost in the depth of the soil; but your heart, dear ——, is destined to know the beauty of God as reflected both within itself and within the visible world around you and eventually the beauty of God as revealed in the face of His Son. Your heart can give voluntarily and freely the tribute of obedience to its Creator. Your will can cleave to God's will voluntarily and thus pay to Him the tribute of loving adherence. Your heart shall cease indeed to beat some day in this world, but only to rest until God calls its scattered elements back again to blossom in His Eternal Springtime. The little drops of water are drawn up by the mighty sun into the clouds, the scattered elements of your little heart will be drawn up by the Mightier Will of God's Uncreated Son until they gather once more to beat with ecstatic and unending joy in chorus with all those other hearts that shall have learned life's supreme lesson, the loving acceptance and adherence to God's Holy Will in all things.

Dear ——, I wish you a happy birthday,

In Our Lady's Heart.

A HOST OF LOVE

MOTHER DEAR:

This little note is to bring you my greetings for your Birthday.

There are some sentiments of the human soul so deep, so worthy of reverence, that, like the Consecrated Hosts, one hesitates to touch them. Such a sentiment, my Mother, is my love for you, and as it is my priestly privilege and duty to daily hold my God within my hands, so now is it my privilege and duty to touch with deep reverence upon that sacred subject of a Mother's love and loveliness.

A Mother's love, the Mother's love that you have given me through the years, has it not been a gleaming host of love to be consummated only by Death — nor yet by Death, Mother dear, for a Mother's love, because it is truly spiritual, transcends the boundaries of Time, and becomes, in God, eternal.

O my Mother, a host of love you have been to me and will be forever, and I, by reason of God's boundless mercies, by which I am His priest forever, according to the Order of Melchisedech, I, too, Mother, will ever have and be to God and God's Mother and you, just a host of love. Forever, FATHER PAGE.

GOD'S HARP

DEAR BROTHER IN CHRIST:

In your letter, your first letter, do you remember you asked me to give you some thoughts on the recitation of the divine office? This letter is the answer to that request.

O my Brother, to understand what our privilege is in chanting, even though it be in silence and alone, to understand our privilege it would be necessary for us to be lifted as was dear St. Paul to the angelic choirs of heaven! And herein lies, I think, our difficulty. If we but knew the gift of God, the glory of the duty that Christ through Mother Church imposes on us and which makes us one with that great symphony of praise that goes up to God in His High Heaven from His universe, both animate and inanimate, both terrestrial and celestial, then would our lips tremble with loving rapture as God's Son touched the cords of our hearts and sounded the score His Spirit wrote in the long years ago!

My Brother, kiss your breviary with a reverent prayer to God's Holy Spirit when you take it up. May Mother

Mary's hands place your heart as a harp in the hands of Christ, especially the Christ of the Eucharist if you are in Church, and then His fingers will touch the strings and His love and yours ascend to His Father in a single hymn of loving gratitude, adoration and petition.

Let me add a final recommendation: study the psalms; you will be rewarded a hundredfold in the deepening of your devotion to them.

I had hoped to see you during the vacation period, but what matters, I meet you daily

In Mary's Heart.

ALWAYS AND EVERYWHERE

Dear Sister in Christ:

I have just checked up on my Christmas mailing list and have discovered that your name is not there. Well, there are compensations awaiting us always when we accept Life's little crosses sweetly, and one of your compensations, I trust, shall be this note just for yourself. There are now so many friends for me to remember at Christmas time that a special letter to each would be out of the question. It is only God Who can give His children individual service always and everywhere!

The ramifications of this last truth, at least so it seems to me, are among the sweetest consolations of the spiritual life. To realize we have Someone always and everywhere with us, Someone Who always cares and always thinks of us, Someone Who is always ready to help us and send us a special note of love—what a consolation, what an oasis in this desert where the sun of selfishness so soon dries up the waters of friendship, excepting only such friendships as are hidden from the dust of the world in the deep well-wounds of Our Divine Friend!

Nor is this Oasis of God's dwelling with us and

within us a mirage, a figment of our imagination, a suggestion of complacency and self-love. No; nothing is more reasonable, nothing more logical, for love tends to union, and only those who are wilfully blind can doubt that God loves us, can fail to find the Light that shines in the darkness and illuminates every man who comes into this world. God's indwelling by grace in our souls, God's abiding with His friends, is the logical outcome and immediate conclusion of that Infinite Love that brought His Son to earth and that shall, please God, eventually take us, sinners, but not as sinners, to Heaven. Our soul is the goal of God's love, even as God must be the Goal of our affection.

Therefore, dear Child, set all the sails of your soul-craft to catch the breezes of Divine Love. Direct your course to the only harbor of abiding peace, the Port of Divine Union, and remember though we may imagine at times that we sail the open sea, we really never pass beyond the breakwater of Christ's arms and to find anchorage we need only cast our wills into the clear waters of God's grace and let them come to rest upon the pure white sands of His Most Holy Will.

ALL IN ALL

My Dear ——:

Digging away at my letter pile I come to a letter from one who claims kinship with a "leisurely Catholic." From the viewpoint of correspondence I must be the latter, for I am months behind in mine. However, it is the patience of my friends that is alone notable in this.

Sunday last could have been a leaf from the diary of Autumn, today Nature's fingers have clumsily but happily turned over too far and given us a day from March. Tomorrow, I suppose, will find us turned back to the proper seasonable page. Life, our life, is like the weather, is it not? Bright days, dull gray days, rainy days, days of high winds in the tree tops, days of murmuring breezes of grace within our souls, days of storm and days of peace, days of brooding loneliness and days of feverish activity as if our souls, like the gardens of the world, were being prepared for Spring. And, after all, is this not true? Only our Spring is to be eternal and our blossoms will remain in the garden of God forever.

Which thought prompts a further one; though all the world loves the Springtime yet not all souls in the world are prepared to pay the price of worthily growing so that they may be found pleasing and ready for God's strong hands to pluck them and transplant them to where the sky of tomorrow's evening melts to gold to make a sunrise in Heaven.

So, ——, whatever the weather, whatever the season, let us go forward with confidence to the appointed tasks that God's Adorable Will holds for us. After all, that is really all that matters — just that we fill our place in the loving design of Our Heavenly Father, just that through rain and sunshine, we walk hand in hand with Christ, Our Blessed Lord, just that through faithful cooperation with His Divine Spirit we come to that perfection of living wherein life is very full because God has become truly All in All.

VOCATION TO SACRIFICE

Dear Sister in Christ:

A day late as usual, but, just the same, with heartiest greetings for your birthday.

We enjoyed our little visit at ——. Somehow the seldom-had pleasures of life never lose their freshness, and their remembrance carries a fragrance that sweetens the daily bread — our daily bread of sacrifice.

Speaking of sacrifice, surely a mother's vocation is a vocation to sacrifice, if ever there was such. At the altar of love, sanctified by God's grace and consecrated by the Sacrament of Matrimony, a true mother stands hourly and ceaselessly offers up the sacrifice of all she has and is that the precious heritage of life may be extended through and in her own life to countless generations yet unborn. And, even as the Sacrifice of God's Own Son was sweetened by the depth of His Love for His Heavenly Father and for His brethren, so is the sacrifice of a true mother made lightsome by her consecrated love for her husband and her little ones, who are themselves living pledges of the abiding character of their parents' affections.

Moderns do not reflect sufficiently on the spiritual values enshrined in a true home, else they would be more skeptical of the present day propaganda so subversive of those ancient and God-given guarantees of family peace and security. Indeed, this superficiality of thought would not be possible were these bland prophets of a better world accustomed to listen to the happy voices of children and search for wisdom in the eyes of little ones.

That is why, dear ——, I am so happy over your little home. Were you and —— great novelists I would rejoice in your successes; were you great sculptors I would admire your marbles. But you have done more, far more than clothe thoughts in pleasing words; you have done better than give to images of fancy the validity of stone; you have been collaborators with God in bringing into the realm of actuality *living* masterpieces destined to adorn His and your eternal Home! Masterpieces so precious are these that He has already purchased them at no less a price than the Precious Blood of His Son Divine.

That is why, dear ——, I bless you on your birthday, and ask the Divine Sculptor to make your own soul more beautiful in grace as you labor joyously to perfect His image in the souls of your little ones. Nor shall I forget to ask her who mothered God's Son to aid you who mother so faithfully His wee brothers and sisters.

God bless you, therefore, dear ——, and may He draw you ever more closely to Himself while through you He continues the beauteous designs of His eternal Love.

FOR THE LOVE OF GOD

My Dear Child:

Your note of last week brought me happiness, for it serves notice that the grace of God is working in your soul. There is no surer sign of spiritual light than unselfish interest in the welfare, spiritual and material, of others. The soul that by loving aspiration tends upwards to God has need to balance and support its higher altitude by putting down deeper roots into the soil of our common humanity. Thus, here as elsewhere, the paradoxical nature of the spiritual life is evident, and the more nearly one approaches union with God so much the more closely will one be concerned with the welfare of one's fellow beings. And so I am pleased to see your growing attachment to Our Blessed Lord accompanied by a renewed interest in the lives God has brought into contact with your own.

How simply and clearly the remembrance of this truth serves to differentiate the wheat of true holiness from the chaff of false piety. It is better, of course, to leave judgment of the interior life of others to the One for whom each soul is as an open book; nevertheless there are times when it is necessary for the regulation of our lives for us to reach practical conclusions as to the spiritual caliber of others. In such instances I know of no safer method than the test of the attitude and activity of a soul in relation to its fellows. Fraternal charity and unselfish interest in others is one of the hardest virtues for self-love to simulate successfully. The real article costs too much and the imitation wears thin in short order. I believe that is one reason why the Master designated fraternal charity as a sure sign of His discipleship.

However, in the practice of fraternal charity there are many things concerning which it is well for you to be on guard. Genuine fraternal charity has three characteristics that distinguish it; it must be constant, disinterested, and universal. And this is but another way of saying that it must be like the charity of Christ, the Master.

How constant an element was the charity of His Heart in relation to mankind; neither lack of appreciation nor positive malice could change His friendly attitude and His willingness to help and pardon all. How unselfish and disinterested was that charity that even from the Cross was concerned with securing the welfare of His enemies. How universal was that love that envisioned not alone the men and women of His own land and race but those of every land, of every race and of every century, both young and old, rich and poor, just and unjust, and planned to envelop all these without exception in the red mantle of His Saving Blood!

And so, dear Child, as the winds of March are singing through the bare treetops as if to wake them from their winter sleep, I rejoice that the winds of God's grace are moving across your soul and rousing your mind and heart to fresh endeavor in the service of your fellow beings for the love of God.

A LITTLE WHILE

Dear ——:

I had forgotten about the remark to which you referred in your note. After all it was very much to the point. We are indeed replaceable, and the sooner and more deeply we realize this truth the better for our peace of soul and consequent union with God. In one place only God wills that we never consent, even for an instant, to being replaced, and that is in His Grace and His Son's Sacred Heart. Beyond that, speaking for myself, there are a few hearts and lives in which, apart from God's Holy Will, I would not wish to be replaced, and yours is one of these.

Thus, you see, for me holy indifference is not anticipatory in character — as long as God leaves me my dear ones I will hold them dearly; when and if He takes them — so be it.

A little while I must be brave,
For He Who takes is He Who gave,
And I know well when all are gone, —
So will the dark — and in the dawn,
I'll watch in glad surprise
Christ-rise:
And all I love, now quite a host,
(So gracious is the Holy Ghost),
Will come with Christ, and smiling say,
"We only hid —
as we were bid —
a little while away!"
Meanwhile, each wave upon Time's shore
Whispers Love's pledge "forevermore!"

Asking Our Lady to bless you, and to secure for you the grace of finding God in all His creatures, and all whom you love in God.

THE FIRST MISSIONARY

Dear Sister:

I promised you some time ago that I would write to you in the beautiful month of St. Joseph. This letter is the fulfillment of that promise.

St. Joseph, dear St. Joseph — all can find inspiration in his life and virtues. Yet it seems to me none can find greater inspiration in his life, or more powerful aid in their own, than missionaries who turn to Joseph and make the protector and guide of the Holy Family, the protector and guide of their lives. For Joseph was the first missionary, the first to carry Jesus and Mary into a pagan land. Let us study briefly some phases of his life.

The most important thing in any life is the purpose back of its living; by this above all else will our individual lives be measured and weighed by God. Now Joseph's life had one purpose, the service, the loving service of Jesus and Mary. For their sake he toiled and planned and prayed, praying that he might fulfill with the utmost perfection the sublime obligation that his vocation involved. We know, too, how fully his prayer was answered. Jesus, God's Son, chose to be born in the utmost poverty, but one consolation He gave unto Himself, the love of a perfect Mother and the care of a perfect man.

We recognize, of course, the fitness and reasonableness in this design of God, and we should likewise find added joy in this — that the supreme consolation that the Christ-Child took unto Himself He has deemed, in His love, not too great a gift to share with us. For we, too, have Mary for our Mother and Joseph for our Guardian and Guide.

One could write volumes on the missionary vocation and its exemplifications in the life of good St. Joseph. But when we had finished writing, all we had said would be summed up in this: like unto Joseph we are called to be exiles from home for the sake of advancing the interests of Jesus Christ, and like unto Joseph in exile we may have his one and only consolation, the knowledge and possession of Christ's love and His abiding presence.

OUR GREATEST FOE

DEAR SISTER:

I am answering your letter promptly, because I feel

I can point the way for you to carry on with greater courage and perfection, on the battle-lines of God. Your note indicated that you at times feel what we all have experienced — discouragement. Now discouragement is the greatest foe that we who serve The Master have to contend with. Other foes we have; other weapons are at the disposal of the spirits of wickedness. But of our foes or of the weapons our foes may use, none is more deadly than discouragement, for courage is of the essence of good soldiering, and we must be good soldiers of Jesus Christ. Therefore, I write to put you on your guard against our greatest foe.

If you analyze discouragement, my Sister, you will find that it is rooted in a lack of two of the most beautiful virtues of Christian life, Faith and Humility. If we have Faith and Humility, we can always say, paradoxical though it may seem: "Yes, I know I can do nothing of myself; but I can do all things in Him Who strengtheneth me." We must never give way to discouragement, because to do so gives courage to our enemies and tends to lessen the morale of our fellow soldiers in Christ's Army. When we feel its subtle influence stealing into our souls, even as the deadly gases of modern warfare come upon their victim, let us learn to put on our gas-masks promptly, which means nothing more or less than to take refuge in the protective armor which God has given us. It means, in simple language, hiding our weakness in the strength which is of God and in God. It means "putting on the Lord Jesus Christ," as the Soldier Apostle Paul recommended to the Christians of the first century. And having put on Jesus Christ, we will have all the strength of God at our disposal; we will have courage and confidence not in self, but in God.

O how foolish is that soul in the religious life that places confidence in its own virtue or strength! — for our virtue and strength are as the grass of the field that bows before the slightest breeze and is prostrate in the storm; whereas the weakest soul that takes refuge in Christ will be as a mighty oak, battered, perhaps, but unconquered by rain or wind. Only souls that are filled with foolish pride try to stand alone. Stand alone I pray you, Sister, but let it be alone with Christ.

OUR PEACE

Dear Brother in Christ:

Your brief note brought me happiness in the knowledge that my note had done the same for you. I am trusting this letter to reach you for the beauteous Feast of the Resurrection, to add a wee "*Pax vobiscum*" to that Supreme One that Jesus, Our Peace, will give you from out the silence of the White Host on Easter morn.

O my Brother, we who are priests need only the realization of what His Presence in the Eucharist means, in order to make us contented and happy anywhere. I have had a few cares, a few trials, a few crosses to bear during the years of my priestly life, but I thank God for them, and especially I thank Him for that grace which I know is also yours—and indeed is offered to every priest by the Divine Master—and that is the grace of taking my burdens to the feet of Jesus Eucharistic, and having them disappear, dissolve as did the morning mists over the sea of Galilee when Jesus stood on the shore and spoke in the Eastertide sunrise to the disheartened fisherman.

Let us, beginning at Easter as we kneel before Jesus in the Sacrament of His Love, let us daily thank Him, you for me and I for you, for the grace of our Eucharistic devotion. Let us beg Him to increase that devotion constantly, till the hour the veils shall part and we possess Our Peace not by Faith and Hope, but by Love made perfect by His Merciful Love and Our Mother's prayers.

LIKE GOOD ST. JOSEPH

DEAR BROTHER IN CHRIST:

I have just opened and read your note of the 8th and am answering at once. Never hesitate to remind me of forgotten obligations. I only wish I might, like good St. Joseph, know and fulfill all my duties faithfully even unto death. The more one studies his life, the more one becomes convinced he had found the secret of peace, the road of peace and walked thereon in virginal yet loving union with God's Son and God's Most Holy Mother.

Though St. Joseph was not, theologically speaking, a priest, yet when I think of priestly models, after Jesus, our Great High Priest and Mary, Mother of Priests, I place their faithful guardian first. I have written "theologically speaking" because in a wide sense, especially if it be true that Joseph performed the Circumcision of God's Only-begotten Son, then must the humble Carpenter of Nazareth be counted as sharing very closely in the exercise of priestly privileges. At any rate, blessed is that priest of the New Law who shall have even remotely approached to the height of St. Joseph's sanctity, and followed humbly in his footsteps which were ever so intimately united with those of Jesus and Mary.

Let us ask this special grace for each other during this blessed month, that we may each of us labor as Joseph labored, live as Joseph lived, love as Joseph loved, and die as Joseph died in the arms of God's Own Son. Perfect love of God, virginal love of Mary, with the courage of a clean heart and a grace-fortified will, Joseph must be our model both in the hidden obscurity of our little workshops and the open places of our pilgrimages. May we know when and how to flee the world as Joseph did. May we, like him, hold the presence of God's Son and God's Mother as our lifelong and chiefest consolation. May we, like Joseph, take Jesus whither He would be carried, and may Jesus take us whither we would wish some day to arrive— Nazareth-town of Heaven with Mother Mary to welcome us and bid us rest a while by the fireside till the evening meal shall be served.

THE LOW ROAD

My Dear Child:

Do you suppose that possibly part of God's design in making His children wait for the things they desire is to increase their joy in the final attainment? Certainly this is the effect in many cases, and always this will be true when what we have prayed for is something worthy of prayer.

What mysterious depths the subject of prayer involves! Think, for example, of Jesus, Lord of the Universe, urging His disciples to pray to the Master of the Harvest that He send laborers into His vineyard! The harvest is indeed His, but He demands prayers; prayer is the first form of cooperation He requires. When we would have expected Him to send His disciples into the fields, He tells them instead to pray, and then, in answer to their prayer, He will send laborers into His own harvest!

What a lesson we find here of the importance of prayer in the economy of salvation. Jesus wants our zeal directed toward souls, but He wishes us also and as a matter of first importance to recognize the place of grace in the work of salvation. He wants us never to forget that in Him and in Him alone rests for the laborers the inspiration to begin, the strength to maintain and the supreme grace to finish well all works of apostolic zeal. Only God's grace can make real laborers for His vineyard, and the avenue to this grace as to all others is that of prayer.

Be happy therefore, dear child, in this, for though you will never reach the mission fields in person, you can, and please God will, visit them daily by the hidden road of prayer. Through God you will reach the first-line trenches and there by God's merciful designs, angel hands will distribute the precious graces your impetrations and sacrifices shall have won.

To me one of the most consoling features of doing things for Jesus, is this: He always knows, He always sees, no matter how minute the action. The greatness of His Love transmutes the smallest gesture of my devotion into gold; while the greatness of His Love for others, especially for His Missionaries, makes Him hasten to translate the least sacrifice made for them in terms of divine generosity.

See, child, how sweet a thing it is to serve so good a Master, and how easy it is to help others by walking daily with Jesus and His blessed Mother on the lowly road of prayer.

VIA DOLOROSA

My Dear Child:

I do not know just when I shall visit ——, but when God wills it I shall make it a point to see you. A cross like yours cannot be carried alone, and why should you attempt to do so when Jesus is so ready to share it with you?

It is easy to understand the plans of God when these for the moment coincide with those of our own fashioning. Perhaps you are not aware that self-love can forge plans so surreptitiously as to deceive all but souls very deeply grounded in humility. It is quite another story when God's will for us is obviously different from that we would have chosen. This latter is your case, and the only sensible advice that I can offer is simply the old but always sane counsel of embracing Christ's holy will and making it your own by, and in love. If this does not lessen the suffering it will at least supply a powerful motive for sustaining you on your via dolorosa.

After all the measure of our sanctity—that is of our nearness and likeness to God—depends not upon our having our own will on earth but on our following in the footsteps of One who did not His own will but the will of the Father Who had sent Him. Not when God's will grooves into mine but when mine fits into God's is there reason to be assured of the genuineness of my affections for my Heavenly Father.

Since these things are so, and it seems to me one cannot deny them, I would recommend you to rest content with your present situation and seek therein, day by day, your sanctification. If God denied you His love, then, indeed, you would have cause for grief; but when He merely denies you a specific manner of manifesting your love, then you owe it to Him to smile even through the shadows of self-love's disappointments. Since you cannot be a missionary in ——, be one in spirit like the Flower-soul of Lisieux and God's Holy Spirit will bear the fragrance of your love and unselfish sacrifice everywhere.

Asking Our Lady to bless you.

QUO VADIS

My Dear Child:

I can grasp quite well your reaction to the biography of which you wrote. It is true no one can doubt the sincerity of —— ——'s soul or fail to admire the natural virtues her life so amply illustrates, but let us be mindful of the first purpose of our existence which is to love and glorify not our fellow creatures but our Creator and Heavenly Father. This is why, personally, I cannot enthuse over any life that has not achieved this first and highest end. That is why a life like that of Mother Rose Hawthorne carries the warmth of the spring, while a life like that of —— —— has about it something of the coldness and bleakness of winter.

It is true, of course, in the physical order that winter glorifies God as well as spring or summer, but it is the sunshine that makes all seasons glorious, and the sunshine of our spiritual existence is faith in, and love of God. I may be a little fanatical on this point but surely logic is on my side; for when God has proposed Himself as the legitimate Object of our affections, how piteously insignificant all other achievements become!

We must, of course, admire the natural virtues in these great ones of the earth. In their respect the words of Our Blessed Lord relative to the greater wisdom of the children of this world in their generation are verified. Their industry, their single-mindedness, their patience in adversity, their modesty in success, their tireless devotion to the causes they have espoused, excite our admiration and are surely worthy of emulation. Yet when such as these minister to a suffering humanity and fail to recognize the greater Glory and the higher Beauty beyond, they seem to me as travelers who tarry at a pleasant wayside inn and miss the glory of the sunset.

I want you, dear Child, to appreciate and enjoy the wayside inn of our humanity but not to rest permanently within the limits of its satisfactions. One by one your fellow guests must go before you, or you before them, out into the twilight alone. When that hour comes for you, I want the Voice that calls you to be the familiar voice of a Lover long expected and lovingly awaited: I want you to be able to go forth into the twilight not as one ending a pleasant visit but as one beginning life.

APRIL

April weeps; her tears are not tears
of despair, but of expectancy.

SHOWERS

DEAR ——— :

Your last letter told me that it has been raining, and that the rain has dampened your ardor. Really, Child, this will never do. Shall we not be as unflinching in the service of God as worldlings are in the service of self?

Men of the world, pressing forward toward their chosen goal, turn up their coat collars when a storm breaks, pull their hats down firmly, and hurry on. Showers of adversity may not stop their progress.

Shall such as these put us to shame? Our dear Lord, Himself, remarked this fact, and His comment on it was—"the children of this world are wiser in their generation than the children of light." Let Him not recall His statement as He looks down in love on us!

Courage! Were there no showers, there would be no flowers in the spring. Brave hearts love the rain of adversity for what it accomplishes within the garden of their souls. The fairest virtue-flowers only open in full glory when they have received their full share, not only of sunshine, but of rain as well. This is God's law. Jesus did not exempt Himself from it. Upon His ears fell a rain of blasphemy, upon His back the cruel rain of the scourges, upon His face (one shudders to think of it) the blows, aye the spittle of barbarians, and every blow as it fell, every mouth as it struck tore His Blessed Mother's heart as well as His.

Shall the servant be greater than the Master? What seek you, Jesus or His Crown? Nay, if you seek His Crown, behold it is composed of thorns that thirst to drink His Precious, Precious Blood.

Courage then, Child. After the shower comes the rainbow of Eternal Love, and at the end of the rainbow no fabulous gold, but a very Real Heart that burning with Divine Love has been shining down on you all the while, though you knew it not.

For love of Him walk joyous of the rain that beats against your face the while.

THE STREET VENDOR—AND CHRIST

DEAR SISTER:

I received your letter today, and am answering at once for I want to help you if I can in your little difficulties which are indeed to be expected in the Religous Life. I am so glad you mentioned them, for if you only spoke of the joys, how should I know the trials except on general supposition.

Now listen—.no cross, no crown; were there not sacrifice involved in the religious life, what would be the special merit in living it? In the eyes of men and angels, aye in the sight of God, the religious life is held in high regard because of the sacrifice such a life demands, sacrifice for the sake of a hidden love and an Invincible Lover, Christ.

The Religious Life bespeaks a Divine Romance—a Romance involving a poor, weak little creature and an all-rich, all-powerful Great Creator. The world like a street vendor holds out its little tawdry attractions—the movies, a dance, a visit, a ride. God holds out just His silent aching virgin arms, His pierced hands, His wounded loving Heart. O, if He were only visible, all were easy, but if all were easy, where would be the glory of persevering, self-sacrificing love?

Steal, my child, into the silent chapel when your heart begins to grow weary of life or lonely for the old home. Kneel very quietly; try to let the silence sink into the depths of your being, and when all is silent within, ask yourself slowly these questions.

Who loves me best? Where is He? Why is He here? Has He ever wanted consolation? (Gethsemane.) Has He ever been tired? (The Way of the Cross.) Did He go on? For whom?

O child, the longest film, the longest ride, the longest visit, the longest life, all, all these must at last come to their ending. How sweet will life be in its ending for the soul that has lived for God! Not in the joy of Christmas or Easter is the glory of your life, but in this, that you have come to Eastertide by way of Calvary; in this, that for the love of Jesus you have crucified yourself.

I wish you this grace that you may so grow in the true love of Him, that you will come to crave suffering, trials, loneliness — the Cross. When it grows too heavy, seek Jesus, your Lover, in the Blessed Sacrament. He and Mother Mary will help you, for they know just what each heart throb costs.

When there is anything as reasonable as to serve Jesus, anything so profitable as to suffer for Him, anything as sweet as to love Him, I will counsel you differently. Till then let us rejoice to be His, His let us hope and pray forever.

AN EASTER GLORIA

Dear Friend:

Does your heart want to sing at Eastertide? I trust it shall this Eastertide at least. The world laughs, or at least politely smiles at us — but let it laugh or smile — we are Christ's and Christ is risen triumphant in our hearts.

I love Thee and I glorify Thee, Jesus, my Sweet God, because Thou has triumphed over my cold rock-like heart. I glorify Thee and give Thee thanks for all the glory Thou has wrought over field and mountain, sea and glen, but most of all, Beloved Jesus, for the glory Thou has revealed within the hearts and souls of manly men, and noble women, and little children's eyes. Thy beauty rests upon the sea at dawn, the fields at noon, the hills at twilight, where the thrushes sound the taps of dying day. But in the souls, by Christian faith and hope and love made fair, the souls where dwells Thy Spirit's living breath, ah, there, Beloved Jesus, Thy Beauty shall not die, nor pass, but ever be more gloriously revealed unto Eternal Light. Glory, therefore, Sweet Jesus, to Our Father be, and to His Son, Our Saviour, which Thou art, and to Thy Spirit, All Eternal One.

Ever, as in Thy Mother's Heart. Amen.

TO A YOUNG MAN

DEAR ——:

I am sorry I missed you at the train last Saturday—but it could hardly be helped without shirking my duties here—so I know you will understand.

Now that you are at a distance, I am going to say some things I might hesitate to say if you were here. First of all, for some years now you have been a source of consolation to me. Because of a growing feeling of confidence in your reliability, I have come to feel like a captain looking over his fellow officers and saying to himself—"there's so and so; we can rely upon him." God has given you special gifts of both nature and grace. Remember they are from Him—make use of them gratefully, faithfully. That you may do this—be faithful above all else to prayer. The man who prays persistently, perseveringly, will never be a proud man, and proud men are the ones that take the most disastrous falls.

That you may pray well, try to realize in a practical way the personal and individual interest of God in you and in your life, and all that this interest of God has brought to you. Our God is very near to us—so near that we need only turn inward to hold converse with Him. As near in His Humanity as the nearest Church; nearer in His providential care than our own heartbeats. Speak to Him, listen to Him, obey Him, and your life will be founded upon the safest of all foundations — union with the Holy Will of God.

As for your relations with others, I know well you have left your heart here at home. It is, I believe, well placed. Leave it here. No man is fully worthy of the love that a noble and clean-hearted girl gives him. No man who understands what such love is will challenge my statement. God has in His infinite generosity dowered you with such a love. Strive to be worthy of it — that is the particular gratitude God asks for such a gift.

My Love is Christ and Mary, and I shall ask my Love to keep you — my brother — always true to your love and thus true to the Divine Love which giveth love to you and all the world.

THE REAL TEST

Dear Sister in Christ:

I am very much pleased with your spirit. Nothing so fully reveals the depth of our spiritual life, the reality of our love of God, as the spirit of cheerful conformity to His holy will in the varied and multitudinous events of life. It is easy to deceive ourselves when God's will, as it were, conforms itself to our will, and skies are blue above us and sunshine in our hearts; it is easy at such times to deceive ourselves as to the depth of our spiritual life. In reality such conditions offer no testing worthy of the name. The most selfish child behaves and smiles when everyone is waiting on its whims.

The real test of a soul is found not in sunshine, but in storm. Like the seaworthiness of vessels, so the spiritual value of our souls is proven only by the way they stand up under the wind and the waves of the open stormy seas. To me, the sea and the things of the sea have always had a very deep appeal. I love to think of our souls as sturdy yet lightsome craft, blue of hull and white of sail, smashing head on into seething seas, smothered for a moment, but always lifting their heads bravely up again and plunging onward toward the shores of Eternity and the Port of Heavenstown. The words of New England's sublimest singer often echo in my heart—

Build me straight, O Worthy Master,
Staunch and true, a worthy vessel
That shall laugh at all disaster
And with wave and whirlwind wrestle.

Make these words a daily prayer unto the Beloved Master-builder of your soul, dear Sister, and fear not but that He will bring you safe through all life's stormy seas, safe home to Marystown and a mooring in the Harbor of His Eternal Love. I bless you.

"RESURGAM"

DEAR ——:

Back of the main altar in the parish where I spent many happy years there is inscribed a single word, "Resurgam"; in English, "I shall rise again." It seems to me, dear ——, that this one word sums up the deepest meaning of a life of Faith, and the life of Faith is the only life to live.

A life without Faith, what a hopeless thing it is! In reality, there are few lives absolutely void of Faith; it may not be much more than faith in self, or a blind, vague groping like that which we make for a door knob or electric light tassel in the dark; but, nevertheless, we know the knob or the tassel is there, and so we search with confidence. Thus, or so it seems to me, many of our separated brethren grope; they believe in the Truth, the Way, the Life, and they search with confidence in the dark. May Our Blessed Lady bring them safe to the gates of Paradise and the Light of the World.

But we walk, or certainly should walk, joyously in

the sunshine, confidently through the shadows, unerringly through the night, for we know in Whom we have placed our Trust and that never, never shall we be confounded.

Now all this is but a preface to the one thing I write to tell you, which is this: God has taken one dear to you. You cannot follow her out beyond the starry spaces, but her soul sends back across the great frontier one message to you and to all who mourn beside a Christian's grave, deep in your soul faith transmits that message at once so simple and so sublime, "Resurgam — I shall rise again."

O Blessed Word, coming first from the lips of God's Eternal Son, finding echo in the deepest recesses of the human soul, breathing consolation to the dying and those who watch beside them, bespeaking the ultimate yearning of all creatures and all creatures' confidence in the ultimate will of their Creator that they shall live again and greet their Saviour and their dear ones face to face.

This, dear ——, is the full message of the Eastertide, for Love Undying has in death won us Life, and so we may well brush aside the tears of mourning in the exultant joy of our Faith in His Resurrection which has made it possible for us to walk down through the Valley of the Shadow of Death fearing no evil and up again beyond to the Sunrise of an Eternal Easter morn.

May Our Blessed Mother lead us safe thereto.

IDEALS

My Dear ——:

I want you to know how pleased I was to learn through your good sister ——, of your persevering efforts to hold to your ideals amid the adverse surroundings in which you at present find yourself. "God be praised" is all that I can say; "God be praised" for that gallant little band of souls that refuse to purchase questionable pleasures, earthly popularity and human companionship at the price of the unquestionable displeasure of God, Heavenly estrangement and the loss of Divine Friendship. God has paid too much, too big a price for our souls, to sell them so cheaply. Let us not defraud the Divine Purchaser of what He has bought and paid for with the coin of His Heart's Blood.

I know you will say perhaps that this involves a great deal of will-power and the sacrifice of much that is dear to human nature. Very well; as a priest who is no longer young in God's service, let me assure you that in the end those who surrender their ideals are the unhappiest of mortals even in this world. It is not possible to break ourselves loose from God's Commandments without enslaving ourselves promptly in the arms of the world, the flesh and the devil. Some worldlings sneer at the supposed slavery of the children of God, but those who still maintain some vestige of untrammeled reasoning will confess that no one follows the pathway of their unbridled fancies but soon finds himself enmeshed in an ever-increasing network of chains forged in the fires of hell. It has been my happiness, as it is the happiness of every priest, to release many such a soul from its bonds, and I have never released one who was not ready to admit the fact of his slavery and that his indulgence had brought him neither lasting peace nor happiness.

Therefore, I write to you who are still only a little girl facing the highroad of life, and say to you, please be wise enough to profit by the experience of those who have traveled the road ahead. Please turn a deaf ear to the hawkers and fakers whose tents and pavilions line the way; please carry the treasure of your physical and spiritual integrity with care; please answer the onslaught of the three highwaymen of humanity with a tightening of your hand on the staff of the ideals of your childhood which your good mother placed within your hand, and answer calmly and bravely to their threats and entreaties, *No Surrender*.

May Our Blessed Lady keep you to your Journey's End.

"THE MISSING LINK"

Dear Brother in Christ:

This is a somewhat tardy answer to your after-Christmas letter.

I am so glad to learn that you find happiness in the service of others. No man really should enter the Priesthood of Jesus Christ unless he is at least firmly resolved to seek his own happiness in giving happiness to others rather than seeking it in personal gratification, however legitimate its source may be. Our Divine Model and Exemplar said of Himself, that He came "Not to be ministered unto but to minister to others" and how can we be truly "other Christs" unless we make His policy our own standard?

Of course, all this is at variance with the accepted code of paganism, both ancient and modern, but that is the best proof that it is truly Christian. Our Master clearly foresaw the struggle between the two ideals that would be perpetuated through the centuries. He did not compromise nor seek to avoid the issue, rather did He indicate and define it, and crystallized its meaning by the simple yet profound declaration, "No man can serve two Masters."

If you will, dear Brother in Christ, it is Christ Who is really the Missing Link necessary to restore the union of man with His Creator. He it was Who by His Incarnation and Redemption restored once more the intimacy that God had willed to have with His rational creatures. This intimate union Christ now continues to exercise by means of His Mystical Body, of which we are called to be the priestly members.

Let us strive, therefore, both by prayer and practice,

to perfect ourselves in the spirit of sacrifice which is Christ's spirit, and may His Holy Spirit perfect our souls and make of them so many links of a golden chain of love, binding Humanity's heart to the Heart of Humanity's Saviour in the bosom of Mother Church.

Pray for me, my Brother, to the Mother of Our Lord.

OUR GROUNDS OF HOPE

My Dear Ones in Christ:

Before the purple shadows shroud our souls in the memory of Christ's Passion, I am taking advantage of the kindness of my Superior to write you a word of greeting for the glorious sunrise of another Easter morn. I would like to write to you individually, but this year that will not be possible, so I ask you to be contented in sharing this one letter knowing that I hold you all with all love in the Hearts of Jesus and Mary.

Easter means the triumph of Faith and Hope even as Calvary meant triumph of His Love. We are aware that our little lives will presently be submerged beneath the waves of Time. We know, though we are reluctant to admit it, that the relentless hands of Death will snatch from us our dear ones. Where then is our ground for lasting contentment, hope and happiness?

O souls that are dear to me, it is because Faith speaks to us of God's eternal love as revealed to us in the life and death and Resurrection of His Only-begotten Son that we must find the sure ground of our hope, our contentment and our peace.

It is because Jesus Christ demonstrated by His Resurrection that He was what He claimed to be, God's Eternal Son, and therefore Master of Life and Death, that we may look calmly to the future and walk bravely into the shadows of the valley of Death, confident in His Power and His Will to conduct us — who believe in His Name — safely through that valley to the eternal hills and the City of His Father which He has willed should be our Eternal Home.

I think we do not reflect enough on the joys God has prepared for those who love Him, and this is one reason why our present difficulties seem so burdensome. One of the sweetest joys of Heaven will be without doubt our reunion with those we love.

I am very well and very happy in the service of God's Blessed Mother.

LIFE MORE ABUNDANT

My Dear ——— :

Sometimes the little surprises of life furnish us great joy; now this note will certainly be a big surprise and consequently I hope will bring you at least a little pleasure. You have done silently so many favors for me, I feel you are entitled to both the surprise and the pleasure.

One of my favorite themes in directing souls who are, as we say, "in religion," is the beautiful religious life of many souls who are, as it were, in the world; and conversely, I love to point out to souls whom God's Will holds in the world that they have nevertheless the opportunity to live lives of intimate union with God; and what but this union with God is the End of Religious Life and Religion? Christianity if it reveals anything reveals this — a God not only loving His creatures but seeking as well their love in return. No matter who we are or where we are — our fundamental happiness will depend upon the degree in which we shall have responded to this demand, this seeking of God.

If religious who think they have trials and troubles could take your place for a day, it is my guess they would return to their convents with great satisfaction and kneeling in the silence of Divine Love illumined by that wee flame men call Faith, thank the Giver of all good gifts for the many mercies and great love their lives cloister.

But you, too, my dear Sister in Christ, have the same Divine Lover waiting you; the doors to His Home are seldom closed, the doors of His Heart are always open. How blessed is the soul that must grow weary at times of men's words, and even her own thoughts, who has learned to seek and find and listen to the Eternal Word of God. We have only lived on the surface of life till we have entered into the crypt of our own soul and found God waiting us there! Yes, and because the depths of our own souls are sometimes such dark places, so musty and dusty with but the faint memory-ray of the graces they once held, God in His ineffable tenderness has given us those other crypts — the often dark and dusty chapels where the Light of the World waits so patiently to pour His blessed sunshine into the cold and famished souls of men.

That you may have many friends and many consolations is my wish, dear ——, but that Jesus may be your Chief Friend and your Deepest Consolation is my prayer.

BEYOND THE VEILS

My Dear ——:

Jesus, it would seem, has been forging one by one — and swiftly of late years — the links that are to bind you closer to Heaven. It is, of course, the vision of Faith that alone makes it possible to see things in this light when one of our dear ones has slipped through the veils of life. But, thanks be to God, we have been granted that vision, that gracious gift of a Heavenly Father, and in its light we can walk with quiet confidence even to the edge of an open grave and stand there sorrowing but not despairing while the earth claims back its clay.

There is a profound fitness in the choice Our Blessed

Saviour made of the Resurrection as the final proof of His Divinity and the ultimate pledge of our own resurgence from the grave. Death had mocked at man from that sad hour of the primeval sentence. Death still mocks at earthly Power, Pleasure, Beauty, Pride, but Death can no longer mock at those happy children of God who by Faith and obedience to Faith's authentic voice clothe their souls in robes of immortal glory.

Death remains, indeed, the ultimate and effectual barrier to any merely earthly Utopian program of life. Death must always mark the margin of worldly achievement. It is only Christ Who has been able to achieve beyond that frontier, Christ and those who have become members of His members.

But since Christ has granted us this participation in His triumph, why should we not build for ourselves mansions in Heaven? Why, for example, should not you and —— plan for yourselves and the little ones now so much of your every heart beat a home upon the eternal hills? Time, to be sure, brings its inevitable separations but when fathers and mothers have made of their lives fair partnerships with God, then surely there remains for them just as inevitable reunions beyond the veils.

Thus, dear ——, do I conceive of your living your life, thus do I pray you may achieve in God your high vocation both as wife and mother, thus do I trust to find you happy in eternity. Perhaps, then at least, we, bachelors of God, will have time to rest at the firesides where Divine Love burns brightly, and bless the friends of our youth. Asking Our Lady to keep you and —— and the children ever beneath her maternal mantle and promising you my prayers for ——'s soul.

THE POT OF GOLD

My Dear ——:

I am ready indeed to share your sorrow and could

have wished the privilege of visiting your dear mother before her death. Whisper those words so pleasing to a Heavenly Father, "Blessed be God's Holy Will."

For the preservation of interior peace at times like this it is quite necessary for souls to take refuge in the living-room of Faith. God has meant us to live therein always but it is often only when the storms of life arise that souls are willing to seek such shelter and study more intimately God's design for life. When perforce souls do so, they suddenly discover hidden beneath the somber draperies of trial, or concealed from casual observation by the shadows of disappointments, a wealth of precious gifts.

In the present instance, your dear mother dying without special consolation was thereby given a final grace of more perfect configuration to her Suffering Redeemer. Surely it is a special grace to be like Jesus in even a minor detail of life; and dying is not a minor detail but an event of supremest importance.

God, however, is ever graciously mindful of human limitations and that is why, though the privilege of special attention for your dear one was not granted, yet now she shall have the greater privilege of the Holy Sacrifice, and I am sure, if she be waiting without the gates, as the Precious Blood pleads for her, Divine Love will open wide the heavenly portals.

"Blessed are they that mourn for they shall be comforted," our dearest Jesus has promised and surely with Mary and Martha we will not fail to proclaim our faith in Him who is both Everlasting Truth and Love Eternal. Having wept Himself, Jesus will be slow to condemn tears, but why not let the sunshine of His love break through the clouds of the present moment and arch your horizon with a rainbow of bright-hued hope?

Even though you must still wait for the pot of gold at the foot of the rainbow, purchase in the present moment the gold of Christ's love with the pennies of cheerful sacrifice and loving resignation.

Asking Our Lady to bless you always.

FATHER

Dear Brother in Christ:

Two of your . . . friends have brought me news of your dear father's death, have asked me to say Mass for him, and to notify you of their request. With their desires it is a pleasure to comply.

It is always a pleasure to me to offer the Holy Sacrifice for a father's soul. How could I love the Heavenly Father from Whom all paternity proceeds and not reverence those reflections of His Image and refractions of His Attributes which are given to men in the life and character of every noble father?

I think we who are priests should be especially devoted to the fathers through whom we have received the gift of life and to the office of fatherhood in whose spiritual functions we have the privilege of participating. It is ever in the spiritual elements of fatherhood that the reflections of the Divine Paternity are most clearly discernible; and, since this is so, how jealously we should guard those characteristics of our priestly life which bring to us from faith-guided hearts the sweet and holy title of "father."

Moreover, you, as a shepherd of souls, even more than I as a religious, have the obligation of being truly a father. And since you are such, striving always for the material as well as the spiritual well-being of your people, going before them in sacrifice, counseling them first by example and then by preachment, guiding them gently yet firmly, strengthening the wavering, confirming the strong, hastening the slothful, and checking those whose unguided zeal might lead them from the safe path of devotion—because of these things, I know, it is pleasing to the Heavenly Father that you should claim with humble gratitude the sweetest of titles given by men to men; yes, given by men to God. That is why from the depth of my heart I whisper to you with the murmur of my pen moving across the white surface of this note, "God bless you, Father, and may Our Heavenly Father keep your daddy for you unto eternal years!"

HEAVEN OR HELL

MY DEAR ——:

I have heard from Father —— that you are intent upon studying for the priesthood in a religious congregation. If this is so, and you can meet the essential requirements, I will be glad to arrange an interview. But first let me state the requirements, and then you can decide for yourself whether or not you wish to go further.

As regards mental capacity, all communities today are looking for the best. On this point the most satisfactory thing will be for you to submit your scholastic grades. Sound judgment is undoubtedly of greater importance than scholastic standing, but unfortunately only time and experience can reveal this important factor in a candidate. Teaching communities, like our own, demand both high scholastic standing and good judgment.

Secondly, normal health is required to meet the exactions of the years of formation and then of the active apostolate.

Lastly—and most important of all—what have you in mind? Why do you desire to be a priest? If I could look into your soul and read the answer to these last questions, I would know at once how to advise you wisely. I am going to be a bit blunt, therefore; please remember I have many duties waiting me. I will give you a personal questionnaire to submit yourself to. If honestly you can answer in the affirmative to its questions, then by all means go forward towards the glorious goal of the priesthood, and I, or any other priest, will be only too glad to help you. But if you in honesty cannot answer these questions in the affirmative, especially the first one, then in God's name and for your own salvation do not go ahead. Here they are:

1. Is the love of God the fundamental purpose you have in mind in aspiring to the priesthood? (Don't go into the priesthood to save *your own soul,* choose matrimony or a monastery for that.)

2. Do you know what human love is — I mean in an honest way — and are you ready to renounce it permanently?

3. Read Kipling's "If" and decide whether or not by God's grace you can, as we say, "take it." By this I mean can you put up with hard obediences, misunderstandings, treatment — at least subjectively — unfair, uncongenial companions, monotonous assignments, separation from relatives and friends, etc.?

My dear boy, Christ's priesthood and the religious life are the most wonderful things in the world but only to souls who are capable of living in the high altitudes of grace. If you love God supremely you can be supremely happy therein, and that is almost heaven. But if you don't love God at the beginning of the journey, the chances are you will not love Him at its end, and if you do not love God at the journey's end, that will certainly be hell.

I hope I have not frightened you, but the priesthood and the religious life never needed real men and real lovers of God more than at the present moment — when the world is waiting for the sunrise.

THE HOME FIRES

My Dear ——:

I know you will pardon this note when I tell you I am one of your brother's closest friends. Indeed so much are we of one heart and mind in the blessed service of Christ and Our Lady that perhaps better than anyone else I may say I know his soul; and knowing his soul, I feel I know yours, which he has told me often was so like to his as to be identified with his own in Christ.

First of all, I need not remind you of the tremendous privilege of being the sister of a priest. This is a vocation in itself! For all men need the kindly touch of womankind, and we priests must seek that ennobling inspiration under Mary Queen in our mothers and our sisters. Nay, more, in the faithful performance of that vocation which is truly yours, you are, day by day, inscribing not only your brother's, but your own name as well, never to be effaced, within the crimson glory of His Sacred Heart.

Do all, therefore, that rests within your power to encourage your brother to perseverance in his brave resolve to spend himself without reserve for Jesus in the mission fields. Only a living Faith can inspire such action. Only an abiding Hope can dictate such a policy. Only a Love pure as a mountain stream is capable of such devotion. Such Faith, such Hope, such Love, I wish you, and indeed am already aware that you possess.

I know of no greater sacrifice you could make unto Jesus crucified for the advancement of His Kingdom. I know that you have made this sacrifice in a spirit of deep, spiritual joy, and therefore, I congratulate you with all my heart.

Time marches onward, our souls pass onward, to judgment and Eternity. How happy you will be, when you meet Jesus, that you banked all His precious gifts, and above all your priestly brother within the shelter of the Sacred Heart. Be not afraid, but rather rejoice in the supremeness of the sacrifice, for the greater the gift, the greater the love that inspired it and the surer the rewards awaiting at the bench of an

All-just Judge. Be not afraid, Jesus never wishes to take back His gifts; He only wishes them to be appreciated as truly gifts of His Love, and then placed swiftly for safe keeping within His bleeding wounds. There, my dear ——, they will be safely kept for you in life, and given back to you in death, and death will thus be sweetened in anticipation of eternal joys.

In the Sacred Heart I know your brother meets you and greets you day by day. In the Sacred Heart the leagues of the sea and the miles of dust-stained roads mean nothing. There, in Christ's Heart, your generosity has won you a permanent abiding, there you will be always one with your brother, there you will help to keep the home fires burning until God's soldiers are all come Home. Please pray to Our Lady for me.

THE GENTLE COMMAND

Dear Brother in Christ:

The New Testament pages are thronged with scenes that reflect the glorious Love of the Sacred Heart falling like the rays of a dying sun across a winter's evening; but few of the New Testament pictures are more soul-stirring than that scene in the glorious First Eastertide when the Risen Master gave to poor penitent Peter both the opportunity to atone for his threefold denial and the gentle command to feed His lambs and sheep.

Three times, so that it might be more deeply impressed upon His Captain's soul, did the Divine Commander reiterate that charge. How His gentle words surcharged with love must have burnt their way into the mind and heart of Peter. "Feed My Lambs, Feed My Sheep." We can almost hear the whole soul of Peter crying out, "O gentle, forgiving Master, I will indeed feed Thy flock and care for it. I will feed it with Thy Own Flesh and Blood. I will guard it at the price of my own life. I will envelop it in the red mantle of Thy Own Precious Blood."

O my brother, as you stand at the altar morning by morning, and nourish your own soul at the Mystic Wounds of Christ, and then turn to feed the lambs and sheep of Christ's flock, hear those words of the Gentle Commander echoing in your own soul. The Master was speaking to us all, all of us who should be the officers of His Army; and to us has come the Gentle Command born of Love, that we should feed the little ones, yes, and those who are no longer little but old and gray and calloused by the rough hands of Life's tribulations, that we should feed them one and all with His Own Flesh and Blood — for Divine Love would not leave us orphans nor could the Good Shepherd leave His flock without adequate provision for its nourishment and care.

Let us, my brother, carry out that Gentle Command of the Master with loving gentleness and patient thoroughness — let us feed the flock of Christ.

WHAT PRICE GLORY?

Dear Brother in Christ:

It gives me great happiness to know that my brief words of encouragement have been helpful to you and I will be only too glad to continue to write you from time to time.

I have seen enough and learned enough during my years in the priesthood to know that once out in the actual field of the missions, one comes face to face with the grim realities of the unending war between God and Satan for souls. It is not a dress parade, it is not the place for dreamers, but for soldiers — men who are willing to give as much and suffer as much for God and His interests as thousands of others have done for personal interests or for country. It is a real fight, and well you know it.

Very well, therein lies your glory! Just because it is hard, discouragingly hard at times, just because the odds seem against you and you fight, as it were, alone; just because you have to suffer and battle and battle and suffer, just because of this you shall be glorified by Our General in the Victory Parade that ends forever this little world of ours.

What price glory? For us the same Price the Master paid in His Passion and on His Cross! And when otherwise? We want, if we love Him, to share His lot, to pay His price, to drink His chalice.

May Our Lady help us both in the battle and give us the victory that God has promised to her arms.

NO SURRENDER

Dear Sister in Christ:

If I mistake not, I promised this letter quite some time ago. At any rate it is better to keep our promises tardily than not at all. Would that even tardily we might give God all we have promised Him. On this point especially, even though we never succeed, we must never surrender; that is the all-important point, that is the grace we must ask for humbly and perseveringly. May Our Lady of Good Counsel help you in making your novices realize the importance of this truth and in putting it into practice.

The great danger, as you know probably much better than I, the great danger in the religious life is the surrender to mediocrity. Such a surrender is really more than a danger; it is a failure, a defeat for God's side, a victory for the world, the flesh and the devil. The very essence of the religious life is the unending lifelong pursuit of sanctity, a battle to death and unto death with self in its various ugly manifestations. The rules of our warfare are clear cut, the method of successful combat not so difficult to comprehend. The trouble rests not with our weapons but with ourselves.

We fail to obey Our Captain's orders; we begin to slack up in our drill, neglect the minor details of good soldiering, and finally we find ourselves in very truth imprisoned in mediocrity, and hence, by that very fact, a failure in Christ's army, a sorrow in His Heart.

No surrender, therefore, is what we must not only practice but preach as well, dear Sister, in a position similar to yours. No surrender to anyone but Christ and surrendering to Christ means, if lived up to, conquering all the world.

Let us pray for each other, dear Sister in Christ, and kindly ask your novices to pray that Our Lady's servants may never lower her colors except in salute to their Queen.

RIPENED WHEAT

My Dear Child:

May this letter add an extra though modest measure to the joy of your Easter-tide. While we are young — and, indeed, some are always young — Christmas is the center of our spiritual year. But for those of us who find our shoulders yielding to the weight of Life's burdens, to those of us who are growing old, the spirit and message of Easter assume a growing importance and mark a date no less vital than Christmas on our spiritual calendars. It is not that we have forgotten the joys of our childhood in grace, but rather that we find it more consoling to look forward to the hope of the future than to look back over the road we have travelled. Our trust is vested in God's Mercy rather than His Justice. Our life fits better the rôle of Magdalen at the tomb than that of Mother Mary beside the manger.

Meanwhile it behooves us in the daily resurrection of our powers to devote ourselves to the task of preparing for that last and final slumber whose waking will mean so much to us. Life for the thoughtful Christian is a rehearsal for death, or let us say, a rehearsal for deathless life, that life which Our Redeemer has pledged us in the might of His Power and Love. To such souls as these the things of Faith are living, almost tangible realities; the Christ of the wheaten veils thrusts aside each morn the stone of care from the portals of their souls; graces like gentle mists refresh the well-seeded fields of their conscious hours, while angel wings form an invisible bower about their repose.

This, dear child, is the life of Faith, the risen life to which your Faith invites. You in a special degree have need of cultivating this manner of living, for you are a missionary, and missionaries perhaps more than any other class of Christians, must seek their consolations in the things of Faith.

Thank God then, dear child, for the appreciation of the things of Faith which He has given you. In the end, these are the truths that really matter. When evening comes, as come it must to all, it is not past pleasures that will prove your consolation but the memory of the labors and sufferings that you bore for Jesus, and the blessed hope these tearful sowings may rightly inspire that your ripened wheat will be found worthy of the granaries of God.

JOY IN SUFFERING

My Dear Child:

I should have answered your letter before this, but I trust the delay will be forgiven. It pleases me to learn of the deeper interest in the missions the adoption of missionaries as spiritual brothers has awakened in your community. We need the specific to hold if not to arouse our interest, and the remembrance that a particular missionary is being aided by our prayers and sacrifices somehow makes it easier for us to pray to God, and to die to self.

This practice which has received so sweet an impetus through the example of Little Thérèse is but the logical unfolding of the consoling dogma of the Communion of Saints. May your prayers made eloquent by a generous measure of conformity to God's Holy Will assist your spiritual brother in China to make of the inevitable trials of his life not only a high road of salvation but a veritable pathway to heroic sanctity.

You have asked me to choose a spiritual motto for you. This is a pleasure but a rather difficult one because there are so many ways of saying "I love you" to Almighty God, and that after all, is the only worthwhile message and meaning that religious existence can bear. However, since I must choose, I shall give you one that will serve to remind you of the abiding Presence of Jesus in your soul. Let us make it then, "Jesus in Thy sweet Presence I place all my confidence."

The remembrance of His Presence in your soul will bring you both warmth and light — the warmth of love in the light of faith, and, by His grace your soul will be as a living-room with your heart as its hearthstone and Christ's love as the fire burning thereon.

Jesus came, child, to cast fire on the earth, and what is this fire, save that Pentecostal effusion of His Holy Spirit whereby that flame of love men call zeal is implanted in our hearts? O blessed remembrance of Christ's Presence which is all sufficient for our manifold needs! The soul aware of this hidden gift can still suffer, indeed must suffer more deeply than ever, but there will be eventually, if the soul corresponds to grace, a joy in suffering which apart from mystical elevations is, I think, the nearest approach on earth to the bliss of Paradise. This bliss, dear child, I shall ask Our Lady-Mother to give you in the Heart of her Son Divine.

MAY

May brings lilacs for
Our Lady's lap.

MARY AND MAY

DEAR FRIEND:

It was good of you to call to see us when you were in town last week. Even though your visits are brief, they are appreciated. I would rather breakfast with a friend than with the morning paper — for the friend will speak to me of the generosity of God, the paper only too often of the meanness of the world.

May is coming and May is Mary's month. The bluebirds, her little pages, have been whispering the glad news from tree to tree in the orchards, and every tree has promised to be in perfumed bloom for her. The robins, proud in the livery of her Son, have been broadcasting the news from the cedar tops morning and evening. The brooks have been singing to themselves over the glad tidings. And mother earth is hastening to put on her best green to do honor to the Mother of her Creator.

I know you love Our Lady — to love her is our Catholic heritage. Others proclaim with us the Divinity of her Son, but only we of the Old Faith have not hesitated to place Him, where His Father first placed Him, in His Mother's arms. If they could only see it so, how Herodlike it is to try to snatch the Child from His Mother. And then as now, how futile is the effort!

"What God hath joined, let no man put asunder." The inspired words treat of the marriage bond, yet they are equally applicable to the union of God's own Son and His Son's own Mother. After the love of God, the love of God's Mother is the most reasonable, logical and beautiful thing in the world. God loved her first, God honored her first, and we but follow in His footsteps. Every true Catholic glories to hail her,

Virgin and Mother, Queen of God's Heart and of his.

You remember when you were here, telling me how the builders of Chartres were guided by this norm — "Would this be pleasing to Our Lady?" If you desire to practice true devotion to God's Mother, build your life by this same guiding law — "Would this be pleasing to my Mother?" Jesus, Our Lord, was subject to her for thirty long years, and the endless stream of miraculous favors granted at her shrines throughout the world prove beyond the shadow of doubt that He still hearkens to her slightest request in the Courts above. "It is in thee, O Mary, that we find all graces and even God Himself."

Slip an "r" into May and you have Mary. Slip the Rosary into your daily life and your May will be truly Mary's. Bind yourself to your Mother, musing on the mysteries of her life and His life, while the beads slip through your fingers. Some day someone will place them in your stiffened fingers — let it not be a mockery of truth. Devotion to one's Mother is not for a day, a month, a year, nay not even for a life, but forever. May you love your Mother as nearly as possible as Jesus did, and may she bring you to Him when Life's little drama is done.

"AND HIS MOTHER'S HEART"

DEAR ——:

Just to let you know you are not forgotten on your birthday by your brother.

A birthday should be a day of gratitude, of gratitude to God, and under God to our parents — to those unto whom we owe the fact that we have moved out of the world of Might-be into the world that Is. Only God knows the number of little ones who would have been had His earthly co-operators been less selfish. We are because our parents were not selfish — because they recognized, as noble hearts molded after God's Heart always recognize—that the purest because most unselfish joy in the natural order is the joy of honest parents in the upturned face of their child. When I see such joy I wonder how the world of men can be so blindly selfish and so selfishly blind. In the person of a little child God still offers to come unto His own, and His own receive Him not. How blessed in His sight is the home where He is cherished and cared for in the souls of little children, where He reigns as in Nazareth—reigns by love—child-love in parents' hearts.

I have said—in the natural order—for as blessed as is your life as a father, there is a greater blessedness still which I know you do not begrudge or deny to me, your brother, the blessedness of being childless that in Christ I may be father to all. So while I pray for you and yours, do you pray for me and mine, for my family, my little ones, the little ones of Christ, all those whom He would gather in His Heart. Their number only He knows—but since He died for their happiness, it surely is not too much that I should live, that they might find that happiness where it alone is found, in His Father's Home and His Mother's Heart.

"THESE MANY YEARS"

Dear Sister:

I think you know your spiritual father well enough to realize what happiness it would give him to be present for your Profession. Few joys are greater in my life than the triumph of God's merciful love in the souls or hearts of those who have been entrusted to my care. However, our supreme happiness must be found ever in the carrying out of Our Divine Lover's most sweet and blessed will. His blessed Will holds me here. Besides I have the joy of being actually poor—too poor to travel because of the needs of His poor who have had so much to suffer the past winter. I sometimes wonder if the average religious appreciates the protection from the fangs of poverty that their vow of poverty has given them! The more a true religious knows of the trials of life in the world, the more will he or she realize the truth of the words of Truth —"My yoke is sweet and My burden light!" Those who think otherwise know not Christ. They do not even know the world!

Now, Sister, I want you to know how I am always with my children in Jesus and Mary. Not only for the few brief hours of a joyous Profession Day, but all through every day of their lives, praying for them and loving them in the Heart of Jesus and His Most Blessed Mother. My prayers, my merits—if there be any—my love is all in the Heart of Mary, and there you may go and claim them in your need. Along with the poor pebbles of my offering, Mother Mary will give you the rich jewels of her virtues and the white, precious pearl of the true love of Jesus Christ.

Hasten then, dear daughter, to the Heart of Mary. She will be smiling down on you and your little big offering. She will smile at your offering, not coldly, but sweetly, for it has been hers already these many years—your heart.

THE GRATEFUL HEART

DEAR ——:

I am glad my letters have brought you pleasure, and I am most grateful for your care of them. In return I am going to let you in on a secret—a secret that all the world should know, but which, strange enough, it will never learn—that secret is the secret of gratitude.

The most essential thing in life is to love God. Without God's love this world of ours would never have come to be, without God's merciful love it would never have been redeemed, nor without God's patient love would the Redeemed World come to its Last

End, its First Beginning, God Who is Love.

Now then, here is the secret—the easy way to love God is to love Him by gratitude. A grateful heart is a loving heart, and a loving heart God never despises. His Son did not spurn the grateful love of the public sinner Magdalen, and almost the last act of His earthly life was an act of gratitude to a convicted highwayman —"This day thou shalt be with Me in Paradise!"

O Child, if we but think, how can we help being grateful to Almighty God, how can we help loving Him. No soul so wretched but what its immortality may yet be transfixed with God's glory—the eternal benediction of His unveiled Face. No heart so abject and so forsaken that it may not find God's Heart open; yes, yearning to receive it and embrace it, after having cleansed it in His Son's Own Blood. No one who is motherless that God will not share His Mother with.

To the Goodness, the Beauty, the Love of God, lift thou a grateful heart and thy soul will soon be an overflowing Chalice of love, which Mother Mary will lift to the parched lips of Jesus Christ, now, and, please God, forever.

MOTHEREST

Dearest Mother:

It is now the very first hour of the first day of thy sweet month of May, and I am here in my little room, writing a note to thee, Motherest, which I shall bear over my heart this morn, when I go to meet Thy Divine Son in the dawn-tryst of the Holy Mass.

O thou who once gave Jesus to the world, thou who bore Him, even before His blessed Birth, to bless His yet unborn precursor, thou who showed Him with ecstatic joy to the humble shepherds and lifted Him to bless those truly wise Kings from the East, do thou now, O Blessed Mother of the World's Redeemer, use thy material influence with thy Divine Son in Heaven that He may bless anew and continue to be patient with me and all priests and with all men here upon earth, whom He has redeemed in His Most Precious Blood.

I know, Motherest, that there is no need to remind Him of His love, for His love is Divine, but our hearts are so cold, Mother, our lives so filled with forgetfulness of God and the things of God, that surely Divine Justice must cry out that we are deserving of the withdrawal of the gifts of Divine Love and Mercy.

Divine Love shared thee with us, Motherest, as thou well knowest, when Divine Love was paying the supreme price of Love upon the altar of the Holy Cross, and in that hour of anguish thou who had brought thy First Born into the world without pain, became again a Mother, the Mother of all whom Jesus, thy Only Begotten, was then making His very own, by that most sacred of blood relationships, the fraternity of His Most Precious Blood.

Remembering, therefore, Dearest Mother, thy own anguish in which thou didst become our Mother at the foot of the Holy Cross, do thou continue to pray for us 'til all men shall become by the grace of a Mother's prayers, men of good-will, and thereby come to acknowledge the Divinity of thy Son, the Truths His lips spoke, and the Church His Will established for the enshrinement of His Truth and His Love.

Motherest, I pledge our soul to labor unceasingly, until death do us unite, for the coming of thy Son's Sweet Kingdom and His Eternal Reign, and that all men may come to know by happy experience what I know so well, that thou art according to the plan of God not only the sweet and true Mother of His Divine Son, but as well, the sweet and true Mother of us all.

Ever, in the Heart of Christ.

GOD'S MOTHER AND OURS

Beloved Brethren:

This is the second Sunday of that month that Mother Church has in a special way dedicated to the Blessed Mother of God. It is likewise the day dedicated by popular appeal to honor the mothers of the land. It will be fitting, therefore, to dwell briefly for a few minutes this morning upon these kindred subjects.

For most of us born in the faith it would be impossible to say when we first began to love, either God's Own Dear Mother, or our own. These two loves have been, as it were, our birthright, and as it was our mother on earth who taught us to lisp our love to our Mother in Heaven, so it was our Mother in Heaven who inspired us with ever-deepening reverence for her, whose unselfishness and fidelity to God's Holy Laws gave us under God, the supreme gift of life.

I think nowhere else than in America could one find such a strange paradox as a Nation, glorifying mothers and motherhood, and at the same time listening with growing eagerness to doctrines subversive of both. God glorified womanhood far beyond the power of man by becoming in the person of His Son, a Babe. The Incarnation of the Son of God added a new luster to that sacredness that belongs to all the mysteries of nature, and especially the mysteries of life. By the Motherhood of Mary, all motherhood took on a new meaning, a fresh sacredness, a permanent consecration. It was for the sake of their little ones that He had become a Little One. It was not only for His Mother's sake, but for all mothers' sake that Jesus had become Mary's Child.

Let us turn, therefore, on this beautiful day in the month of God's Mother, and beg Her, Whose Son is truly God, to claim all the mothers of this land as Her very own, to teach them the sweet truths of reverence for God and His Holy Laws which she learned at St.

Anne's knee, and finally, by Her prayers and shining example to bring them all safely to Her home, which is God's.

A mother's true place is in her home with her dear ones round about her. Whatever else Heaven may hold, this at least we know: that it will be a home where mothers shall find their dear ones and dear ones find their mothers and mankind find its God at home with His Mother.

MOTHER DEAR

MOTHER DEAR:

This is the month of your birth, and this letter bears to you my earthly birthday greetings. I have written "earthly" because on the morning of the twenty-second, while I trust you shall be still peacefully sleeping, I shall, please God, be at His Altar offering the Ineffable Mysteries of His Son's Oblation and whispering your name to Jesus.

Life, Mother dear, is a weaving and we are the living strands running together and then apart, and then together again, please God, when the design shall have been completed.

Once, now a long time ago, you rested a little newborn baby-girl in the hungry arms of a little Irish mother, her soul in the arms of God's Mother, her mother. You lived to place that wonderful body in the silent hands of Mother Earth. The weaving went on, though one strand had parted.

Once, now quite a long time ago, almost forty years, it is, Mother dear! I rested against your joyful Christian Mother-heart and shared its beating while I drank of its pure strength.

The weaving goes on. I see the snow of Life's winter in your hair when I in spirit bend to kiss your brow. I know the strands must some day part again.

God's Holy Will be done. I cannot write much more, my eyes are misting, but, Mother dear, I want you to know though the love of God and of the souls His Son has died for has drawn the strands of our lives apart, the same Love of God will some day draw them together again and, Mother dear, we shall be so happy by God's fireside with all our dear ones round about us, their faces illumined by the brightness of His Eternal Love.

You know, Mother dear, I am always yours, always your son in the service of the

Dearest Mother of All Mothers.

"LIKE MOTHER MARY"

MY DEAR CHILD:

I am writing to you this peaceful Sunday morning from the Academy of the Sacred Heart in —— —— where I am closing a Retreat this afternoon.

On the point of direction, my advice is as follows:

(1) Possibly you have made the mistake of not making a proper distinction between frivolity and cheerfulness. The latter, where supernatural, is the fruit of the Holy Ghost's Presence in a soul, and a very precious fruit, indeed, especially in Community life. Perhaps you did not realize that intense seriousness is compatible with joyfulness in both demeanor and in spirit. In other words, we can be very much in earnest about becoming saints without carrying an habitually grave face. The very realization of God's infinite love, of His Presence, together with all the other gifts His Presence brings, the knowledge we are on the road *Home to Heaven*, that we have His unfailing strength and understanding to fall back upon, these and a thousand other considerations should make us the happiest of God's creatures, and would it not be hypocritical to hide that happiness from our fellow beings? We

owe it to God to manifest to the world that we have found it a sweet and joyful thing to belong to the Lord, Our God. Make, therefore, dear Child, whatever changes are necessary to the end that your seriousness of purpose may have that touch of humble confidence of achievement which is reflected in a cheerful face and manner. Be like Mother Mary, sweetly grave yet gravely joyful, with a smile for God's creatures reflecting His smile upon the mirror of your soul.

(2) Do not try, do not waste time with explanations of past conduct with others than superiors, and with superiors only when such explanations are asked for. To be willing to be misunderstood and thought less of unjustly by one's fellow-religious, when motivated by the desire to humble oneself, is a sign of advancement in that art of hating one's own soul that makes us advance rapidly in the complimentary art of loving God.

(3) Abandon all things—past, present and future—into God, your Heavenly Father's hands, and wait with confidence the manifestation of His loving wisdom in your regard.

Ever in Mary.

STAR OF LIFE'S SEA

Dear Mother:

This is a note of business, of our business—caring for souls. You have doubtlessly received already a request of admission from ——. This note is to attest my belief in her qualifications for the contemplative life. You will find her well disciplined both physically and mentally for the life. Of her holiness you will be the judge. Personally I think she is destined for a place among God's chosen ones if she does not lose courage on the way.

Speaking of God's chosen ones, you will recall my

theory that such souls are few not because God has failed to call many to high sanctity but because there are comparatively few who choose to respond generously to His call. It is certain, of course, that "it is God who worketh in us both to will and to accomplish"; but it is equally certain that we can resist the action of His grace.

More and more I realize how much our souls are like little sailboats offshore! We slip along swiftly by reason of the breeze of God's holy grace; we lose the breeze by our faulty handling of the helm; wise is the skipper, who, having taken aboard the Divine Pilot, is ever careful to follow His guidance.

Whether the sea be calm or rough, whether the harbor lights blaze clear or be shrouded in mist, whereever you sail, dear Mother ———, remember your Divine Pilot and fear not, and in the hour of need when the racing waters bare white fangs along the sides and your little craft seems loath to lift its head from the trough of the sea, do you lift your eyes and through the wrack find the beacon God has placed in His high heaven to cheer all storm-tossed sailors, Mary our Mother, sweet Star of Life's Sea.

Of course, you will see Our Lady only by faith, yet thank God Who has given you such vision. And thank Him, too, for this: that the radiant light of grace falling upon the star-soul of Mary has been reflected through the Christian ages upon the moving ocean of humanity and wrought there its fair reflection in so many, many of her daughters.

Starlight, dear Mother, upon your sailing till you near the further shore, and then the Morning Star to hold your courage till the coming of the Son.

Semper per Mariam.

MOTHER'S DAY

Mother Dear:

It is now another year that God has spared you to me, and I am very grateful. It is not that I cling to my dear ones; I understand God too well and love them too much for this. God is All Loveworthy and we at best are but faint reflections of His radiant Goodness. My dear ones are the stars of my firmament but I am ready to have my stars hidden from me in the veils of eternal light, for I know well that they cannot pass from out His loving care.

You, Mother, were the reflection in the quiet pool of my childhood of that Morning Star whom Gabriel once saluted in God's name: the reflection still gleams in the deeper waters of these maturer years.

You opened to me the wonder-book of Nature wherein I learned to find the beauty and wisdom of God in the heart of the tiniest flower and the voice of the tiniest bird. You taught me to listen, while the lace was still upon the grass, to the matins of the robins and to hearken at dusk for the thrush's bugle call. And I trust, Mother, if God so wills, that I may be with you in the hush of the evening when He shall be calling you home.

As I grew older you led me into that timeless universe where the gifted hearts of men share their treasures with the humblest of travelers. Traversing that world hand in hand with you, I found many things to be loved and some few things to be hated; and—was it in the London of Dickens?—one of the abiding passions of my life, love of the poor.

The love of our fellow creatures can but lead one nearer to God when it is drawn from the example of a Christian mother. And that example you gave so completely that I cannot remember when I began to have a deep respect for womanhood but I feel instinctively that this is part of the heritage that came to me in your arms and from your heart. That respect I have never lost, and, please God, never shall lose.

So, looking back over the years, Mother, I realize more and more how much I owe to one whose holiness was veiled in cheerful simplicity, whose courage was contagious and whose intellectuality constituted a challenge never furled: and so I send you this little note to greet you on Mother's Day. Before it is delivered its sender will have joined a host of other priestly sons in lifting a White Message of Love to the Heavenly Father for one of the most precious of His gifts to the children of men — a Christian mother true to her vocation.

EARLY HARVEST

Dear ———:

M——— has told me of the great sorrow that has come to you and your home in the death of a little daughter. There is no answer for these bereavements apart from our faith which offers us the vista of a permanent home beyond the stars where there shall be reunions without the inevitable separations and laughter without the usual sequence of tears.

Perhaps it is because we are so apt to become engrossed in the impermanences of this present moment that God, from time to time, takes from us something of permanent value. And this suggests what I think can prove a source of abiding consolation to you and your dear wife.

Your little daughter, flesh of your flesh and heart of your hearts, was one of the things of permanent value life had brought you. Secure income, prominence in civic life, a comfortable home — these are the things that often absorb the minds of good men to the exclusion of the consciousness that not in these possessions but rather in the sanctifying of their own and their children's souls are the lasting achievements of

Christians to be found.

When the dust of time shall be thickening imperceptibly over all your material objectives, the veils will be thinning between you and the glorious, immortal spirit that has climbed upstairs before you bringing a bit of you to heaven. Then you will understand more fully, what now we know by faith, that God's harvestings, the early as well as the late, are equally demonstrative of His Eternal Love.

Asking Our Lady to bless you.

"IN MARY'S SERVICE"

My Dear ——— :

Your little note gave me happiness, and what pleased me most was the way you ended it with inscribing yourself "in Mary's Service."

If you can only learn by prayer and meditation to realize what it means to be in Mary's Service, how happy your missionary career will be. Knights of old rode forth in search of adventure, wearing upon their lances and arms the colors of their lady-love. In them, at their best, Christian ideals found a beautiful and romantic expression. But my little brother, when after your years of training, your years of page-ship, and squire-ship, you finally kneel to receive the Accolade of Christ's Own Priesthood, then you will have the chance to ride forth in Holy Obedience in the Greatest of All Adventures, the Most Romantic of All Quests, for you will go forth to win souls, souls held captive in the dark dungeons of Paganism, fair souls enslaved in the kingdom of Evil.

Now of all the knights who ride for Christ, aquesting souls, none ride so surely, fight so fiercely, suffer so bravely, receive so few wounds and bring back so many souls to Jesus, as those who love His Mother very especially, wear her colors over their hearts and her sweet image in their souls.

Now you know why it pleased me, to have you inscribe yourself "in Mary's Service."

THE QUEEN'S REGIMENTS

DEAR SISTER:

I received your Easter letter this morning. Even though we have a goodly portion of the liturgical and spiritual way of the Cross, which we term Lent, to traverse, I am answering at once so that this letter may reach you in the sweet month of Our Lady, our Queen's own month of May.

I love to think of the different Religious Orders and Communities of Mother Church as so many Regiments, each with its own particular branch of Christ-work to be done, each with its own distinctive uniform and discipline, yet all marching under the Banner of Christ the King, and all wearing, at least in spirit, the colors of their Queen. Thus the various Communities, by their common love of Mary, become, as it were, in the plan of Jesus, the Queen's Regiments, fighting under her colors for the Triumph of her Son's sacred Cause.

What inspiration you should find, Sister, in the reflection that you by your vows are a sworn and accepted soldier of a Regiment for the Queen — not an earthly Queen who must, perhaps, be seen only at a distance in order to be loved with enthusiasm, but a Queen, who though one of us in all that makes humanity sweet and lovable, is above us in this, that she has never tasted moral defeat in the Battle of Life! What confidence we should have, fighting under her colors — she who is more terrible to the powers of evil than an army in battle array; she who is most gracious to the wounded, for whose sake her Son was wounded; she who is most appreciative of efforts because she so loves the Objective of our fighting — the Cause of Jesus Christ, her Son, Our Lord and God.

Under the Queen's colors, in her beauteous Service, let us carry on, my dear child, 'til she calls us to join her Army Triumphant in Heaven.

LITTLE BROTHER

My Dear Little Brother in Christ:

Your letter brought me great happiness. I will indeed pray for Father ——'s dear Mother and for your own, as well to Our Very Own Mother, Mother of all Mothers.

You ask me to pray also for your perseverance in your beautiful missionary vocation, and this also I will do with great pleasure. I will pray not only that you will persevere by God's holy will and grace until you ascend the flower-decked altar in the midst of your friends to offer with jubilant heart your first Solemn Mass, but I will pray that you persevere until, like your holy Patron, St. Francis Xavier, you shall have consummated your mystical Sacrifice, alone with God, at the altar of the missions. In the First Mass you will hold Jesus in your hands; in the second and mystic sacrifice of a missionary you will be the Host and Christ will break you—even as the Host in the Mass is broken. But always His hands will hold you and place you a loving victim on the golden paten of His Most Holy Will.

To my prayers, little Brother, you must add your own. You must pray in that practical way that will be proven by your cheerful fulfilment of each day's duties. You are not strong physically, but that only gives you a very special claim on the affection and tender care of Our Most Blessed Mother. For you must know, Mother Mary has a very special interest in little candidates for the priesthood. You see, they remind her of her own little Jesus. Turn to her, therefore, little Brother in Christ, just as the little Christ did, and she will care for you even as she did for Him.

Remind her, for she is so pleased to have us do so, of her Jesus, and this especially by the care you take to be like Him in all your actions, even in the minor acts of your heart and mind. The years will slip away and you will be grown into Christ's Manhood and come unto His Hour, and God's Mother and yours will stand together watching you from Heaven as you continue His Sacrifice on earth.

MARY'S MYSTICAL HEEL

MY DEAR CHILD:

I was pleased to receive your letter and more pleased to know you are carrying on so bravely in the front-line trenches for God and God's sweet Mother. There are so many beautiful and encouraging truths to suggest to missionaries that it is hard to choose from among them. However, since Our Lady's Month is approaching, this time, at least, it will not be hard to decide. Sometime when "the going," as we say, "is tough," slip away yourself alone with God, and reflect upon this thought: as a Sister on the foreign missions I have the privilege to co-operate in a very realistic manner in the fulfilment of my Heavenly Father's plan announced in the Garden of Eden, when He declared: "I will put enmities between thee and the woman, and thy seed and her seed: she shall crush thy head, and thou shalt lie in wait for her heel."

Reflect, dear child—is it not the murky kingdom of Satan that you see around you? Of course his kingdom is to be found here in our dear land and other Christian lands, but here, ordinarily, his face is veiled and his satellites, outside of Russia and Mexico, must generally work under cover. But in the mission field where you are working, one sees the kingdom of darkness in full sway with laws of the True King unknown or at least unacknowledged, blasphemy substituted for the chant of God's praises, and darkened intellects sinking ever more deeply into the mire of ignorance and the revolting slavery of the flesh. Now, into this fortified kingdom of evil Jesus has sent you and your fellow religious, Mary's mystical heel for the crushing of the serpent's head; Mary's seed, between whom and the spawn of hell God has placed implacable enmities. You, Sister, and your companions are Mary's soldiers and God has promised you the victory if you but remain faithful to your high vocation, faithful to your Mother and your Queen.

Forward then with courage, Sister, to the attack. God wills it; He is with you. Bury your weakness in His strength in your daily Communion; fortify the little fortress of your soul by fidelity to meditation, and remember, it is not many beautiful thoughts God asks of you at such times, but just that like the purest of human love you rest your heart and your will affectionately and tranquilly in His pierced hands.

I have permission to send you some little things that may be useful to you. Don't be afraid to simplify your prayer, and remember distractions will trail us as long as we live — unless we can learn to love God to distraction, and to this we should aspire!

"THE LEAST OF THESE"

My Dear Child:

I am trusting this note to bring you my greetings for a glorious Eastertide. As a missionary Sister, you and your companions have, of course, numerous and special sacrifices to make in the service of Our Blessed Lord. You will remember, however, a Divine Lover counts and cherishes the least of these, and though at times their cumulative weight may seem crushing, yet how happy you will be, and how blessed, when the hour comes — and the Bridegroom, and finds you waiting to spread before His eyes the heaped pearls of a life of immolation.

Once a religious grasps this truth, once a soul has ascended to a spiritual altitude from whence the world spreads out below in a vista of great fields whose most precious harvests are crosses, then indeed will the foreign missions be revealed as the richest sections of that immense panorama, for on the foreign missions especially crosses attain rapidly a luxurious growth.

Nor does it matter much whether these crosses come from without or from within; both fulfill their purpose, both are crucifying to human nature, and both for the love of Jesus are to be embraced and borne with quiet fortitude, and in so far as possible, even with joy. This last thought suggests to me a final observation, the value of prayer to God, the Holy Ghost.

I know of no shorter road to the riches of the spiritual life than to put one's hand in Mother Mary's and ask her to entreat with you the graces and the gifts of her and your Divine Spouse. The Holy Ghost is the Divine Font of all true devotion, and those who have discovered the streams of grace that flow therefrom are well on their way to the kingdom of God; they need never thirst, they need never faint or be famished.

So dear Child, I recommend to you daily prayer to the silent Divine Guest of your soul. Ask Him so to strengthen you that you may be able not only to walk blithely in the way of missionary immolation but that as well you may be humbly and in Him a source of inspiration to your companions, till the evening falls around you and the least of these your gathered sacrifices will be a pearl to gleam forever at the feet of God.

IN REMEMBRANCE

My Dear ——:

You need not be concerned in regard to the tardiness of your letter. The bonds of real spiritual friendship rest upon a surer foundation than that of correspondence, and besides I am well aware of the duties that crowd the daily existence of religous engaged in nursing.

Only one thing is essential to you whose high vocation it is to tend the bruised members of Christ's Mystical Body, and that is the remembrance that these suffering members are indeed truly His. Being mindful of this you can play the part of Mary even while fulfilling the duties of Martha, you can kneel before Jesus even while you wash and bandage the feet of the lowliest and least of His brethren.

This mystical but real extension of Our Divine Master which His Divine Spirit brings to pass in the souls of the faithful opens to you the very privileges of the Blessed Mother in the years of Christ's Infancy, and of Our Lady and the faithful disciples when the shadows of the first Good Friday were deepening for the second time. The remembrance of His Presence can bring you everything, can make you patient, long-suffering, courteous, sympathetic in the treatment of the afflicted bodies of men. I think of this truth occasionally when I minister to souls in the Sacrament of Penance, but it is easier I believe to be mindful of Christ when our labor is physical rather than mental. In the latter case, the best we can do at times is to begin with an act of union and then plunge ahead into the duty that waits. Even so great a master of the spiritual life as Saint Ignatius of Loyola found such a course necessary during the early stages of his studies. However, Ignatius loved God to distraction while we love God with distractions which is quite a different matter.

Go forward therefore, dear Sister, with confidence, wasting no time in nursing the wounds of self-love but rather doing all that holy obedience permits you to heal the ills of Christ's Mystical Body; and that you may do this the more efficiently do not fail to ask Our

Blessed Lady to live in her virtues within your very heart.

CHALLENGE TO SELF

DEAR ——:

I think I promised you this letter some time ago on the occasion of my visit following your Profession. Now I am fulfilling my promise. It is fortunate for some of us that there is a Purgatory wherein we can pay off our debts without contracting new ones. For while our desires make promises easy to make, our human limitations make them difficult, at least at times, of fulfillment.

If there is anything that the world scoffs at, it is the vows of religion. How could it be otherwise, since the vows represent a challenge flung to self, and, in their valid acceptance, involve not alone the loss to the world of another possible devotee but a rebuke to its philosophy of life? "Eat, drink and be merry; don't cheat yourself; be yourself," variously phrased but carrying always the same theme-note of cheating death by indulgence—the world chants its program with the monotony of a street hawker. To be sure, not always as crudely as this; indeed, sometimes with a subtle intellectual appeal calculated to deceive even the elect. But God, dear ——, has given you the grace to hear another voice out of the silence of your own soul, a voice that invited not to self-indulgence, not to life leading to death, but to death leading to life, to the way of self-denial, to the path of the self-abnegation of religious consecration.

It may seem that I leave no middle ground, no middle way to be followed by souls who are not prepared to walk by way of Calvary. And perhaps I am wrong in what I am now going to say, which is that there is no middle ground for real Christians, and that it is the attempt through the ages to make one that brought about the conditions leading to the disasters of the sixteenth century no less than the difficult situation facing civilization today. Long ago St. Paul proclaimed that those who are Christ's "have crucified the flesh and its concupiscences," and he was writing, let us remember, not to religious but to the Christian community in general.

But, you may say, what of the laity, what of legitimate enjoyments in the world? My answer is this: both by nature and, I trust, by grace I am hostile to puritanical extremes. Once and for all I cry "God bless all honest recreations provided for His children by a Heavenly Father's love." Yet, let us remember, recreations, as all things created, are but stepping stones to God; and long experience has taught me that anyone, whether in the clerical or lay state, who sanctifies his soul consistently, does so by the exercise of a steady discipline —and discipline is crucifying. In many instances this discipline may reach no heroic heights, but in proportion as the soul is possessed of peace the discipline is constant and exacting.

Such are the exactions of life, as we know them, that no one can hope to sail his little soul-craft much beyond the breakwater of youth without carrying the ballast of Christian self-discipline. No one crosses safely the passion-currented waters of mature life without a constant adjustment of his course by the compass of Divine Law; no one avoids the deadly reefs of grievous sin except by sailing close-hauled to the wind of God's grace. And to do these things requires, if not heroic self-denial, at least a steady discipline of one's whole being. God made us for the open, turbulent sea, and you by your vows have engaged yourself to seek no port of rest save that of His Heart; to lay no course but under His command; to value no cargo but the gold of His Love.

I send you Our Lady's blessing.

JUNE

The thorn completes the symbolism
of the rose.

THE JUNE GRADUATE

Dear Friend:

This is your feast day and I must not let it pass without writing to you.

Your career so far has been one of the bright spots in a very happy ministry — for I am indeed very, very happy in the service and love of Jesus Christ. Never forget a faithful priest shares the consolations as well as the sorrows of his Master.

Your Senior year should be a golden harvest year, in which you reap the fruits of the former years of toil. But as you live it, I want you to weigh quietly and prayerfully the reason for your being, and then decide how best you can save your soul while promoting the Honor of God. God, Our God, has a chosen work for each of His children to do. One is meant by Him to reflect His Image in a home where little children shall come to find faith and hope and love. One is intended to teach by example His principles of justice in the busy marts of business, one to touch the bodies of men with His healing touch, and another is called to the supremest art — the care of immortal souls.

Pray God then to guide your every step that you may come to know how best you may serve Him — only in serving Him is there any lasting happiness. No man is so unhappy in the long run as the man who thinks only of himself. He lives in a windowless house and his energies are quickly exhausted from lack of air. His only monument will be in lifeless stone. He who lives for self may not expect others to live, not to say die for him — and yet Christ died for him.

O the Mystery of the love of God for souls — who can comprehend it as revealed in the Open Heart of Christ? Do you know what the greatest tragedy in this world is? The failure of men to appreciate the love of their Creator. May the month in which you will be graduated find your heart beating in harmony with the Heart of your sweet Saviour, and may He teach you to comprehend ever more and more the depths of the riches of His holy love.

In His Service ever.

IN THE HEART OF CHRIST

Dear Madame:

M—— has told me of your generous resolve to give her up to God and the Blessed Mother. I offer you sincere congratulation on this grace of generosity which God has given to you. To be generous with God is a rather rare grace is it not? And yet it is the very highest prudence and the very deepest wisdom. It is the science of sanctity, it is the wisdom of the saints. No one has ever had just cause to regret being generous with God. His gratitude is both infinite and eternal.

Not being a mother it is impossible for me to fathom the depths of your sacrifice, but in the Heart of Christ we learn many things, and deep in the Heart of Christ, close to that innermost shrine wherein His Blessed Mother's name is written, there is written the names of the parents who have with breaking hearts given their dearest unto Him and His. The stars shall fall from the heavens, times shall corrode away all human lettering from lifeless monument and tomb, but the names that are written in the Heart of Christ shall glisten fair forever. O how joyous to find one's name there in the Eternal Dawn.

Yes, dear Madame, you have been generous with God. But remember always God has first been generous unto you. It is He who first gave you the sweet white lily you now lay at His Blessed Mother's feet. It is He who has preserved this flower of your heart.

It is He who has given you the strength to offer it back to Him. It is He who will return it to you in fullest bloom and beauty when these short years are passed. Blessed are those gifts which God Himself preserves unto the eternal years.

May the sunshine of God's blessed grace and the love of His Son's Sacred Heart lighten your steps on the way that you have yet to walk. You do not go alone, behold the Mother of God walks silently yet sweetly beside you. How sweet to walk with Mary unto the Heart of God,

Where may we abide forever.

THE GARDEN OF GOD'S LOVE

Dear Child of Our Lady Immaculate:

It does seem very, very evident that the Queen Immaculate is taking care that you fulfill your childish vow without delay. And I am very glad also that you shall be entering for the beautiful Feast of that Holy Spirit Who first breathed into your soul the love of God and Mary. He is Mary's Divine Spouse. He is to be yours—the Spirit of Infinite Purity, Mercy, Truth, Peace. Ask Him to give you these for your dowry; these and that ever growing love of Jesus which He alone can give.

What a wonderful plan God offers us—and alas how few there are who avail themselves of its privileges. God not alone wills to take us to Heaven hereafter—but even now to make a Heaven in our hearts—Paradise once more by the indwelling of His Sweet Spirit within us. What blissful vistas of hope, what mountains of strength, what vales of consolation open up before the devout soul in the contemplation of this Reality—the Truth of God's familiar, loving Presence in our souls. Our first parents walked with their Creator through the gardens of Paradise—their children, with souls resplendent in the Blood of the Lamb, have entered into even a more intimate relationship with God — He dwells with them — yes, within the gardens of their souls. The Kingdom of God is within us! How fervently should we pray for the coming of that Kingdom — for its extension — until He shall reign in every soul created to His image and for His glory.

This then is the lifework of every Christian, the coming of God's Kingdom in his soul. And if this be so of Christians in general, how much more so is it the lifework of those who aspire to live for God alone.

Enter then, dear Child, into the garden of your soul; invite the help of the holy angels and especially of their Queen; build about you the wall of silence with the stones of prayer and the mortar of sacrifice — when the wall is well built, lo you will find your garden fragrant with the scent of the virtues. The white lilies of purity, the blue violets of humility, the red roses of the love of God will be growing there. There you will find rest — there you will find peace — there you will find God and glorify Him, and His Sweet Spirit shall seal the gates thereof until the eternal years.

"AND THE HEART OF JESUS CHRIST"

Dear ——— :

I have been thinking of our conversation concerning the need of cultural education of Catholics. You will remember, as we talked, before me on the table was "Another Life" of the Poor Little Man of Assisi. I think that little coincidence is symbolic of my belief.

I will grant you that culture is beautiful and, when it is Christianized, elevating — but I will not grant you that culture is the special means ordained in this day and age, or any day or age, for the bringing of a nation to the feet of Jesus Christ.

Fishermen the Master chose in the beginning in overwhelming majority for the first Apostolic venture. God wished not His Divine Wisdom to depend on the niceties of human progress. His Truth is Eternal, His Truth is One, fitted to pierce with Divine Love every honest heart, be it of princely scholar or of peon beggar. He will not have Eternal Wisdom bound round, fettered by the changing hands of human scholarship. That is why the Poverello has done more for the conversion of this enlightened world of ours than all our modern scholars. The word of Truth is not in human wisdom. The little things and lowly of this world God has chosen to confound the mighty and the strong.

Give us more humble priests that will let God's Spirit work within them like the Sainted Curé of Ars. Give us more humble, faithful practicing Christians like unto Mat Talbot. Give us just a few more lay brothers like Frère André of Mt. Royal. Give us just one soul athirst for that Supreme Truth and Beauty which is God—just one more little Francis of Assisi. Give America a few unlettered saints and they will bring this great and beloved Nation of ours into the arms of Mother Church—and the Heart of Jesus Christ. Scholars win applause, saints win souls.

THE SINGING HEART

Dear Sister in Christ:

I congratulate you sincerely on your reception of the Holy Habit, and I trust and pray that you will wear the uniform of Christ Crucified not only exteriorly, but that you will also clothe your soul in those beautiful virtues of which His Sacred Heart is the Supreme Exemplar and Source.

Not only do I recommend to you all the virtues in general, but I will go further and recommend to you one virtue in particular—I want you to strive especially to cultivate the virtue of the singing heart.

You have never heard of the virtue of the singing heart? Well, there is such a virtue, and you will find it mentioned in both the Old Testament and the New. The Old Testament puts it thus—serve God in joyfulness. The New is more descriptive, recommending us by the inspired pen of dear St. Paul that we should be filled with God's Holy Spirit, singing and making melody in our hearts to God. (Eph. 5.)

Now that, dear child, is what I mean by the virtue of the singing heart. I want you to beg of God's Holy Spirit so to fill your soul with gratitude for life and Faith and Vocation and all the other countless gifts of His that descend in such a steady downfall upon you that your heart cannot help singing, singing even in sleep as do the brooks of a summer night, singing always a song of grateful love for God.

Some hearts are naturally singing hearts and God's Holy Spirit plays upon their heartstrings melodies that charm the angels of His Kingdom. Some hearts find it harder to sing, but the harder it is to sing, so much the more the merit in singing. In love God made this world of ours, and set it moving in sweetest harmony with music of Heaven. Man has brought many a discordant note into its Divinely planned orchestration since then, but our part is simply this: the Master Musician listens and catches the notes of each instrument, and though they be numbered only by Divine Intelligence, He hears our heartbeats and He only asks that ours be in harmony with His and Mother Mary's.

OUR HEART

Dear Sister:

The eastern sky was afire this morning as I hastened over the hill to say Mass, and my heart, too, was afire with grateful love for the Good God Who is generous and loving with all His creatures but, it seems to me, with none more so than with His priests. Does He not come to them—unworthy though they be—morning by morning in the spiritual Sunrise of the Holy

Mass, lifting Himself in love over the crimson waters of His Most Precious Blood? I know you will say, "Yes, but He comes to me too!" Yes, Sister; He comes to you because He loves you, because He has a Sacred Heart that loves all the world of creatures, and loves His priests with a special love because it was and is the plan of His Heart to take the hearts of His priests and make them other Chalices to hold the love that overflows from the Chalice of His Heart and bring that love unto the famished hearts of men. Through His priests Jesus wills to multiply His presence on earth, and thus gives glory to His Father and promotes the Salvation and Sanctification of mankind.

Cease not, therefore, Sister dear, to pray for the priests of Jesus Christ. Theirs is a vocation, the very sublimity of which makes it difficult for selfish humanity, both in attainment and perseverance. At their hands the Good Shepherd will require strict accounting for His lambs and sheep. Blessed will they be, if they can echo the words of their Master—"I have glorified Thee upon the earth: I have finished the work which Thou gavest Me to do." Shamed will they be, if accepting the honors of the priestly life and earthly rewards, they shall be found to have been wanting in promoting the very purpose of their existence—God's glory and the salvation and sanctification of immortal souls.

Despite all the shameful tendencies of this modern age, despite the pitiful abrogations of human minds from Divine Truth, of human wills from Divine Law and of human hearts from Divine Love, O how easily would the world of human hearts be led back to its Creator and Redeemer—back to the Heart of its God—if only the priests of Jesus would give themselves with complete devotion, disregarding all things else, to the eternal interests of their own and their people's souls.

To this end, let us consecrate our soul, Sister, to the

Heart of Jesus, Our Heart, that the Heart of Jesus may hold sway over all souls and firstly, as He wills, over the souls of His Priests—

Semper per Mariam.

"CHILDREN'S VOICES"

DEAR ——:

I am very happy to know that another little voice can now be heard in your little home. Children's voices in a happy home—how pleasing they must be to God. Have you ever reflected on what a chorus of discordant notes ascends from this earth to its Creator? I have stood at a hotel window high up above the theater crowds of New York and listened to the roar of waves of humanity breaking on the shores of pleasure; now my ears could catch but a little part of the raucous noise of a great city, while God hears every heart-beat of the teeming million of His creatures, hears their lies and their blasphemies, hears their wicked schemings and their cheap perversions, the blackening of good names and the besmirching of innocent souls, hears the crudities of the street corner and the inanities of club-rooms and the sibilant tongues that lisp adder-like in the drawing-rooms. But, thank God, the Creator Who listens to the abuse of God-given powers, listens also to the chanting of His Glory, to the praises of His saints and to the earnest words of honest hearts, to the fiery words of lovers of truth and the heartfelt pleadings of the champions of the oppressed, to the hymns of His cloistered virgins, and to mothers singing their babes to sleep. And I think I know our Good God well enough, to know that the voices of little children at play are to God, Who sees His gifts outraged, as the gentle rain pattering on the parched soil or lulling, by its droning on the roof, a suffering soul to sleep.

Praise God for children's voices, for the little voices

that echo in your home and heart, train those voices to sing always of God's goodness and might and power and tender love, of the Glory of His Mother and His saints, and you, dear ——, will be promoting in a most exquisite way the Glory of God, for you will be training a little choir for the Symphony Supreme and Eternal of Heaven, and may He Who has said "Suffer little children to come unto Me for such is the Kingdom of Heaven" keep us always little children, and as little children let us trust Him, love Him, praise Him, that we may be found some day worthy of His Heart and Mother Mary's arms.

THE HEARTHSTONE

Dear ——:

I was so glad to hear from you, especially since your note reflected, as a mirror or a well-polished panel might, the light of a fire burning on the hearth. Now your heart is the hearthstone and Divine Love the living flame thereon, and I rejoice that you have learned the most precious lesson Life can teach us, which is this — nothing can take the place of the fire of God's Love within our lives.

Other flames there may be, other sources of heat, but all other means of heating are going to fail us sooner or later, and we are going to find ourselves very cold and very much alone if we have barred Jesus Christ and His Mother and His dear ones from our fireplace. God wills every human heart to be a living room and in the living room an open fireplace with a cheerful blazing fire, and His Son as the Guest of Honor, or better the Host, and we as the relatives and friends of the Host gathered there for warmth and consolation at the close of each day. Make your heart, dear ——, such a dwelling place, first for God, then for those whom God has committed to your loving care, —— and ——, and all the rest of us, and then how abidingly happy you will find yourself.

Summer will pass, and autumn finish its colorful painting, and the fields without be enfolded in the white mantle that heralds the coming of winter's reign; so too with our lives, they have their springtimes and their summertimes, their autumns and their winters—but if within our souls there are hearthstones where God's Love sends forth Its undying flame, then there will always be warmth and light and love in our hearts and the winter of life will find us waiting for God's eternal spring.

GOD'S POEMS

Dear Brother and Sister in Christ:

This is to say how happy I am in your happiness in the coming of little Anne.

The more we have found life worth while the more we should rejoice in seeing the gift of faith conferred on others, and if, besides, one has had the God-given privilege of parenthood, how reverently should one face the problems Christian Parentage involves. Joyce Kilmer wrote himself immortal by his Poem that points out that only God could make a tree—and this is true—but Christian fathers and mothers have, under God and with God, created far more gloriously than trees or poems or all other works of the wide universe, excepting only God's angels. After all, a child's soul is a poem writ by God, to be read and loved by men. This thought I am enshrining in a little poem which I dedicate to Our Little Anne.

God's Poems

I looked into a baby's face,
And lo, I thought, I saw a trace
Of Mankind's first primeval grace,
In long lost Paradise!

Set in a mount of white and pink,
Two jewels flashed that made me think
I had gazed off from this world's brink,
Yet I saw but her eyes!

Still well I know I was not wrong,
For what are children but God's song,
Fair poems that to Him belong.
These we must not despise!

GOD'S VIEWPOINT

My Dear ——:

I was so pleased to have a real letter from you, and thus to catch a glimpse of your inner life. You may smile at the last phrase but the truth is there, nevertheless, for the inner life of a married man—is it not, by the design of God's love, his home and his dear ones! How quickly would the troubles of men and nations disappear were this truth recognized and accepted by the peoples of the earth. Let humanity but accept its God and put in practice the teachings of His Son, their Saviour, and what happiness would follow for all.

You wrote of my happiness and that you thought I would always be happy. I hope you are right; this much at least is true: I know the secret of happiness. The question is, will I live according to my knowledge? If I do so live, even in suffering, even in darkness, I shall be happy. I try always to see things from what I may reverently term God's viewpoint, and when one learns to do this, one sees everywhere His beauteous design, save where sin has rent it, and even where sin has intervened one sees the tireless fingers of God—like the fingers of a mother—busy, ever busy, mending His children's thoughtlessly torn garments.

Everywhere I find God's Love, and the results thereof; why, therefore, should I not be happy? And, after the altar, perhaps nowhere is His Love more fully revealed than at the altar of a Christian home where love that He has made sacramental unites an earthly trinity to chant together His Glory and to live through the years a mystical sequence of His Son's joys and sorrows.

Life, my dear ——, is a reverent thing, a thing of infinite value and of well-nigh infinite beauty once God's viewpoint has become our own. As a child at His Father's knee we see His plan as He sees it, at least to this extent, that as a picture puzzle partly put together we can see that the picture is to be a thing of beauty, and that Our Father's hands are always guiding ours to its completion.

Therefore, dear Brother in Christ, you will not mind if a priest who is growing old recommends you to see and to teach your little ones to see life through the eyes of God. Do this and I promise you a generous share in the future of the happiness that is now yours, the music of God's grace in your soul, His strength in your will, His light in your mind, His love in your heart, His peace in your dear little home. Jesus, Himself, will dwell therein, for you are gathered there in His Holy Name, and His Most Blessed Mother shall keep you and yours safe through the heaviest storms of life and the darkness till the night is passed.

THE INFANTRY OF CHRIST

Dear Father ——:

Last week's *Pilot* brought us the story of your brother's funeral, and I feel I owe you a brief note of sympathy as well as a Mass for the repose of his priestly soul.

To have a brother of mine follow me into Christ's Priesthood was a consolation I did not merit. Blessed be His Holy Will. So long as my brothers walk worthily in their high vocations to Christian fatherhood, I shall be content. God must have pure and brave and generous hearts in the strongholds of the nation's homes as well as at His altars. America will never be on the road to peace till her homes as well as her churches are places of prayer and praise and loving sacrifice.

But let me return to my theme, your priest-brother. Had God given me a priest-brother, I would have wished him to be like ——; and had God chosen to call him early from the vineyard, I would have rejoiced in my brother's good fortune. I would have smiled, I think, through the tears!

Why should we not rejoice when a priestly soldier's death finds him faithful at his post of duty? Diocesan priests are the infantry of Christ. They are a most essential part of Christ's army. Upon them rests the work of holding and consolidating the ground won by the more mobile forces of the Church Militant. Their work, like that of the "dough boys," is too often overlooked, their contribution undervalued, their sacrifices unappreciated; but not by their Supreme Commander.

He always understands, He never forgets, and when across the silent valleys and sleeping hillsides the clear notes of His buglers sound taps for one of His own, why should we not rejoice? Our brother has been called home from the strife, home to rest, home to live and to love and to pray for us close to the Heart of God.

CASTLES IN SPAIN

My Dear ——:

At this time of the year with the long vacation just beyond the white-muslined orchards of the Maytime, I suppose you are busy building Castles in Spain. There are people, plenty of them I know, who condemn the practice of daydreaming, but I am not of their number. Surely many an honest and even heroic deed owes its inception to the inspiration of an hour of indolence. The fields seem but idly sleeping in the warmth of the Spring sunshine, yet already the seeds of September's harvestings are stirring beneath their brown Franciscan robes. The dreams of good men and of noble women — even their daydreams — are the seeds of the world's noblest achievements. What we must remember is that these seedlings of fancy must be duly transplanted into the garden of reality, into the field of actuality, there to grow and bear fruit in and by the grace of God.

Build, therefore, dear child, your Castles in Spain; build them with high walls, upon the strongest of all foundations — the adorable Will of God — and about the most beautiful of cathedrals — that of the Sacred Heart. Then be ready to execute the humblest of details as the Master Builder assigns them to you day by day. Be not petulant when He makes changes in your blueprints. Far beneath the sky-musing towers must repose the solid foundation stones of the ordinary virtues, and remember besides, the Divine Architect always marks accepted plans with the impress of the Holy Cross, always crowns the finished buildings of His children with the emblem of triumphant love. The final fruition of your dreams leave in His pierced Hands, I know no other place of equal security.

Castles in Spain, cloud-cities, torn apart by changing currents of events, how often we have watched them and remarked their gossamer futility! But the dream castles we place with loving reverence within the Sacred Heart are not subject to changing breezes but only to the gracious regiment of God's Infinite Wisdom and Love. In that world of peace, I place you, dear ——, and all whom I love, knowing that when the breath of God shall have swept away the plans of His creatures' creation, I shall thus find you incorporated in the Eternal Design of His Love.

ABIDING ARMS

Dear Sister:

Believe it or not, I have just finished reading your letter and there is still unopened Easter mail on my desk! It is because you are a missionary that you are receiving this note.

I finally reached —— and received the usual cordial reception. I cannot recall just what I preached at the Ceremony but it must have been on the necessity of loving God, for that is the thought that underlies my convictions on being happy as a Religious or indeed in any other way of life.

If we love God deeply enough—which we cannot do, absolutely speaking—but deeply enough to fight self and overcome self, then we come eventually to enjoy a certain inner peace despite all the turmoil that reaches us from without. Spiritual toothaches are, nine times out of ten, little more than abscesses upon the root of self-love. Hence, when we kill the root we establish peace.

God has blessed you, it would seem, with a naturally cheerful disposition. Thank Him for this gift; ask Him to supernaturalize its activity and utilize both the gift and its possessor in their entirety for His greater glory. Ask the Divine Spirit to make your joy like that of Mother Mary and to prepare your heart in joy for its future participation in Our Lady's sorrows.

The knowledge of God's love should make us cheerful under all circumstances and conditions, for God's love, when recognized and claimed, makes the lowliest beggar a prince and enthrones the sufferer with Christ, on the Cross here, it is true, but hereafter with Christ in Glory.

Therefore, dear ——, as you minister to the afflicted members of Christ's mystical Body, let your heart be a contented brook that goes its way; now across sun-drenched stretches of meadow, now through cool shady woods and again under dark stone arches of bridges, yet always onward and always singing. The brook cannot analyze the sense of joyfulness its music conveys to men, but you can analyze your happiness and that very process will but deepen the current of your song. For God is Love, dear Sister, and Love has reached down to us abiding arms through the Incarnation of His Son Divine.

GOLDEN EMBER

My Dear ——:

It was a pleasure to hear from you, especially so since I trust I can help you. I enclose my solutions to your friend's difficulties. For your guidance I add what follows.

In general, I believe, it is better to allow time for God's grace to prepare the ground somewhat as Nature does the harvest fields during the winter and spring. The finest of June roses have a background of long culture and I warn you not to force the unfolding of this precious soul that God has committed to your keeping.

In the second place, what we need in God's service is not forced plants but workers whose vocations have been the logical result of years of cultivation of the things that are of God. God's interests suffer when His officers lack that abiding enthusiasm for His Cause which results not from temporal advantage or passing emotionalism but from that quiet steady current of spiritual forces which channel within a soul ever deepening convictions as to the privilege of God's service.

Thirdly, as regards the dominant note or motive in Christian life, it would be but a superficial examination that would assign so great a rôle to fear. Hope is in reality the great underlying source of the energies of Christian living. And in this connection I am going to quote you some lines I wrote lately because they say what I wish to say just as I would wish to say it:

What then is Hope?
Hope is a flower growing in the dust,
Hope is the sure expectance of the truths that must
Await the sunrise of Eternity
For demonstration; the e'er recurrent surge
Of Faith upon the cold, damp sands of Doubt.
Hope is a lantern breeze-tossed but not out,
Hope is a smile upon the lips of pain,
Hope is the buoyancy that Christ's Sweet Name
Does stir within the hearts of men; the urge
To nobler being that can break a thousand bars.
Hope is the instinct guiding in the dark,
Hope is the hidden spring that sends the lark
To carol in the clouds while all the world
Is rapt in slumber.
Hope is a stairway leading o'er the stars:
Hope is the golden ember mid the ash
Of dead desires,
Whereat the fires
Of each tomorrow's cheer must still—
By Grace's breathings and man's own good will—
Be lit.

Such, my dear ——, are my conclusions and I think they will be found to be likewise the just reflection of Christian life in its universal aspects. Fear—other than that reverential fear which is Hope's bodyguard—is a craven thing, and no craven thing has motivated the hidden but no less heroic lives of millions upon millions of Christians. Fear did not give us the Crusades, Chartres, or the Franciscan Movement. And if you counter that these things are not normal manifestations of Catholic life, then I answer, all honest living is a crusade, every soul is a Chartres, and Francis of Assisi sang a song older than the Canticle of Canticles and newer than Gertrud Von Le Fort's Hymns to the Church — the rhythm of Divine Love beating upon the shores of earth and awaking answering echoes in the deeper shells of self.

THE ROAD TO PEACE

Dear ——:

It seems likely that your vocation is to be that of the Holy Cross of Suffering, and your only cloister that of a careful conformity to God's Most Holy Will. Perhaps I am wrong in this surmise, but whether I am or not really does not matter, as long as you learn to rest your will in the will of God even as a child rests its hand calmly and with perfect confidence in the hand of its father.

Many of us find this road to peace only late in life: and as for the world, need I comment, it would seem this road (which is for nations as well as for individuals the way to peace) seems the last to be considered, and then taken only sorrowfully and painfully when the ways of human leaders have proved disastrous.

However, we must strive amid the uncertainties of the times to work out our own salvation. We cannot, of ourselves, save the world, but we can at least save and sanctify our own souls as our initial and essential contribution to this greater cause.

That is why I would urge you, dear ——, not to plan for tomorrow but to take the opportunities God gives you today and weave them lovingly according to the pattern Duty at the moment shall furnish. So at the end of the day — even as a child — you will have something to show your Father when He comes to take you home from school.

Asking Our Lady to bless you.

THE HEART OF OUR CAPTAIN

DEAR BROTHER IN CHRIST:

When this note reaches you it will be the glorious Month of the Sacred Heart, June, the Month of Our Beloved Captain. If there is anything that ought to bring consolation and joy to the heart of a missionary, above all else, that Thing is the remembrance of the Heart of his Beloved Captain.

Down through the ages, men have followed men to countless fields of battle, but no one ever followed such another Captain as we follow. What a goodly company they would make, the great commanders of the centuries, and what a mighty army their combined legions would form! But greater than all these and vaster than their united forces is Our Captain and the Christian hosts that have followed Him and still follow Him, undauntedly down the dusty high roads of the centuries!

In comparison with Our Captain all others are as if they were not; measured with His hosts, the armies of all others are as little companies. Jesus Christ is by Divine Right the Commander of Commanders, the Captain of Captains, the Lord of Hosts forever. And not only is Our Captain the Mightiest of captains, He is the Most Gracious as well, the Most Patient, Most Unselfish, Most Forgiving, Most Loving, Most Lovable! If men have followed other leaders with enthusiasm even unto death, how much more reason have we to follow Our Captain, seeing that He for love of us has made Himself a voluntary Victim in atonement for our transgressions.

If you think along these lines, my brother, your heart will grow warm within you, and you will not find it hard to answer His Love, the Love of the Heart of the Beloved Captain with the complete love of your own.

I am never tired of reminding my spiritual family of

this consoling truth. Lavish your love and service upon creatures, and what one of them can fully comprehend and measure your giving? Pour out your love in service of the Master's Heart, and behold, He counts your every heart-throb, He weighs each ounce of sacrifice, He remembers every tear. The more unselfish creatures are, the more God-like they will be, but the most unselfish of creatures is but a blurred image of the loving unselfishness of God, and the unselfish love of God for us is poured out upon this world through the open Heart and Wounds of Jesus Christ. And your Vocation, my brother, is to hold your heart daily as a golden cup up to the overflowing Chalice of His Heart and let your heart be thus filled with love and grace to be borne carefully and patiently to the thirsting souls that sit amid the shadows of Life's Bethsaida, and have no one to carry them to the life-giving waters of its pool. Courage, therefore, my brother! Renew your resolution at the Master's feet, your spirit by His Spirit, your heart by His Heart. There will never be on earth anything more glorious than the occupation of the angels, the loving service of the Beloved Captain and His Sweet Mother.

THE TRAINING CAMP

DEAR ——:

I was very much pleased by your last letter. It revealed to me that you are profiting by your training, to the end that you may some day prove a true and faithful soldier of Jesus Christ. I was especially pleased by the note of earnestness in your comments, and withal your happiness in your vocation.

After all, these qualities should be characteristic of a true priest and particularly of a missionary. Jesus needs men who are at once dead in earnest and at the same time cheerful and happy in the pursuit of their high enterprise. Were our country at war, how earnestly we should give ourselves to the work of preparation to fulfill our duty unto her! Shall we do less for Our God?

Wars between the nations of earth come and go, leaving their human wreckage behind them. But there neither is nor can be a truce or cessation of the war between God and His enemies for the possession of the immortal souls of men and women.

It is for participation in this unending War of wars that you are now in training. Only Christ, the Commander, knows to what degree the salvation of hundreds depends upon your willingness and preserving endeavor to become like unto Himself.

There can be no question of a truce with such an enemy. There must be no deliberate weakness where immortal souls are at stake. We cannot afford to fail when Jesus has so trusted us. Give yourself, therefore, dear brother in Christ, ever more unreservedly to your holy environment, that it may mold you yet more fully to the image and stature of the Perfect Soldier. And because this work is one of love, never let a day pass without slipping into the Commandant's Quarters, and kneeling there in silence, beg Him to inflame your life, your heart, your soul, ever more completely with the glorious crimson of His Heart and Love.

They fight best who love best, and it is our duty to fight for the Cause of God's Incarnate Love—and God's Sweet, Sweet Mother Mary.

THE DEEPENING MYSTERY

My Dear Brother in Christ:

Just a letter for the anniversary of your Ordination that I may add one wee note to the *Magnificat* of your priestly soul on that day.

Sometimes I wonder when thinking of this Gift Ineffable which Jesus has given us, sometimes I wonder will we ever comprehend how great a gift it is?

Surely not on this earth, for I know your own soul will have found what every true priest finds—the Mystery of His Priesthood and of its powers growing deeper and deeper as the years pass by! With us who are priests of His Heart is it not like unto the honest scientists who peer into the mysteries of the natural universe; the further they advance in knowledge, the farther and deeper stretches before them the expanse of the reign of His laws. So, too, as we grow in the knowledge and love of God and His holy ways, so does the wonder grow in our souls at the lengthening horizons of the Kingdom of Love!

After all, the Priesthood is the sublimest Romance, the greatest Adventure, the divinest Profession on earth—for it is the Romance, Adventure and Profession (if I may so speak) of God's Incarnate Son.

Therefore, dear Brother in Christ, I rejoice with you as you pass another milestone on the pilgrimage of life, and as I lift my Chalice—which is likewise yours because it is His—on your anniversary, I will ask Our Father in Heaven to make us both more worthy in His Spirit to drink of the Life-Blood and the Heart-Love of His Son.

LETTERS OF CHRIST

Dear Brother in Christ:

I received your Easter greetings this morning and before that I trust you had the letter you desired. What a gracious charity at times a letter is, coming like a kindly breath of air on a sultry day or a channel of light through the cloud banks, and bringing to a soul in need the blessed gift of courage and inspiration in the realization that someone is thinking of him, someone is interested in his well-being and expecting him to carry on bravely for Christ.

Missionaries are, as you are well aware, notoriously poor correspondents, but for this they may well be forgiven in large measure because of the preoccupations and exigencies of their lives. They might well answer our remonstrance with a reference to this beautiful truth — missionaries are letters of Christ, living letters addressed by God's Divine Son and bearing the message of His Love and His Truth to the nations afar off. Sealed by His grace, canceled by His Precious Blood, these living letters fulfill the most valuable of purposes — the salvation of immortal souls.

So, dear Brother in Christ, we must be patient when our friends on the missions are slow in answering the effusions of fraternal charity, and though Christ has not found us worthy to be ourselves addressed to the Far East, let us find consolation in this, that the greatness of His Heart's love makes Him welcome even the best intention inspired by His grace. So there remains for us, stay-at-homes, the privilege of addressing ourselves to His Most Sacred Heart.

SINGING RIVERS

My Dear ——:

I thank God and Our Lady for the gleams of consolation that have been conceded to you, and I thank you for the card and note. I wish you would try the enclosed verses to the Holy Spirit as a wee Pentecost novena. I am sure if you do so — childlike — the light will grow stronger.

Thanks for the offer of the life of Damien, I have seen a copy here, but I think I can say now with simplicity I no longer need books other than my trinity of books, the Bible, my Crucifix and — for me the always open Book of Divine Love — the Eucharist. My river runneth full and, please God, shall sing under the dark arches of its journeyings and beneath the tears of tomorrow's rain as well as under the sunshine of this my life's early afternoon. Indeed I must sing for I have a double burden of song to carry, my own and that of another brook which it would seem lost its way but only for a while and only that under God's grace, it might sparkle the brighter under the caress of the morning and run the faster and sing the more happily until it loses itself in the arms of the Sea.

Asking Our Lady to bless you.

ROSES FOR REMEMBRANCE

My Dear Son:

I must not let this month of Our Blessed Mother pass without the long-promised letter to you. I need not apologize for not writing sooner as you are aware of the many duties that crowd the doorway of my daily existence. I do not regret crowded portals, but I do wish I had more efficiency and stamina, and greater zeal for the work at hand. I have just been reading Margaret Yeo's Life of St. Charles Borromeo and his ability to get things done is a revelation of the efficiency of true sanctity. Read all the lives of the saints you can lay your hands on. I know of no more pleasant means, apart from the sacraments, of learning to recognize our own limitations and the limitless Goodness of God. The lives of the saints are truer than fiction stories, and each reveals the sublimest of romances — that of a soul and its God.

In the Month of the Sacred Heart, as the full tide of the summer heat sweeps in over the Eternal City, a gracious Providence will direct your steps to cooler if less sacred haunts. But wherever your superiors decide to take you and your comrades, cling to that inner consciousness of God's Presence which is the joy and the strength of God's servants. Hold to this practice of God's Presence, even though the awareness is but a constantly renewed functioning of Faith carrying on amidst the shadows of the night. Compared with the brightness to be, this is the night; but faith whispers of the morning, and if we strive to love God with generosity, even this present darkness will be fragranced by the roses of His remembrance; and for this fragrance, should we not be ready to endure the thorns?

Asking Our Lady to bless you.

ISLANDS INVISIBLE

Dear ——:

I am just about to go West to give a little retreat in the —— Monastery, and while there will speak to Mother ——, whom I know very well, concerning the possibility of receiving you. When I know the answer I will write to you.

However God may decide, I would urge you to realize that we can attain to highest sanctity anywhere in the world, in the active as well as contemplative life, on the one condition of our being willing to give to its attainment the fullest measure of devotion. In such cases when a soul is held in the world by circumstances beyond her control, or immersed in a world of duties created by Holy Obedience, God Himself stands ready to build an invisible but nevertheless real cloister round about the heart, within which the soul may lovingly abide amidst the currents of external activity. Thus in East Boston or the Sahara Desert a soul may have its Carmel and become very much like one of those islands that lifts itself in serene majesty in the midst of a turbulent stream. All about there is agitation, activity, cross-currents, but the island itself maintains and reflects the peace of solitude.

May God give you this peace and within this peace grant you, dear ——, that union with Him which is its ultimate source.

Asking Our Lady to bless you.

JULY

In July, Nature seems to pause in twilight sleep before fruition.

"SUNRISE"

Dear ——:

You do not know how much pleasure it gave me to learn you have begun to go to Mass daily. Now at last, you have hit upon the right solution to all your difficulties, as the mists dissolve before the rays of the morning sun, so will all your trials find their answer in the light of the *Light* of the World.

Daily Mass, would that we all realized to the full and vividly, what graces await the fervent soul in the awakening silence of the morning. No pool of Silhoe is This—nay but a very Ocean of mercy, of strength, of consolation, of love and that Love Divine. Only think, in Holy Mass Jesus not only adores for us, pleads for us, blesses us—in the Mass Jesus waits for us, yearns for us, begs for "the alms of our love."

Pray God's Holy Spirit, therefore, that He may give you the grace to appreciate the spiritual Sunrise of our daily Mass, and may the Son of God uplifted to awaken, to enlighten, to bless, to warm all hearts, find your heart uplifted to meet His in faith, in hope, in love.

One thing more, as you hasten along the empty streets in the quiet of the morning, as the early Christians did—thank God for the gift of Faith in His Son and His Son's Holy Church.

HOME-COMING

Dear ——:

I am going to miss our daily tramps and I know well that you are missing the home God gave to you. There is perhaps this advantage in leaving home; the deeper appreciation that absence brings. And there is the joy of returning, the joy of finding again the peace and love and consolation that home enshrines for the honest-hearted man.

I want you to remember that there will be no town or city on your route wherein you may not find yourself at home. Mother and father, brothers and sisters will not be there, nor their abiding memories—the essentials of a home. But in every town you will have a Home where you may find your truest Brother and your own true Mother. Kneeling in the silence, close to the Veiled Throne of Jesus, you may be one with those you love—for they too are close to Jesus—they too abide within the shelter of His watchful loving Heart.

O, what a gift God has given to us; a Home everywhere and that Home His very Own. Only a God of Infinite Love could plan so wondrously for His creatures' consolation. Only a God of Infinite Power could condescend to such depths of self-annihilation as the Real Presence entails.

Seek then, between the calls of business, the silent appeal of your Brother. Answer that call, and kneeling alone in your Father's Home, ask Jesus to keep you and those whom I know you love so deeply, deep in His Heart, until the home-coming, which will be without a tinge of sadness, for it will be for good—forever at home with God.

Please God, we shall meet ere then and walk many a mile on the home road together.

Please remember me to Jesus whenever you are at home with Him.

THE CHALICE

DEAR ——:

How I wish I could win you for the Service of His Heart. I could—were I only a saint—win you as Ignatius did Francis! But what I cannot do myself, perhaps one far more greater will do for me, and so I shall ask Our Blessed Lady to claim you, you who stand in the vigor of young manhood looking with clear eyes out upon the world.

There are two ways of looking at the Priesthood of Jesus Christ, both give true views, but one will surely make a humble man draw back, while the other reaches down into a real man's heart and makes him at least wish he had the courage to give.

We can look on the Priesthood as God's supremest Honor, excepting only the unique Honor of Mary's Divine Maternity, and this it truly is. What greater Honor can be conceived of than that of being powered to bring God from Heaven to earth, and men from earth to Heaven. The Mother of the sons of Zebedee asked for her two sons the places to the right and left of Christ's throne—she did not know God's Plan—she did not know that her sons were destined to a higher Honor than that she sought for them. She was to live to see her sons hold God enthroned within their very hands. This is the view that makes a man who knows himself draw back, but listen.

The Priesthood is not only the Supreme Gift of God to a man, it is also the supreme gift of a man to God. In a true priest, God has given, man has given—the result is a work of Love, Divine and human. The Priesthood offers man the supremest way of giving all to God. This is what Our Lord meant when, turning to those same sons of Zebedee, He asked them quietly, "Can you drink of My Chalice?"

That is what the Priesthood really means, a chance to drink of the Chalice of Our Lord, a chance to add your life and blood to His life and Blood; a chance to lift His Chalice to your lips and the chalice of your soul to His lips; a chance to give till there is nothing left to give—till the arms of death receive you from the arms of the cross and lift you to the arms of Jesus and His Mother Mary.

At death, all chalices save one are empty—pleasure, position, passion, pride—that one is the chalice of consolation of a life that has given generously to God.

I shall pray that His Holy Spirit enfire your heart with a love of Jesus Crucified, with a love that shall want to give as well as receive, with a love that will dare to aspire to high things for Jesus, with a love that shall achieve high sacrifice—the sharing of His Chalice, and of His consolation—in His Mother's Heart.

"WE PRIESTS"

DEAR ——:

Today is the Anniversary of our Ordination. I trust you remembered me in your Mass as I did you in mine. How swiftly the years have flown. It seems but yesterday that That Great Day was dawning. Though the years have slipped between—we are still young, are we not, still newly ordained? I hope so, still with our first fervor and zeal and innocence—preserved for us by the Blood of Christ!

The Blood of Christ! How closely one in spirit should we be—we priests—seeing that morning by morning the Same Blood purples our lips, crimsons our hearts, purifies our souls. Why should we not be one in heart, and mind and soul, we priests of Jesus, nourished by the Blood of His One Heart. Why should we not be joyous, we who have such a daily pledge of His undying love. Why should we not be holy, we who are inebriated with the Life Blood of God's Holy One. "I know Thee, who Thou art," cried out the evil spirit, "Thou Holy One of God!" Every priest should be able to win like recognition from the foes of God and Holy Church. There is a mysterious force in real holiness; it can win recognition even from the devil, not to say from men.

But I am wandering. What I want to ask is this: have you ever felt, after the Communion of the Precious Blood, a sense of humility, born of the realization of the greatness of His giving and the littleness of ours? O, if ever God, who is Generosity Divine, has been generous, it is with us, His priests, He has been generous. Others, Christ has made His children. Of us — He has made Himself.

With feeble recognition and thin gratitude we answer all this Largesse of Almighty God. Like James and John, He has invited us to drink of His Chalice — we have and shall do so faithfully day by day. It has all been very sweet thus far, and I trust we shall grow stronger so that we may drink the dregs of bitterness and trial as unhesitatingly as we have supped of the depths of devotion and consolation. Are you prepared for this? We priests must be preparing for Gethsemane even while we dwell on Tabor. When we shall have emptied Life's chalice — we shall be given another brimming one — overflowing with eternal joy.

May the Blessed Mother give us both.

TRUST GOD

Dear ——:

Your letter of —— reached me safely and I am hastening to answer the same. O child, when will you begin to realize what the Precious Blood of Jesus Christ has done and will do for you? A soul that is fearful is a soul that does not know what the Precious Blood of Jesus has done for it — what the Precious Blood of Jesus will do for it as often as it has need. Now it is a strange paradox that oftentimes as in your case one who is sincerely desirous of honoring God and sanctifying his soul dishonors God and risks his salvation by lack of confidence in Him whom confidence most pleases because of His attributes of goodness and of mercy.

Do you stop to realize how you like to be trusted by those you love — do you not think that God too wishes to be trusted by those whom He loves with a love that has found expression in the bloody Sacrifice of His Most Beloved Son? Distrust men if you will, but do not distrust the God who made man to His image and has used His Son's Precious Blood to restore that image to its pristine brightness.

O, how a soul pleases God that trusts Him with a childlike faith. Such a trust is not presumption for it is childlike, and what is childlike is Godlike and what is Godlike pleases God. Is that not the story of the little Thérèse? Did she not just climb up in God's lap or, rather, insist like a child that she be lifted up? And so God stooped and lifted her up to His Sacred Heart, and refuses her nothing because she delighted that Heart by an absolute trust which paid homage to that Heart's boundless goodness and infinite mercy.

Cast yourself, therefore, dear child, I beg you, into the ocean of God's mercy. You will never sink for the arms of God will hold you, His Precious Blood sustain you, His Mother's Heart keep you and, clothed in radiant glory, you will come safely to the eternal shore and rest thereon forever. The soul that truly trusts God will always do its own part. It will live in God and for God, and in Him find strength to pass bravely through all the storms of life. Ever in Our Lady.

THE DOMINANT NOTE

DEAR ——:

Your letter brought me happiness in the knowledge of your own. The appreciation of the sublime truths of Our Faith brings inevitably a strange blending of sorrows and of joys in our lives. Temperament undoubtedly plays its part, environment has its influence, but when all is properly weighed and balanced, measured and placed in proper perspective, it seems to me, in the final assembly the dominant note in a Christian life should be that of joy.

Now by joy I do not mean that joy of childhood which has so largely a physical basis, nor do I mean the joy of grown-up children in the exultation of smoothly functioning bodies, nor the joy of earthly possessing, or earthly achievements; no, the joy I mean, and which I hold to be the characteristic note of real Christian life, is the spiritual joy that is born of Faith and Hope, and is the outward manifestation of Love Divine.

To worldlings this thought of spiritual joy means nothing, but so for that matter do their ideas of happiness mean nothing, or little or nothing, to me; and whereas Time strips them with inexorable fingers of their joys, Eternity keeps mine for me.

To return, the dominant note of a Christian's life should be joy. It should be joy, because his life is a gift of God, of a God of Supreme Goodness, Beauty and Holiness, Who is infinitely happy within His Own Being, and Who willed that eventually His rational creatures shall come by obedience to His laws, faith in His Son, love of His Spirit, to share the happiness of His Kingdom forever and forever. A true Christian, therefore, should have ever a singing heart, a spirit that serves God with joyfulness, for, like the ceaseless murmur of the sea, his heartbeats should be repeating over and over, "God loves me, God loves me, God loves me," and I love my God.

I am aware, of course—and here is where the difficulty arises for human nature—I am aware that trials of all sorts await us along the road of life. Original sin did a real job on this little globe of ours. Like a shiny new car smashed up on its first trip, this world will never be the same. From thence onward constant repairs have been necessary. But Faith has always its answer for this, and for all other objections. Yes, human nature needed repair and needs repairing still; human nature has slumped sadly into the mire and still sinks therein, but human nature has had its Repairer in the

Person of God's Own Son, and God's Own Son still abides upon this globe of ours in the Church that He established and that He promised He would be with until time should be no more.

We have, therefore, no need to walk alone, to bear life's burdens alone; against us stands the world, the flesh and the devil, but with us stands Our God, and God is good, O so good, dear ——, to those who trust Him, to those who try to answer, even though feebly, His Love with love, His Generosity with generosity, His All with all. Therefore, dear ——, let us go forward in Faith, in Hope, in Love, our hand holding to His Pierced hand, our hearts in the keeping of His Mother's.

TO A BROTHER PRIEST

Dear ——:

Last week I had a long train-ride to make along the banks of the Merrimac. The promise of the Springtime was everywhere wooing Nature to come forth in all her beauty, and along the river banks especially the gleaming white of the birches amid the dark background of the evergreens caught my eye. Whenever I see the white birches I think of the Mother of God, and that day as I journeyed and mused I thought of Our Lady and of her children, her children whose souls are kept gleaming fair because, like the white birches, their roots draw life-giving nourishment from the waters of a River. Now the River that nourishes immortal souls is the Stream whose Source is at Calvary, whose Spring is the Heart of God.

I suppose it will be only in Eternity that we shall come to recognize fully our debt to the Blood of Jesus. In that Life beyond when we shall possess and be possessed by God, shall see Our Sweet Redeemer face to face, then, I suppose, we will at long last realize that we are indeed a purchased people, and looking upon the glistening wounds of Christ we shall glimpse the munificence of the Price God paid for our salvation, and in consequence the debt we owe to Jesus and to His Most Precious Blood.

However, we must not wait until Eternity to pay our debt to God. We must begin now to prove our gratitude to Jesus, to pay our debt as best we may unto the Blood of God. Our souls must be golden chalices holding with care the graces His Blood has won for us. His Life-Blood coming to us morn by morn in the Chalice of His Eucharistic Heart must circulate in our souls to nourish, to strengthen, to purify, and then, even as the chalice of the daily Mass is always somewhere uplifted, so let our hearts be always uplifted by sacrifice, uplifted to God for His greater glory and the succoring of His creatures, and then consumed by unceasing prayer and self-denial.

Such a program is indeed trying to the earthly in us, but oh! so refreshing to the soul. Let us find consolation in the remembrance of the natural fatigue and repugnance that Our Beloved Master felt in the midst of His sufferings. Let us draw strength from His weakness, light from the shadows of Gethsemane, Blood from His Sacred Wounds.

You remember the old song that was old when we were young—"Drink to me only with thine eyes—the thirst that in the soul doth rise doth crave a drink divine"? Well, often I have thought of how a Divine Lover has answered that soul thirst, not figuratively, but really and substantially. Morning by morning our lips meet the lips of Christ's Wounded Heart and His Blood seals our soul until that other Sunrise when Jesus and His Blessed Mother shall come for us across the Great Frontier.

Till then let us keep faithful tryst with God—and Mary.

THREE NAILS

MY DEAR ——:

You are preparing to make your final vows. God be praised! I join the saints and angels rejoicing as yet another soul fastens itself to the Holy Cross of Jesus. May the nails never be withdrawn till the angels do so after your death and then, as with Jesus, the place of the nails will be gleaming apertures of light that shall enhance your glory forever in the courts of the Lord.

The world, at least a goodly portion thereof, thinks of vows as a cowardly serfdom—a surrender of man's noblest prerogative—his freedom, his liberty. As a matter of fact, just the opposite is true—to give back to God the most precious gift God has given us, to take our wills, yea, and all the other powers of our souls and bodies, and by a single act donate to God everything without reserve, our all, to be used at His good pleasure—this is in reality the supremest exercise of our God-given freedom. For no man can give more than all, and by the vows you will freely make you are giving all to Him Who is your All as He was your Beginning and will be your End and the Road Between.

But let us come down to earth. If this letter is to really help you, it must lift you up, but it must also put some concrete foundations underneath, else the elevation might be to no purpose. Many have taken vows; not all have kept them. The sixteenth century witnesses thousands of men and women putting aside their promises to God, and broken vows have not been confined to any one century by any means. Would that it might be so. The truth is this: vows will be kept only while love, Divine Love, reigns in the soul. The nails did not hold the Saviour to the Cross; Love did, His Love for us. The three nails by which you will seek to be crucified to the world will hold you to the

Holy Cross only so long as love for Jesus remains dominant in your heart.

I shall say Mass for you on the morning you make your vows, and my intention shall be this—that the love of Jesus Christ may never have a rival in your soul.

Ask Mother Mary for the same grace for

FATHER PAGE.

THE ONLY ANSWER

DEAR ——:

There are times, at least a few of them, in our lives when we are asked a question to which the wisest of us can give but one only answer—God's Most Holy Will! Such was the question you asked me today. Such is the answer, the only answer I can offer you —— dear, it is God's Most Holy Will.

To be sure, even this answer does not completely satisfy our natural craving for knowledge and explanation and understanding. It is rather an appeal of Faith to Faith. It is adequate only to souls who pay to their Creator and Redeemer the supreme tribute of an absolute trust.

Brother dear, I want you to give to God, your Heavenly Father, this perfect tribute. He it was Who gave you to —— and —— to you, He Who blessed your love and made it a sacred thing by the holy Sacrament of Matrimony, He Who gave that love the power of life, and has now sealed it even as His Own Love was sealed by the embrace of Death.

Time heals many wounds, Brother dear, but Faith alone can take the bitter sting from out them ere they heal. And so I shall pray, my Brother, that the only answer will be sufficient unto you, and your Faith sufficient to lift the eyes of your soul up from the shadows of the valley of Death to a hilltop crowned by the glorious Sunset of Divine Love, upward to Divine Love crucified, and may she who stood within the shadow of that Throne of Love put her mother-arms around you and give you courage to await the Sunrise of Eternal Life. Amen.

"IN THE BLOOD OF JESUS"

My Dear ——:

With what joy I write you this letter in the Blood of Jesus. I am writing in my room with Our Lady at the foot of the Cross and I can almost feel the Precious Blood falling on my hands as I write, for am I not a priest, and am I not writing to one who is so soon to be a priest and hold the Precious Blood lovingly aloft before the eyes of the world in the chalice of his virgin soul!

When I have written this, it would seem, dear Brother in Christ, I have said all that need be said of the priestly vocation. To be a priest is to have the vocation of being not "another Christ" but Christ! And what was Christ but a Living Chalice uplifted night and day—yea, and to be so uplifted through the centuries for the Glory of His Father and the salvation and sanctification of His creatures.

So you are to be a chalice, my Brother, a chalice for Christ, with Christ, in Christ, and you will find it sweet, I am sure, for you will be generous.

When a priest is generous with God, or even tries to be, he is bound to be happy. This truth holds true in all vocations but perhaps in no vocation so assuredly as in that of the Priesthood, for when a priest tries to be generous he is dealing directly with God and God is divinely generous.

Be, therefore, dear Brother, generous with Christ; ask Him to make of your soul a Roman chalice, with the broad, heavy base of humility, the straight stem of singleness of purpose, and the ample, wide cup of generosity. Ask His Holy Spirit, as well, to adorn it with the virtue-gems that shall delight both God and His angels. And as for me, I shall daily ask Our Blessed Mother to keep your chalice and mine and the souls of all priests, our brothers in Christ, chaste and holy and thus less unworthy of the lips and the Blood of Jesus Christ.

TODAY'S CHALICE

DEAR BROTHER IN CHRIST:

Your letter was a consolation, for though, as I trust you realize, I do not mind being forgotten, I am always glad to learn that the souls whom I love are not forgetting Jesus. To keep Jesus always in the picture is, I think, about as solid and satisfactory a recommendation as can be given to anybody, above all to a priest and a religious. You see when Jesus is, as we say, "in the picture," then our souls are bound at least in some degree to image Him, to reflect His character and hold His graces, and when souls hold God's graces they are bound to be fragrant, at peace with God and, consequently, as far as that may be possible, at peace with all the world.

It would seem, thus early in your career, Jesus has taught you a most important truth which most everyone recognizes in theory, but comparatively few are prepared to put into consistent practice. Long ago the Master declared, "No man can serve two masters," yet despite the obviousness of this truth, most of us spend the major portion of our lives trying to effect a working compromise. We are ready to serve God, but on our own terms. We want to please Him, but not at the cost of our own feelings. We desire Jesus to reign, but are not ready to dethrone self. We aspire to sit at His right hand and His left in His Kingdom, but today's chalice we are loath to lift to our lips!

My brother, I am at present preparing a novena in honor of St. Theresa of the Child Jesus. My study reveals ever more clearly to me that the true greatness of this saint of our own day is to be found in her heroic generosity with God. In her soul, despite all her tender and deep affection for His creatures, there was only One Master to be obeyed, One Goal to be sought, One Beauty to be entranced by, One Lover to be loved. Jesus was All to Theresa, and that is, no doubt, why today Jesus grants all to her prayers.

Brother, so dear in Jesus and Mary, we know the Way; let us from henceforth take It. We have the Truth, let us embrace It; we are close to the Life, let us enter and dwell therein, that thus our daily chalice of priestly renunciation shall be sweeter to the lips of our souls and Jesus be our All in all.

THE PRIESTLY PROGRAM

Dear Brother in Christ:

By the time you receive this letter God will have given you one of His greatest gifts, a participation in the priesthood of Jesus Christ. You know I share your happiness, the while I pray that at the end of your stewardship you may give Him back His gifts with abundant interest.

To receive the sacramental configuration to our Blessed Lord that Holy Orders confer, is, in very truth, a surpassing privilege. To live up to what that configuration implies is, thereafter, a supreme duty. Christ, our Blessed Master, was exalted among men by and on the Holy Cross, and if there be any other pathway to ultimate glory it is yet to be discovered. Therefore, dear Brother in Christ, from the first set yourself to accept with love all the sacrifices that priestly living entails. Nothing worth while in this world can be achieved without sacrifice, and the path of every noble life is paved with the stones thereof.

I feel humbled when I think of the generous spirit of sacrifice that animates countless Christians in the more hidden walks of life—the fathers and mothers, the brothers and sisters, the aunts and uncles, whose lives are beautiful in the eyes of God by reason of the uniform weaving of the strands of unflinching faith and unselfish love into the fabric of their daily existence. Oftentimes so simply have these souls accepted the burdens of Christian living, that they do not realize the heroism of their program. What a sweet surprise awaits them in the judgments of the Master!

Our priestly program must, therefore, be based squarely on the foundations of sacrifice, the oblation of all we have and of all we are for the glory of God and the salvation of immortal souls. This may seem and possibly is platitudinous, yet be persuaded, dear Brother, that upon the basis of oblation alone and in proportion to the degree and perfection thereof, can we, God's priests, hope to find happiness and abiding peace.

Meanwhile, though the laity may legitimately seek consolation in the holy bonds wherewith God has willed to knit human hearts together for the furtherance of His Divine purposes, our consolations must be sought primarily in Christ. Only while He reigns undisputedly over a priestly heart can that heart have peace. Only when Jesus reigns in us can we hope to advance His reign in others.

Thus, the priestly program of life, unnatural and strained as it must indeed appear to many outside the Faith, is, in truth, a logical conclusion from the premises of the greatness of God's giving to the sacerdotal heart. "Generously you have received, generously give," Christ told His chosen ones. Generously we have received, generously, let us pray, we may learn to give to Him Who has chosen us from all eternity to be such vital elements in His mystical body, and consequently so closely united to His Sacred Heart.

We shall pray for one another through the years, dear Brother, that the Bridegroom when He cometh may find us, His servants, watching, and in our souls the rich fruition of His grace.

FINAL VALUES

My Dear Child:

Here are my recommendations as regards your reading. The rugs and draperies of the soul's living room are the result in large measure of the weaving of the yarn of thought upon the loom of personality. Moreover, the yarn of thought is composed in substantial measure from the twisted threads of our sense impressions and particularly of our reading. Consequently, the importance of our choice of reading in determining the character and the quality of our soul's adornment.

How logically it follows from this that indiscriminate reading means a great many cheap and worthless threads woven into the tapestries of our soul. That is why I could not be faithful to my obligation to guide you to the best of my lights if I did not insist on the necessity of selectivity and discipline in the matter of reading. Eventually the fruit of our thought-looms must meet the examination of the Master of the House. Could I truly care for souls and yet be indifferent to their preparation for His inspection?

But let us carry the thought further. The more valuable a piece of art the more reasonable the practice of having it displayed by itself alone. Masterpieces are frequently and with reason given the distinction of being placed by themselves; and herein lies the justification for those who prefer to devote all their energies and faculties to the perfecting of one masterpiece, a masterpiece for which they have a Divine Model. These souls are like the merchant of the Gospel who, having found one flawless pearl, disposed of all other possessions for its purchase. They are artists who have glimpsed one image of such transcending glory they cannot rest until they have recorded their impression upon the immortal canvas of their souls. They are lovers who have seen with the eyes of faith the ineffable beauty of Christ's face and now cannot be diverted by the loveliness of creation.

It is because these things are true, dear child, that I would urge you to be selective in your summer reading. Read with a purpose—that of beautifying and enriching your soul. Do not weave into your tapestries of memory strands that will be inadequate to the eventual testings of God; and even if you do not care to convert the living room of your soul into a chapel with a single altar piece, at least I would wish you to recognize the wisdom that has its source in final values.

Asking Our Lady to bless you always.

CIBORIUM

Dear Sister in Christ:

I want to thank you for your letter which was forwarded to me from Notre Dame. It is both consoling and humiliating to realize one's words have proved helpful to another. It is consoling because the spiritual benefit of others is the fruitage desired by the writer; humiliating because this fruitage brings with it ordinarily the grace of a fuller realization of the inadequacy of one's own efforts and abilities to the result achieved. Moreover, one should be happy to recognize this inadequacy of self because one may thereby predicate with some reason a greater measure of God's grace in the activity in question. Was not St. Paul thinking along these lines when he proclaimed his willingness to glory in his infirmities that thereby the workings of God's grace might be the more manifest in his regard?

You tell me God's Will has placed you in a hospital. Very well, so long as He gives you the grace not only to recognize but to embrace lovingly His Holy Will what could be more desirable! In the process of our sanctification there are, I believe, two fundamental graces: first, ability to recognize God's Will in all the varied events of earthly existence, the little as well as great, the painful as well as the joyous; and second, the other and certainly rarer grace to realize and remember that back of the present and perhaps painful moment is the infinite tenderness of Divine Love and a Divine Lover.

These two fundamental graces I shall ask Our Blessed Lord to grant you, dear Sister, till the night is passed and in the morning down between the little white garden plots wherein souls are watered by tears and weeded by the fingers of pain shall come not the Little White Host in a golden ciborium but the Chaplain-in-chief to lift you, a frail little flower-host, and place you in the golden ciborium of His Sacred Heart.

In that hour, remember me to Jesus and to Mary.

THE BEGINNING OF WISDOM

My Dear ——:

I owe you an apology for the tardiness of this letter. These days hold for me a multitude of duties and July brings a host of its own. However, hiding behind other duties is a poor defense, yet one more understandable by you than by the general run of men.

When we met last you spoke of the element of fear in Catholic life. I know this is a common charge made by those outside the fold, but honestly, I believe it is one of the charges having the least foundation in fact. Undoubtedly there are Catholics constrained by fear from breaking God's laws, but shall we condemn men for using common sense? Such fear is truly "a beginning of wisdom," and is not the beginning of wisdom something highly desirable in this crazed world of ours wherein the wisdom of man is so largely devoted to preparations for self-destruction?

Actually, however, my long years in God's service leave me with the conviction that the average Catholic is motivated in his or her life by neither base fear nor perfect love, but by the first movements of love which are abetted by the reasonable fear of losing God and at the same time hindered by the difficulty, to creatures dependent as we are upon the tangible, of loving an invisible Being with an absolutely unselfish love. The charge, therefore, of the motivation of our lives by fear, is, if craven fear be meant, absolutely false; and if reverential fear be meant, will be found upon analysis to be translatable in terms of love not—yet—made perfect.

I honestly believe the average Catholic loves both God and the world. The resulting attempted compromise constitutes his difficulty, the resulting struggle, his life, the resulting victory for God or the devil—Heaven or Hell.

To me, the formula of life is quite simple—recognize God's love and give God love for love.

THE PRICE OF VICTORY

My Dear Sister in Christ:

I wish this letter to bring you fresh courage in the Service of the Master. When you receive it, it will probably be July, and July is the Month of the Precious Blood. For some years now I have tried, at least in a feeble way, to practice special devotion to the Precious Blood of Jesus, and I hope this will please you.

We owe everything to the Precious Blood, do we not? The forgiveness, so oft repeated, of our sins, the salvation of all the souls we love, the radiant virtues that make us love them—all that makes living worth while for ourselves and for all the world, has its source in the red fountains of Our Saviour's Wounds.

What a terrible trial life would be to thoughtful souls, were it necessary for them to carry always with them throughout life the deepening encrustation of their sins and failures! Yet the Merciful Love of God which has provided so wonderfully for our spiritual cleansing and refreshment is so little appreciated, so often forgotten or even abused. Let our souls in humble gratitude be like the singing brooks of the springtime, and let the burden of their song be "Glory, glory, glory to the Blood of Jesus Christ!"

It has struck me forcefully that devotion to the Precious Blood should appeal particularly to priests, to us who have the sublime privilege of lifting the Chaliced Blood Divine to our lips morn by morn. Do you pray, my Sister, that devotion to the Precious Blood may increase among the children of men, especially among priests, for the consolation of the Heart of Jesus.

The Heart-throbs of Jesus send the Precious Blood circulating through His Mystical Body. May your heart throb in unison with the Heart of Jesus and bring His Life-Blood to me and to all the world, and when my lips are purpled by the Wine of Virgins I shall whisper your name to the King.

Courage in the Mother of the Precious Blood—His Blood was the Price of Victory, and we must be prepared ever to pay the same.

THE WOUNDED

Dear Brother in Christ:

Though we have never met and may never meet on this side of Heaven, yet your letter served to make us in one brief quarter of an hour old friends.

Your life has indeed been one that it would be hard to explain humanly speaking, but thinking in God—there is here as everywhere a solution to the problem. The trouble is—so few of us do our thinking in God!

A case like yours has a very close parallel in the warfare of Nations. How often does a young officer hardly reach the front lines before the fine vision of his dreams is rudely ended by a screaming shell, or changed to the dull dream of unending pain. In such cases which are of daily occurrence during war-days—we take such losses as part of the inevitable price of victory. We must count them as the same when they come in the ceaseless conflict between God and satan for the possession of human minds and wills and hearts.

To be sure, even deep Faith does not remove the necessity of Faith. Faith is here but a star-shell that gives us a glimpse of the truth. But that glimpse is sufficient for us. By it we can see that every soldier, even though he fall before the first attack is launched, has contributed his bit to the eventual Victory, has fulfilled his duty, has given his all.

Possibly this last statement requires qualifications—even a badly wounded soldier can give something more—his suffering, and if God wills it, his life; and you, a soldier of Christ, can give to your Commander one thing more—your life for the Sake of His Sacred Cause.

Make then this offering, my dear Brother in Christ, and if, as well may be, Jesus chooses rather to send you back once more into action, then you can go with even greater confidence within the Shelter of His Most Holy Will.

I will join your prayers to the Queen of Victory to this end.

WE ARE BROTHERS!

Dear Brother in Christ:

How I rejoice with you in the *Magnificat* your heart will be singing in these days of holy joy and exaltation.

Jesus loves you. He proves it by giving you, by sharing with you, His Own, His Very Own Priesthood. How can you ever repay Him? *Quid retribuam Domino? Quid retribuam!*

You know already the answer. God's sweet, sweet Spirit has breathed the words: "I will take the Chalice of the Lord and will call upon His Holy Name, I will call upon His Holy Name and be saved from my enemies!"

O my Brother, do not drink the Chalice of the Lord only at the visible Altar, but let your soul be His temple, your heart His invisible Altar, and there drink the mystical chalice of Our Lord's sufferings, sacrifices, humiliations, disappointments. If you only pray, pray perseveringly to His Spirit and to His Mother, all will go well. You will grow in the love of Him until that happy day and hour when the bitter wine of man's ingratitude and coldness will be sweet to the lips of your soul because it was once, and is still, the sponge lifted to His.

I shall pray for you always, and you must do the same for me. God has given me, these many years, the grace to recognize that neither race nor color counts with Him and consequently should not count with us; we are brothers—we who share His Priesthood, we who have Christ as an Eldest Brother and His Blood as the Sacred Bond of our amity.

JOYFULNESS

DEAR BROTHER IN CHRIST:

Your note, though tardy, brought me pleasure. I am so glad that you are happy, spiritually happy in God's service. There is no simpler proof of the spiritual health of a religious than the joyfulness of his spiritual outlook. Of course, we must make a clear distinction between that joy which is the result of natural causes and that which we must presume is the fruit of the Holy Ghost, but once this distinction has been made, we can honestly say that we are happy in God's service; then, or at least so it seems to me, we may rest assured we are not losing ground spiritually, that we are instead going forward and that indeed God is with us in the battle.

To serve God in joyfulness was the inspired counsel of the Psalmist; it remains an inspired counsel for God's servants in every age and clime. And why should we not be joyous—we who carry the vessels of the Lord, we who are, indeed, ourselves vessels of election chosen to bear His Name unto the Gentiles together with the precious cargoes of His grace and His eternal love? Vessels, perhaps—yes, certainly—destined to suffer, but nevertheless joyful because we are aware this suffering will but make us more like unto Our Master, dearer and closer to His Sacred Heart!

O, how happy all priests and especially missionary priests should be! Undoubtedly to some this declaration will seem just an effusion of emotional devotion, but I know you, dear Brother, will look more deeply and will understand. Do you recall the famous instruction of St. Francis of Assisi to one of his little brothers "in what true happiness consisted"? Once we shall have found the true love of Jesus Christ, nothing will be so sweet as to share His Crucifixion; and who, day in and day out, has a better opportunity to do this than a missionary? It is precisely this chance of suffering, this opportunity of conformity to Christ and Him Crucified that makes the missionary vocation so attractive to truly generous souls.

Whether we look, like the Israelites of old, back over the Red Sea of God's mercies of the past to us, or regard the pillar of smoke, the cloud of flame, and the Heavenly Manna that now is ours, or look forward to the Promised Land of God's eternal reign, we should be joyful—we will be, if only we look ever more steadily upon the endless manifestations of the Merciful love of the Creator and ever less fretfully at the constant revelation of our own frailty and nothingness.

Let us, my dear Brother, go forward joyously to the battlelines where God's enemies must be met and God's Queen will give us the promised victory.

BLOOD FOR BLOOD

Dear Sister in Christ:

I gave you a special commemoration in my Mass this morning by reason of your Anniversary, and I want this note to carry over a bit of your joy into the days to be.

Our real joy, as the years advance, will be found to rest ultimately in the abiding love of Our God of which the Precious Blood of Jesus is both the Pledge and Seal. How blessed a privilege is yours — to have the Blood Most Precious as your title! Let it constitute, as indeed it does for all mankind, your title to Christ's love and Christ's title to your love. He has purchased your soul with no less an offering, and you are happily giving your Lover Divine that which He has purchased. Give Him all, dear Child; in that lies the secret of happiness for consecrated souls.

And while you strive to give Jesus all, remember, as did little St. Thérèse, those other souls He has likewise purchased but has not received! Remember the harvest fields where the ripened grain awaits the harvesters who come not. Herein rests the essential unselfishness of true contemplatives. They rest at the feet of Jesus, but they are not inactive there. Like Queen Esther, they have a petition for the King. Their petition, however, is not for the salvation of one race but for all races, all peoples; for not one but all these were beneficiaries to that contract between Divine Justice and Divine Love sealed on Calvary in the Blood of Christ.

Go forward then, dear Child, in your God-blessed

pathway of life, and when the stones bruise your feet, the thorns pierce your flesh, offer the answering drops of your blood, at least in spirit, in the living chalice of your heart to the chalice of Christ's Heart, pledging Him blood for Blood!

ONLY BY FAITH

My Dear Child:

The ways of God are at one and the same time simple and complex, hidden and yet revealed; and herein—as ever—the paradox of our Christian heritage is continued.

God's ways with men are simple because they proceed from but one source, His Love, and are revealed because they would conduct men to but One Goal which is Himself. God's ways are complex because there are many paths leading to the One City, and God's ways are hidden because they must breast the hills of difficulty and disappear from time to time in the forests of doubts and the mist-filled valleys of human tribulations. It is only by Faith we can keep the road in these circumstances, while on the back-trail the light of experience grows dimmer and dimmer against the coming night.

That is why to us as well as to all Christ's missionaries the lantern of Faith is so necessary. Without our lantern we must surely lose our way in the darkness, without Faith's vision we should walk blindly even in the light! Did not the Master speak of eyes that saw not? How many, alas! there are, even in our own dear land, who are aware of all things visible yet in these visible things do not find their ultimate purpose—their testimony unto God?

It is the gift of Faith that enables one to find God in all things, in all the multitudinous events and varied circumstances of life. I shall never forget the impression a venerable parish priest of Montreal left in my mind years ago by the simple remark, "Father, I touch the hand of God a dozen times a day." We all touch God's hand, dear Child, a dozen times a day, but sometimes we lack that sensitiveness of Faith which made the old French curé so conscious of the identification.

Since, therefore, it is your high destiny to light the way to God for others, it seems to me, I could ask no more valuable grace for you in this month of the Precious Blood than that of an increase of Faith. This then, I shall ask for you, a Faith so clear and strong that like the headlights of a modern locomotive it will channel a stream of golden light through the fog and bring not only you yourself but a whole trainload of precious souls into the Station where headlights are no longer necessary because of the Radiance of Unveiled Truth.

"BLUE PRINTS"

My Dear Child:

Your note brought me much happiness because it reveals a lively interest in the welfare of others, and where the Second Commandment is being carefully observed, I have little fear that the First and Greatest will be forgotten. I was especially touched by what you wrote concerning the little lady of the streets whom you tried to befriend. God reward you—as indeed He will—for such sisterly interest. Girls of this class are, I am convinced, more often than not victims of their environment and of economic injustices rather than wilful rebels against God's law—more sinned against than sinning—and my own soul cries out against the hypocrisy of a civilization that pays the homage of respect and at times adulation to the man who pays for his sinful pleasure and scorns the woman whom hunger rather than passion has led to selling of her virtue. There is no greater, deeper shame in our so-called civilization than the economic injustices that make these things not only possible but realities of every great, proud city of the world.

However, in the search for souls we must—lest we fail to obtain our end—work with a degree of prudence. Prudence is not a favorite virtue of mine, but I keep its alliance for fear of being outflanked by the enemy of all good. How many wonderful works undertaken for God's honor have come to naught because of a lack of prudence in their apostles! How many temples of zeal have been toppled into the dust by reason of the refusal of their builders to consult the blue prints of experience! So, dear child, as you press forward in your effort to be all things to all, do not forget to beg of the Divine Spirit Who is so much in our thoughts these days to give you a generous measure of those two virtues of Prudence and Fortitude which serve to balance most happily an apostolic life such as you at present seem called upon to live.

You can count always on my prayers and I count most assuredly on yours.

AUGUST

In August, like a queen going
to her death, our gardens
put on a last brave beauty.

SUNSET

DEAR FRIEND:

Silently the heat of midsummer has come upon us, and strong is he who does not wilt spiritually as well as physically beneath its dead weight.

The last time I wrote you it was to commend you on the "discovery" of daily Mass, now I want to urge you to complete the promise of the morning with an evening pledge of love for God-on-earth. I want you to learn to love Jesus abiding with us. I want you to know the peace that awaits in the deepening dusk of the sanctuary illumined by the fluttering flames of the vigil lights and the steady glow of His Heart's love and our Faith.

There is something magic about the earthly Home of Jesus at eventide. Everything seems to lend itself to simple, heartfelt prayer. It is like that accentuated silence that reigns in a big factory when the great motors have ceased their daily toil, the shafts and belts their monotonous singing and the time clock has run out its evening Angelus so sweet to the ears of the children of men.

In that wondrous silence of our Altars there awaits for you peace and refreshment of soul such as you may find nowhere else. Search elsewhere in the desert of this world, in the end you will turn back to the Oasis where the sweeping wings of the angels take the place of swaying palms, and the Heart of Christ is the Fountain, clear, cool, inexhaustible, whose waters murmur as they flow a ceaseless invitation to the world-weary traveler—"Come unto Me all ye who labor and are heavily burdened and ye shall find rest for your souls." In His Service, ever.

CARRIERS OF TREASURE

DEAR SISTER IN CHRIST:

The pyx case arrived safely Thursday. The last one you sent me has served faithfully, holding the Christ Child snugly and sweetly as He was born to the souls He loves so well. But, over a year's steady service had left it just a little the worse for wear, and so I craved a fresh cloak for the Master, and now I have my desire.

The leather will never know it encased its Creator. The silk can never feel the heart beats of God's Son. So they are privileged, yet know it not. What a shame; what a tragedy!

But what a far greater tragedy is enacted in the thousands of sensitive rational souls that are alive to everything but God. A living death—the soul with God so close and yet there be no room for Him, nay they are even too preoccupied to catch the sound of His patient knocking.

Oh gentle, patient Jesus, how long wilt Thou persevere? Oh Divine Beggar, come in out of the cold of the world. My heart is not much, not very roomy, not very warm; I have no sumptuous banquet of loving adoration to offer You, but at least I shall not keep You standing at the door, at least You are welcome, thrice welcome to what little of shelter and peace and warmth there is here.

Speak thus, dear Sister, to the Christ Whom you receive in Holy Communion. Learn to abide in Him and He in you, and little by little there will come a fresh peace into your life, like the peace of a summer morn, a full warmth like that of a summer noon, a brooding contentment like that of a summer's eve when the robins are saying good-night.

The most wondrous thing in the world is the love of God for His creatures. The most astounding thing in the world is the failure of God's creatures to appreciate that love. One thing at least we can do—like the little pyx case let us harbor God, but let us also do what the case cannot—let us be mindful of our high and privileged duty. Where thy heart is, there thy treasure is. May Jesus, Sister, be your Treasure as He is the Treasure of His Blessed Mother and His Blessed Saints.

THE HOST

DEAR SISTER:

You will have to learn to be very patient with creatures—you can learn that from God. I should have written you long ago but the days are not long enough to accomplish all I would like to do.

Since you are now dedicated in a special way to the Blessed Sacrament, I propose the Blessed Sacrament as the Model of your life. Jesus is always the Supreme Model whether in the Manger or on the Cross, and He has not ceased to be the Model in the Sacrament of His Love.

This thought of Jesus here and now in the Eucharist as a Model, has always had for me a very special attraction. The attraction of some souls is the Manger; others, and these in greater numbers, the Cross; mine has always been the Eucharist in which Manger and Cross are united, in which the Little Babe rests humbly under the swaddling clothes, humbly, sweetly, silently, —yes, and crucified by His chosen ones' indifference and coldheartedness in the empty vastness of ten thousand churches. Your heart is only one, Child—but one is better than none, and your one can console His One Heart present in a myriad of Hosts throughout the universe. His Sacred Heart encircles the world with love and is Itself encircled with thorns—your heart resting before the Tabernacle can encircle His Heart with love and thus the world and Jesus Hostia in every part of the world.

As for the virtues of the Religious Life—how beautifully Jesus teaches them to us from out the silent Host.

What are the three great virtues of the Religious Life? Humility, which is the foundation—virtue upon which all the other virtues must rest. Obedience—which is the directing virtue—without which all other virtues would be unbalanced and disfigured. Charity—which is the crowning virtue—the virtue which like the roof of a house is nearest to heaven, protects all that dwell within and makes the dwelling habitable for oneself and others.

In the Host Jesus is humble—so humble only Faith can discern His Presence. In the Host Jesus is obedient—obedient to the word of the most unworthy of His servants, to sinner as promptly as to saint. In the Host Jesus is charitable—Love All-generous, All-patient, All-forgiving, All-loving—giving without measure, giving without limit save only that limit which even God cannot surpass which is Himself.

Look then no further than the Tabernacle for the inspiration of your life, only lift your eyes to greet Jesus morning by morning as He is lifted up to give you consolation, courage, example, love. Salute Him at that moment in the depths of your Heart—"My Lord and my God, my God and my All—host for Host, love for Love, all for All. Jesus, Thou art my All and I wish and will to be all Thine, ever in Thy Sweet Mother's heart. Amen."

MY HEART

Dear ——:

This is the Feast of the Eucharistic Heart of Jesus. There are so many beautiful feasts starring the Church's calendar that it is impossible to have only one favorite, nevertheless this Feast has a very special place in my heart and I feel sure it has in yours likewise.

What has drawn us away from the world and all

that the heart of humans clings to into the silent courts of prayer, the busy marts of service, the altar of sacrifice, save only the Sacred Heart? And where did we come to know and love That Heart save in the flickering silence that marks His Eucharistic Presence? If we are happy today in God's Service, at home in His courts, then this is because there is a Eucharistic Heart of Jesus, because Jesus is still on earth, still lavishing His wealth of love and affection upon the hearts He made to hold and cherish His supreme and holy love.

O, what happiness when human hearts fulfill their Creator's dictate, what joy when creatures love their God! What eternal horizons—gold rimmed like the sunrise—has the soul that has climbed atop the sand dunes of earthly considerations and gazes with awe-filled eyes upon the ocean of God's love.

Let us remember today that the ocean of God's love which once surged in Blessed Mary's bosom now pulsates within His Eucharistic Heart.

OTHER HOMES FOR GOD

DEAR ——:

Now that the excitements and festivities and social obligations that the beginning of your new life involved are over, I am sending you my greetings. Of course I sent you greetings in the Heart of Jesus—Hostia upon your wedding morn, but now I repeat them with a wee bit counsel tacked on. You will, I know, take the counsel in good part, for you know well it comes from the simple heart of a true friend.

Heaven is a Home, God's Home. The destiny of man is Heaven. That man may reach God's Home which is his own through the largesse of God and the Blood of God's Son, all else is given man. Now the Sacrament of Matrimony is intended to sanctify, ennoble and fortify human love that there may be Homes on earth for God, that is, Heaven on earth.

Now I know what a wild flight of idealism this concept invokes, but this, nevertheless, is God's plan, and the only thing that prevents its concrete fulfillment is the selfishness of God's creatures.

Let me say once more, I believe God wishes every little Christian Home to be a little Heaven. How sacred and deep then is the true significance of the Sacrament that makes Homes. It is God's chosen symbol of His Son's ineffable Union with His Bride, the Church, and the immortal souls that make the Church a living, breathing reality in time and for eternity.

Behold then, dear ——, your part in God's vast enterprise. You cannot make all houses Homes, nor all homes parts of Heaven, but this you can do, and this, please God, I know you will do — unselfishly and faithfully fulfill the duties of your God-blessed partnership, and may God ever be at home in your Home, and may He give to you and to your fuller heart the sublime fruition of a son for His Sacrifice and a daughter for His Son's Heart and Mother Mary's Service.

OUR HOST

DEAR SISTER:

This is a day of days for you as the Mantle of Our Dear Lady of the Cenacle slips about you. Had God willed it so, I would have been present to share your joy, but since He willed otherwise, I shall share your joy from afar, and yet not from afar — for we are always near unto the Heart of Jesus, and the Heart of Jesus near unto us, and so in the Heart of Jesus it is possible for us to be always with our relatives and friends.

The life of the Cenacle under the guidance of God's Holy Spirit and Our Blessed Lady's example, centers around the little White Host of the Altar. By His Presence undying in the Blessed Eucharist, Jesus plays Host to the souls He loves so intensely, and the souls that love Him, that answer His love divine with their love, strive to play host to Jesus. In this contest of love they are bound to lose, for they can never match the perfection of God's giving, they can never make so perfect an oblation of self as Jesus has made, and still makes for them. Nevertheless, they can strive, they must strive, and God will bless their efforts—if they be made humbly and prayerfully. Mother Mary will not fail to espouse the cause of their growth in sanctity, and in the end, when the Host comes to welcome them into His Home, then shall they be like unto Him for they shall see Him face to face. It is sweet to lose to God!

Meanwhile, dear Child, go forward with confidence in the purpose of God's Holy Spirit to perfect the work He began so long ago within your soul. Go forward calmly, for the strength of God is within your soul and about you the Mantle of Mother Mary's special protection and prayers. Go forward joyously, for if human love that is sweet and noble is a thing of joy to human hearts, why surely the loving of Jesus Hostia should be the sweetest of joys as He is truly the Noblest and Sweetest of Lovers, and we are His—and He is Ours and Mary is Our Mother.

THE ANSWER

Dear Brother in Christ:

I am so glad that you wrote me of your needs. Here in —— where our people are so numerous and their Faith so strong, we receive many more offerings for Masses than we can ourselves take care of, and therefore we are in a position to help our brother priests in this respect. Write whenever the need arises, and we will take care of your needs, God willing.

Your letter, however, sounded one little note that gave me concern. It reflected a wee bit of loneliness, and loneliness is not good for anyone—not even for a priest. God did not make man to live alone. God does not want man to live alone, even though that man be a priest. That is one reason why He instituted the Sacrament of Matrimony for men in general, and for us, His priests, the Sacrament of Sacraments, the Eucharist that holds His Loving Heart.

My years will excuse my preaching a wee bit to you, my younger brother, or if not my years, my love for you and my sincere desire for your happiness in our priesthood. The answer to our priestly needs, the secret of priestly happiness, the Source of priestly zeal and contentment, the love our hearts — like all other hearts — crave by their very nature, all these things are to be found in the cultivation of a personal devotion to our Divine Lover in the Sacrament of His Love. Devotion to our Eucharistic Jesus is not a luxury, it is a necessity of our priestly lives, for us more truly — if that were possible — than for anyone else is the Blessed Sacrament, the Bread of Life, the Source of Love.

Set yourself, therefore, dear Brother, set yourself if necessary, even grimly, to come by faithfully kneeling at His feet through hours of dryness and distraction to that supreme gift of God, which is a soul aflame with answering love. Do this, and you will never more be truly alone; God will fill to overflowing with His gracious presence your mind and its reflections, your heart and its affections, your life and its activities, and thus Time shall forecast your Eternity and both be filled with God.

Ever in Our Lady's Service.

SOMETHING WORTH LIVING FOR

DEAR ——:

I am sorry — or I would be did I not strive to see God's will in everything — that you have had to wait so long a time for this letter. When one has many things to do, one realizes why Jesus multiplied Himself by the Blessed Sacrament and the Priesthood. He simply did for all what we would like to do for our dear ones.

Please do not hesitate on the pathway of Perfection. It is painful at times, I know. It was painful, yes, crucifying, unto God's Son, Our Blessed Saviour, but He did not turn back nor hesitate because His Purpose had been fired in the flames of Divine Love. All worth-while lives are motivated by a noble love, and the noblest of lives are those that have behind them the noblest of loves, and the noblest of loves, I need not remind you, is the Love of Our God. God, child, and His Love, a God Who is Love, is surely Something worth living for.

This plan of life, I know you have made your own. It was before your mind when you entered the religious life. It must remain and grow more and more dominant as the road unfolds itself to your gaze. Only hearts of strong love have courage for a long road, and you are young, child, and as far as we may judge, you have a long road before you.

But what is a long road but a short road when we walk with one we love, and God walks with you, child, and you must walk with God and hold tightly to His Hand. Then though you may stumble, you cannot fall, for His strength unfailing will sustain you—and the light of His Veiled Countenance light you through the darkest night, His Voice guide you amid Life's mists, His Love bring you safely to your Journey's end—

Home to Mother Mary and, please God, Father Page.

THE MASTER'S CHOICE

Dear Mother in Christ:

I am writing to you for your Feastday, the Feast of dear Peter, that strong yet human fisherman whom Jesus chose to be His first Vicar upon earth. The study of his life can be a source of deep spiritual profit both to you and to those whom Christ has committed to your keeping, and so, I know you will pardon a rather preachy letter, to this end.

How well the Master planned for the encouragement of those who in the years to be would hold authority within His Kingdom when He made of Peter the First Head of His Church. Had He chosen one who had never failed, like Joseph, one who had been faithful in the darkest moments, like John, we would have acclaimed the wisdom of His choice, but would have been discouraged by the comparison. But when Jesus chose the man who failed Him, the disciple who denied Him and sealed his denial with an oath, then indeed we must both ponder more deeply the Master's purpose in order to ascertain His plan of Love.

What courage to superiors who have failed should not Peter's example bring. What confidence of the Master's forgiveness, what encouragement to true repentance for faults, what meekness toward others, what gracious forgiveness to the weak, no matter their station or rank.

The secret of Peter's fall is that of overconfidence, which in turn was the outgrowth of a lack of self-knowledge. Peter never knew until that evening how much of self-love was lurking in his devotion to Christ. The secret of his repentance is simply the triumph of his own humility and the Master's love.

I know, Mother so dear in Christ, that you do not need these reflections, but through you I hope to reach those souls who some day may hold authority in the Community. Teach them, Mother, to be truly humble so that Jesus may be proud of them. Teach them to be proud only of Christ and His mercies because these very mercies are but the fuller revelation of His Love. Teach them to love the lower places that they may find higher ones in His Heart—and Mary's forever.

Pray for me, dear Mother.

My Dear Child:

If I mistake not, this date is close to the anniversary of "your" Pentecost, your Confirmation, Come Holy Ghost!

O Child, we can never love God's Sweet Holy Spirit enough, for is it not God's Holy Spirit who has breathed into our souls the priceless gift of our Faith? I think you are aware I recommend to all my spiritual family the practice of special devotion to the Adorable Third Person of the Eternal Trinity — (indeed, I recommend devotion to Each Person, but the Holy Ghost is certainly the Most Forgotten on earth!). One little aspiration I use is this: "Sweet Holy Spirit, guide and direct all the movements of our souls to the Glory of the Eternal Trinity," and again, "Sweet Holy Ghost, give us the Gift of Fortitude, teach us how to pray, how to live, how to love!"

However, I must not wander from the first purpose of this letter which is to answer your question. Here is the answer. I think you will find it clear and I trust you will follow its direction.

Who are you, dear Child, that you may plan your future so far in advance! It cannot be done and, even if it could be done, it would not be the way of perfect love, the way of the saints in which I think you wish to be led!

Abandon yourself, and, above all, your future into the hands of God, your Divine Lover. Find and follow His Voice as revealed clearly to you in *today's* duties. Dream, if you must, of tomorrow's service, but remember we never live except in Today! and all that you hope Tomorrow will bring you is yours today, i.e., if you are guided by a pure intention to live for God's greater glory. For can we not live and work and suffer for God today! Can we not love God today!

Therefore, dear Child, I recommend to you to be

like your Divine Master, to let yourself be led by His Holy Spirit into the Desert of Holy Abandonment; there you will find rest for your soul, there you will find peace, there you will find Jesus, for in the Desert of Holy Abandonment there is an Oasis His Love has made, and where the Sweet Waters of His Sacred Heart await to cool the parched lips of Life's wayfarers.

Then, please pray for me to His Mother.

THE REST OF US

DEAR FATHER:

It pleased me the other evening to hear you assert that it is not difficult to love God. I do not remember ever hearing this truth expressed as you voiced it, but I subscribe to your conclusion with all my heart. God is just, and since He has commanded us to love Him, this must be something that can be fulfilled by all apart from extreme difficulty and extraordinary effort.

The saints, of course, carry out this Commandment to a heroic degree, but God invites but does not command His creatures to climb such heights, to ascend to such rarefied altitudes. He is a Being of Infinite Graciousness Who loves not only His saints, but the rest of us as well; He is not only a Father, He is Our Father, and as such makes allowance in the perfection of His love for all the imperfection of ours. He has made, He still makes things easy for His children, through the Blood of His Only-begotten, He has made it easier to know Him, easier to love Him, easier to abide in the peace of His Spirit in the bosom of His Holy Church.

When, therefore, we weigh all the elements that enter in, we still, so it seems to me, are justified in being spiritually optimistic. The human contribution is indeed faulty, yet God's contribution is divinely adequate. He it is Who designed our nature, He it is

Who has repaired it, He it is Who has destined it to spiritual flight.

Thus, though it is not likely any of us will break any altitude records, spiritually speaking, yet by the help of His grace, neither shall we crack up our soul-planes. It is not too difficult to learn to fly in the atmosphere of grace, to sustain our flight by prayer and little sacrifices, and though our engines may stall a bit and the controls at times give us trouble, yet, please God, there need be no forced landings save within the ample landing fields of His Commandments where sacramental offering awaits to repair our defects.

So, dear Father, like you, I trust my soul-plane shall come winging home through the twilight, guided by the beacon of Faith, sustained by Hope, destined to make a safe landing and be housed forever in the hangar of Divine Love. Then while the saints receive their well-deserved honors, the rest of us shall joyously thank God that our flight was not too difficult beneath the shadow of His wing.

"ALL DAYS"

My Dear ——— :

Thanks for the remembrance of my Anniversary. Although I ask nothing but God's Most Holy Will, yet it is pleasant when His Will is for our consolation in the thoughtfulness of His servants. We will be more blessed, will we not, when our consolation is found solely in His Will? When this shall be true, then will your saying be true, "all days are happy days." I glimpse the mountain but am still in the valley. I stop too often for rest. I lack the courage necessary for a quick ascent. How many saints there would be if sanctity did not involve heroic self-conquest!

Yet even this side of the higher altitudes of sanctity may we not find rest for our tired hearts, peace for our dusty souls, in the upland pastures where the Master tends those of us who so love Him that we refuse to descend even though to ascend farther seems beyond our strength? After all He is the Good Shepherd and, as such, we can count upon His loving Heart to guide us and His broad shoulders to carry us in safety to our journey's end. What we need most is the humility that asks His aid and the spirit of abandonment requisite for its fulfillment.

All days can thus be happy days if we learn to look steadfastly to God. It is the focusing of our vision continually upon self that leads to pessimism and discouragement. We cannot turn our eyes to the Adorable Trinity and not feel, sooner or later, the warmth and sunlight of God's Love penetrating our being. The thickest clouds disperse at the breath of His Spirit. The darkest night of the soul is but a prelude to the coming of the Light. And through the mists and darkness, just as mariners at sea, we too have a binnacle-light shining in the darkness to illumine our course; we too have the consolation of the consciousness of perseverance amid the tempests.

Pray then, dear Sister, that I may ever hold to my course; pray that I may cooperate yet more consistently with the graces that fall in such generous abundance from the hands of Mary upon all souls but upon none more generously than the chaliced souls of priests.

And what you ask from me, I shall ask for you and your dear Community, for it is a unique feature of loving God that the more one loves Him, the more one truly desires that all others might be partakers of one's Joy. God be your Joy, dear Sister, and may your Joy be with you all days till the shadows melt away.

THE PATH OF HIGH DESIRES

DEAR CHILD:

You may, if you wish, make the heroic act. I think that you are lowly enough to realize it will be God, not you, Who must translate the inspiration into continued reality. However, that you may be doubly sure of bringing consolation to the holy souls, I recommend that you make this offering through and in the Heart of Mary, Our Most Holy Mother. Gift-promises placed in her hands will be just so much the more precious to her Son Divine, just so much surer of being fulfilled with cheerful fidelity along the pathway of the years.

I am glad you have found the heart-path to Jesus. The intellect is a lantern, rather a dim lantern withal (since original sin smoked the chimney), and only faith's counsel keeps us from wandering aimlessly in the gloom. But the heart that Divine Love has enkindled has a pathway of its own — right into the Kingdom of God — and I rejoice exceedingly to know you are running with humble confidence along the path of high desires.

Be not afraid of loving God too much — no one has ever succeeded, though not a few have tried — but, that you may not permit your desires to outrace your capacities, place your hand in Mother Mary's and ask her to run with you in the way.

WITH QUIET CONFIDENCE

DEAR CHILD:

You must not try to carry these burdens all in your own mind — if you do you will just get worn out — and to no purpose. Leave your marital problems *with quiet confidence* in the Sacred Wounds of Christ. The Blood of Christ will there supply an answer. In these cases worrying accomplishes nothing — except possibly to deprive Jesus of the consolation your trust in Him would otherwise supply. When you are old in God's service you will realize how uniformly the element of time enters into the final triumphs of grace. You see God is up against something that He, Himself, has endowed with freedom, the human will, and of His creation God is jealous even to the point of laying siege rather than taking by assault. Besides, as long as God is patient, we can afford to be the same.

So I come back to an old theme song as ancient as the beginnings of God's mercies to the children of men—confidence in God; trust, childlike and absolute—and a singing heart in the knowledge of the adequacies of God's merciful Love to balance the scales of His Justice.

Meantime I shall ask Our Lady to take a hand in your own and your dear one's welfare.

SEPTEMBER

September brings us home again from hill
and countryside and from the edge of
those restless ocean ranges whose
white crests are flung in ceaseless homage upon the
wet hem of the world.

NIGHT

DEAR ——— :

When this note reaches you it will be the sweet dear month of September, sweet because it holds so many Feasts of Our Blessed Lady, and dear to all true lovers of Jesus because dedicated to the Sorrows of His Mother.

When the night of trial and sorrow falls upon your soul — and it will fall because God loves you too well not to cast the shadow of His Cross across the pathway of your life — then, Child, lift up your eyes and through the darkness one light will shine out to cheer and guide your way. Follow that light and you will find it comes from an open doorway, and within you will find an open heart awaiting those that mourn — it is the heart of a Mother, and that Mother, the Mother of God.

Best loved of all His creatures, God gave to her the first place in His Son's Heart and the most perfect participation in the sorrows of that Heart. Mary, Our Mother, suffered most because she loved most, and she loved most because she, before all others, was one with the Will of God.

Accept then, Child of Mary, God's sunshine, with a gay but grateful heart. But remember I have told you before it come to pass, when the night falls, and the wind and rain of trial and desolation sweep in upon your soul — hasten to Mary, you will find her beneath His Cross.

Where may you find,

FATHER PAGE

"BEHOLD THY MOTHER"

DEAR ——:

I was glad to hear from you, glad that you are well, and glad above all that you have decided to give yourself to the service of Jesus Christ. There is nothing so reasonable as to serve God, unless it be to love Him. And in reality they only really serve who truly love. Otherwise the service of God is but a cloaked service of self and He at least is not deceived.

Now you, I am sure, will with God's grace really serve, and to aid you to this end I want you to have a motto, a watchword, a battle cry, that shall constantly remind you of His most blessed service.

Our beloved Pius X. chose "to restore all things in Christ." Francis Xavier had "give me souls," and this too was the battle cry of Don Bosco—the great boy-savior of the last century. Lafayette had "why not?" as a challenge to himself, and the same thought inspired Ignatius of Loyola to fight "for the greater glory of God."

However, as you are my son in Christ, I ask you to come with me. Let us pass into the shadow of the Cross. Pause now and listen. Out of the tremendous silence comes a special last message from His parched lips—nay from His dying Heart for you who are called to be another John—another faithful, loving, single-hearted disciple of the Master. All His love for you is poured out in three brief words that come from out His Heart, "Behold thy Mother!"

If then I might choose for you, I would choose these words of His: "Behold thy Mother." Behold her and your face will ever be turned to the Cross and Jesus. You will not forget Him, nor the reason for your being, and you shall glorify Him and He shall share with you His glory eternal and His Mother's blessed Home.

JUXTA CRUCEM

DEAR ——— :

The prayers you have promised to say for me to Our Sorrowful Mother will be to me a daily source of strength and consolation. How beautifully God wills all things; by prayer we can annihilate time and space, we can help one another, we can kneel together at Mary's knee which was her Son's — Our God's — first and favorite throne.

Not alone from a selfish motive am I glad of the prayers to the Sorrowful Mother. I rejoice for your sake as well, for devotion to the Sorrowful Mother will draw your heart nearer God's, and so, God will be glorified and consoled, as He always is, by and through and in His Mother's Heart. Amen.

We must love Our Mother ever blessed under all her titles, but we are pledged to love her under one in a very special way, and that one is the one that became hers forever as the shadows lengthened on Calvary and like ghostly sword blades transfixed her Mother-Heart.

The world and its children is always ready to rejoice — to drink of the joyfulness of life. We are not of the world, nor are we of its offspring, we who have been born "not of blood, nor of the will of the flesh, nor of the will of man, but of God"; and as true lovers of that God, it is our privilege to share His cup of sorrow, to taste the bitter waters that stream from out His Mother's transfixed and agonizing Heart. "O ye who pass by the wayside, stand and see if there be any sorrow like to my sorrow!" No, Mother, no sorrow like to thy sorrow, for never had Mother such a Son, or such a Son a Mother like to thee, nor any Son or Mother such depths of anguish as the torrent let loose when the Blood of God's Son broke the barriers of God's Justice and swept away the guilt of all mankind.

I have said that we are in a special way pledged to devotion to Our Lady of Sorrows, and perhaps you are wondering why? I will tell you: because we have been the cause of those sorrows. Sin caused His sufferings and thus Her sorrows, and sin has been our achievement, our brave achievement in the sight of an All-patient God. Hence are we pledged in a most personal manner to wipe away those tears, to heal those wounds, to comfort that Heart, and this we can do, if we only will, every moment of our life. By the prayer of affection we can dry Our Lady's tears; with the sweet ointment compounded from the virtues, we can bind up the wounds; by our presence—though it be but in spirit—we can with John and Magdalen console her Mother-Heart.

Let us then, dear Sister, ask Our Heavenly Father for this grace, that come what may we shall be found each morning, noon and night, ever in union with the Sorrowful Mother, juxta crucem, near the Cross, within its shadow. After all, the shadow of the Cross has revealed to us the Light of the World, and the Light of the World shall change our tears to glistening jewels as It has long since the dew of sorrow distilled from out His Mother's and Our Mother's Heart.

Amen.

GOD'S GIVING

DEAR ——:

You are yet a very little, little girl, and it will be many, many a day before you will be able to read and understand what I now write. But I will write now for you, and you will then understand, I trust, at least in some part, how much God loved you even before you could love at all.

You rest now just a bit of pink asleep in your mother's arms—all unconscious of the greatness of God's giving. There is a tiny steady throb within you—that is your heart; there is a greater throb close to yours—that is your mother's heart; there is another throb close beside hers—that is your father's heart; and beyond and around and enclosing your heart and your mother's and your father's is another throbbing Heart which has started yours and theirs on the great journey men call life and which will end only when your heart and mother's and daddy's shall be once more and forever reunited in that place which we call Heaven because it is God's Home.

Meanwhile, Mother Mary will take care of you because you are her Rose. And you will always strive to keep that fragrance which the Blood of God's Son and the indwelling of His Spirit has given to your soul. Sin alone can take away that fragrance and the fingers of Sin must never touch God's Rose and Mother Mary's.

FLYING

DEAR ——:

Life has many mysteries, has it not, and almost the greatest of these is the mystery of suffering, especially the suffering of the innocent and of the just.

Life seems at times like a day of the dying year with its o'ercast sky and a stillness like that which heralds an approaching thunder storm. We wait expecting Sorrow to beckon us unwilling guests unto her spacious home. We wait, and we are not disappointed. Only one ray of light breaks through the cloud barriers—the light of Faith. Its rays fall across our souls and awake an answering gleam—that is Hope. And with Faith and Hope there kindles within our hearts the warming flame of Love, Love of God, which somehow or other keeps this old world of ours from freezing altogether.

What you need now, dear Child, more than ever, is the growth within you of this Trinity of the divine virtues. I once wrote for a grieving soul the following:

Give me, dear Lord, a blazing Faith,
That seeth in the dark,
And give us, Lord, a blithesome Hope
Upsoaring like a lark,
And Love, to bear us o'er life's sea,
As in a mighty ark!

Trust your dear Mother's soul to Him Who created it in love, trust your own soul to Him, trust everything to Him, and thus you will be fulfilling that beautiful precept of the Holy Spirit, "Cast your cares upon the Lord, and He will take care of you."

How happily Christian souls would live if only they would imitate the wee little creatures of earth. Way out on a swaying limb a frail, tiny nest is fastened. Within that airy home little birdlings snugly rest. They do not know of the relation to them of the mighty tree that upholds the swaying branch, they only know they are under their mother's wings and safe. But you, dear Child, know of the mighty Tree of the Holy Cross which surely will sustain you, for it has already sustained Its Creator in the Person of His Son. Rest, therefore, trustingly in the home God has prepared for you. Though the limb may seem to sway perilously at times, it will never break for God upholds both nest and limb by His undying, unchanging and providential Love. Mother Mary watches over her little fledglings, and some day she will teach you how to fly to God.

TO A LITTLE LAD

DEAR ——:

I received your note. It brought me happiness, and made me smile. It brought me happiness because I had found a new friend, little perhaps in size and age, but some day to be big in body and in heart and soul as well. It made me smile because I saw a wee lad sitting at his dresser up in his little room trying to settle the biggest of all questions at the very beginning of a summer vacation.

Yes, ——, the biggest of all questions will always be, "what shall I do with my life?" And in answering this question—we must go slowly, especially at first. There are, indeed, many, many beautiful ways of serving our good God. Every good Catholic is a soldier of Christ, and you have a tradition to maintain, you know. Your father on earth, now in Heaven, was a Cavalier of Christ, his pen was his sword and how it flashed in the sunshine of God's grace and the cause of God's truth!

Always, God calls boys to become real men, pure and true and brave. Mostly, He asks them then to keep the fortress of a Christian home for Him and with Him. But sometimes instead of being inside guards, He calls on them to do sentry duty outside in the cold and the rain, or to ride alone with Him along the highways and byways of the world seeking, like the knights of old, to do good. That is what Jesus Himself did when He grew up, He went about doing good. But firstly, while He was a Boy like you, He obeyed His Mother ever Blessed, said His prayers, and helped all who came His way.

This, dear ——, must be your present plan of action, today to be a good boy, thinking of others rather than self, trying each day to do at least one unselfish act for the love of Jesus; tomorrow you will be a man, an unselfish man, and, if God wills it—and I have a feeling He will—tomorrow's tomorrow you will be more than a man; you will be a captain of God's army, a Christ-Bearer, a Priest of Jesus Christ.

And a soldier of His Blessed Mother.

IN THE FOOTSTEPS OF ST. JOSEPH

Dear Little Brother in Christ:

It was a great happiness for me to be with you on

that morning when you bound yourself to live as a humble servant and lover of Jesus and His Most Blessed Mother. Many, many years from now, when our work shall have been completed and all our promises faithfully fulfilled, may we be together once more in that Home that will be so perfect by reason of God's visible Presence and the knowledge that never, never again will it be necessary for us to leave those whom we have loved in God.

Meanwhile, little brother, let us serve God as perfectly as we can. I want you to do what God wants you to do, and He wants you to follow with cheerful, humble, loving obedience in the footsteps of dear St. Joseph. O how much you can accomplish for Jesus and Mary if only you imitate St. Joseph.

I know God has given you the grace of fervor; never let a day pass without thanking His Holy Spirit for this so precious gift. Now the best way to thank God for His Gifts is by sharing them with others! Strive, therefore, by prayer and good example to encourage others to follow in the same paths and lay bare their hearts to the same burning Flame of God's Spirit.

If you can do this, how dear you will become to the Hearts of Jesus and Mary. Jesus has many, many followers who aspire to carry on His great and glorious ministry to men in the imitation of His Public Life, but all too few who are content to follow Jesus in the hidden toil and prayer of the Thirty Years. But remember this, no one is so close to Jesus and Mary in Heaven today as the humble Carpenter of Nazareth. Love, and love alone, determines the rankings of Eternity. Press forward, therefore, with courage and confidence, following for love of Jesus and Mary in the footsteps of St. Joseph.

GOD'S HOUSE

My Dear ——:

I am not writing to extend my sympathy, for you

have written that you do not desire sympathy, but I do write to point out to you one of the most fundamental truths of the spiritual order in the consideration of which you may come to see with greater clearness the beauteous outline of God's House through the mists.

God, Our Father, has builded for us, His children, the wondrous Home we call Heaven. It was of this House that Jesus spoke when He said, "I go to prepare a place for you; in My Father's House, there are many mansions." Now the spiritual truth I would ask you to recognize is this: that He, Who went to prepare a place for us, expects us to prepare to follow Him, expects us not to seek here on earth for abiding dwellings, or a permanent grasp on earthly things, nor even an unbroken grasp of the hand of the truest and noblest of friends.

God gave you in the friendship of —— one of His most precious and rarest of gifts. Friendships of such purity are fashioned only in the Heart of Christ, fashioned, yea, and refined there. What greater gift after Himself, His Mother and His grace, can God give us than a truly true friend!

However, as I once wrote to one of our spiritual family:

Heaven is Heaven, and earth is earth,
And we come to each by a painful birth!

and all God's gifts outside Himself are given in order to draw us to the best of Gifts, the Goal of Life, the Hearthstone of Heaven, God in His ineffable Goodness and Beauty.

Therefore, dear ——, if God has taken His gifts from you, one by one, it is because He does not wish you to tarry even in desire here on the highroad. It is because He wants you to hasten onward, homeward, to His House, His arms, His Heart, that He has called His gift, your friend, home first.

Hasten, therefore, courageously in Faith, through

the mists that shroud Life's Highway; hasten Homeward to God's House where you will find God, your Father, Mary, your Mother, your friend, and some day see a happy, tired, traveler following, whom friends called FATHER PAGE.

MILESTONES

DEAR SISTER IN CHRIST:

When this letter reaches you, you will have passed another milestone of your religious life. Have you ever found yourself meditating upon the significance of milestones? It is something most travelers do sooner or later as they watch them flash by beside the humming road we call Life. It is well to do so, for there is for each of us a last milestone and a last mile, and then Eternity!

Moreover, there is an important difference between the ordinary milestones and those of the spiritual life, for whereas the former tell us how many miles there lie before us, the spiritual milestones mark with certainty only the hours and days that are past, and give us but little definite information of the number of the years that are yet to be.

Spiritual milestones are a record of the past rather than a certain measure of the future; nevertheless, if we can only remain humble, the record of a faithful past is a trustworthy though not infallible portent of a future faithful unto the Spirit of God's Eternal Love. Our future is molded chiefly of past events which were once ours in the living mold of the Present.

Therefore, dear Child, I am going to recommend to you as the milestones flash by you on the Road of Life, look anxiously neither to the Future nor to the Past, but live and love God in the all-important Present.

This is the only way to live and the only way to love. Living thus, whether the Road ahead be long or short, the years many or few, it will not matter much, for

God asks us only to spin the garments of our eternal glory out of the golden thread of the Present.

Live, Child, and weave
Of grace a glorious garment,
The priceless now retrieve
Before comes Death's disarmament,
So shall your soul be clothed
In Virtue's fairest raiment
And stripped of all you loathed
God shall be yours in payment.

Semper per Mariam.

THE VOICE OF FRIENDSHIP

My Dear ——:

Yesterday a letter from our dear —— told me of your brother's sudden death. This note is but the voice of Friendship speaking to your heart.

I offer you my sympathy not because I think you stand in need of sympathy but rather because it is the prerogative of true friendship to grieve with the friend who grieves. No matter how well we may know the great truths of Our Faith, whereupon we brace ourselves amid the fiery currents of sorrows we cannot understand, nevertheless it is good for us, at such times as these, to have the voice of a friend repeat these eternal verities to us.

Have you ever reflected deeply on the third dolor of Our Most Blessed Lady? In one sense, I think it may well have been her deepest sorrow because it was the sorrow she could not understand! I have long felt these are the hardest trials — the ones we cannot find the reason for! And perhaps because this is so true, Jesus placed such a sudden and unexplained sorrow in His Mother's life in order that we, her children, might learn from her how to search for Jesus in our times of trial and then listen to Him even though — still like

Mother Mary—we shall not understand! In such times we must make an act of faith, heroic, perhaps, but therefore all the more meritorious; we must repeat to ourselves the words of the Boy Christ—and whisper to Him in loving faith, "Jesus, I believe in You, I trust You and I know that even in this Trial You have been about Our Father's business, the salvation of immortal souls!"

Roses require rains as well as sunshine for this unfolding and the rarest flowers of God's gardens are those He has planted closest in the shadow of His Holy Cross where His Precious Blood and His Mother's tears may nourish them. Thank God, therefore, dear ——, for this new shadow that has fallen across your path, and I will do the same while on the Mystic Calvary of my daily Mass I, too, am close to Jesus, His Mother and His Cross.

THE GIFT THAT COUNTS

My Dear Child:

I purposely delayed answering your note till the nearer approach of that Feast Day which God's Mother so graciously shares with you. In the novena I am beginning this evening in her Honor I will remember you, and your intentions will be placed with my own each day at her feet. I am going to ask her to obtain for you as a birthday gift a greater and more perfect love for Christ. Do you ask the same for me, for, after all, that is the gift that really matters; that is the gift that counts.

As we walk "the strands of time" alone, especially after we have grown tired of playing in the sand and of watching the sea fill up our miniature excavations and wash away our sand piles, then it is that the flash of the white sails of a gull or a bit of the torn lace of the foam has a mysterious power to open the inner casements of our soul. Then as the fresh salt-fragrant breeze of God's grace reaches the secret chambers of our being, we begin to realize the sweetness of just loving God, and come to the fuller conviction that only the ocean of His love is vast enough to fill the horizons of our desires, flood the unfathomed depths of our consciousness and satiate the profounder longings of our soul. This is the truth, Child, which makes me ask for you the gift that truly counts, the grace of God's supernal love.

With that grace hidden in your heart, it will not matter whether the tide of earthly joy is in or out. Where the love of God is firmly established, time's tides and passion's currents swirl in vain. Make the love of God, dear Child, the first and deepest foundation of your life. Make it the firm rock on which your feet are braced, the deposit vault in which your treasure is enclosed. Let it be the brightness of your morning, the repose of your noon-day, the coolness of your evening, the starlight of your night. God's love, Child, never forget it, God's love is the only gift that counts. Treasure it in your heart, and God will treasure your love in His, and then you will begin to comprehend with all the saints how sweet a thing it is to love the Lord, Our God.

Happy Birthday—in Mary.

BON VOYAGE

My Dear Child:

I am glad you are to have the opportunity of relaxing, and I know of no better way of doing so than a sea trip. Of course the human elements may prove annoying to one who holds to ideals, but Nature is truer to her primitive regimen. The sea speaks abidingly of God's Immensity and, besides, makes it necessary for us to commit ourselves to His paternal care. The winds spiced with salt spray help to clear away our mental cobwebs, while the mighty throb of the engines suggests continuously the mightier throb of God's compelling love which, having started us on our course, will not cease to maintain and direct our journeyings, till we be safely anchored within the breakwater of Eternal love.

Take along for companionship a good book or two, something that will add a spiritual stimulus to the physical. But, when the company of friends or good books leaves you restless, turn the dial of your attention from the local stations of creatures and seek God. Remember for His happiness and for yours the Divine Lover who accompanies you always. Learn to rest in His arms.

When you return, Our Lady will utilize your good will for the glorification of one of her most faithful lovers. I only wish I could catch in the net of my phrases that elusive spirit of devotion which our Father Moreau possessed in such goodly measure.

Bon Voyage with Mary.

EYES OF FAITH

Dear Father and Brother in Christ:

I am very grateful for the Mass intentions and also for the sentiments that your letter expressed. Please pray that I may prove worthy of my vocation, for that, after all, is the one important thing to ask for a priest. God is indeed "the portion of our inheritance and of our cup," and what a generous portion God is, every true priest comes to realize with an increasing realization as the years raise about his soul higher and stouter walls of peace and contentment.

This last figure may seem an ideal impossible of achievement by some souls, but surely it is in keeping — in perfect harmony with the ordinary designs of God as regards not only priestly but all souls. Why should the faithful servant close his eyes to his own fidelity? I do not mean that he should rest with complacency in this consideration, but I do believe that too many faithful souls fail to draw the due wages of confidence and peace to which their service entitles them and which the Master would rejoice to have them claim. It would be folly for a servant of God to think that there was nothing in his past service but that which merited God's approbation, but it is equally folly, and I believe more offensive to an All-Good God, to consider that the occasional imperfect grain destroyed the essential value of the entire harvest. Besides, a laborer in God's vineyard has only to bring his imperfect and faulty harvestings to Mother Mary in order that they be converted by a mother's love and the grace of God into the fine flour so acceptable to God.

It is because I am so deeply convinced of these truths, dear Father, that I feel the years should add but deeper contentment to our existence as they in turn reveal to us the merciful workings of God's most holy grace. Surely none but the spiritually blind can fail to recognize the thread of Divine Love weaving in and out, in and out, in the pattern of their existence. It is always there, this thread of Divine Love, even in those lives wherein wilful fingers try to ravel or break the thread; but sometimes its strands are visible only to the eyes of faith. God give you the eyes of faith, dear Father; all the world needs them but no one more than a priest.

Always in Our Lady.

WINGS FOR LOVERS

My Dear Child:

Mary, Our Mother, is ever the "Via Immaculata" — the Immaculate Way of going to God. I find assurance in the fact you find this way attractive; it is very lowly and very straight and very sure.

In general, spiritual mortifications surpass in value physical ones — and again those that come from God

— even though through His permissive Will, that is, through creatures, are better than those we choose for ourselves: for example, the bearing with the tedious talk of some visitor with sweet charity. However, if you wish and feel your love would carry you further, then take in general those hidden acts that only He will know of (hence less danger of vanity creeping in) and which withdraw you from the little consolations *outside of Him*. The idea is this — the more our *whole* joy and consolation is taken from just the thought of and Presence and love of Jesus, so much the higher and more truly do we love Him. Jesus' truest lovers — like Mother Mary — *want* no consolation beyond *just Him*. This is what the bride-soul means in the Canticle of Canticles when she cries out, "When I had passed by them, I found him whom my soul loveth: I held him and I will not let him go till I bring him into my mother's house, and into the chamber of her who bore me."

Love, however, must *go before* or else all our running will be with dragging feet. Love wings all lovers, the heavenly as well as those of earth.

In Our Lady's Service.

WAR BREAD

Dear Brother in Christ:

Possibly a note from home — even a preachy one like mine — will be acceptable to you, who are at once so far from home and at the same time so near to Home by reason of your union with Christ.

One Subject, Brother, I hope, shall more and more absorb my life and yours and everyone's, and that is God and His divine claim to our lives and the love thereof. One Object here on earth should be our Goal; not a far-off Deity, not a Supreme Being incomprehensible by reason of His Immensity, and unreachable because of His Omnipresence! no, but God-become-one-with-us by reason of the excess of His Divine Love, God Incarnate and abiding with us to be our Love and Life and Strength and Consolation by becoming in very truth Our Daily Bread — the Sacrament of the Altar.

O Brother, if we cannot fathom the depths of human love in its nobler manifestations, how should we hope to sound the depths of Love Divine! It cannot be, at least on earth. But though we may not comprehend the greatness of that Love wherewith we are comprehended, at least we can abandon ourselves to its divine bearing. We can at least permit the tide of God's Mercy to sweep us out with the Ocean of His Love. Is it not that stranded souls may be reached by the tide of the Precious Blood that you are at this moment so far from your earthly home? Never mind, be not afraid, you will never find yourself stranded on the bar of Divine Justice.

But I am wandering from my purpose, which is this, to urge you to go to Jesus, morning by morning, with loving hunger, for He has willed to be the War Bread of our fighting humanity.

May Our Lady of the Missions be with you always.

HOLDING THE FORT

Dear Brother in Christ:

This letter is just a note of cheer to you who, so many hundreds of miles away, are engaged in holding the fort for Christ and His Sorrowful Mother.

The high water mark of the struggle between God and satan for the possession of mankind was on the top of Calvary at the foot of the Cross, and there, as mingled tides of satan's malice and man's ingratitude receded, they left Our Saviour, triumphant in death, and with Him, all of us who are triumphant through, and in His Victory.

The foot of the Cross thereby became the place of

triumph for mankind, at one and the same time both the place and the means of our spiritual victory.

This letter will find you there at the foot of the Cross, holding the fort with Jesus and Mary. Persevere there, dear Brother; it is the only place in this wide, wide world where we can find lasting rest or peace.

What a strange paradox—the last place in the world one would expect to find peace, there one finds it. The place of suffering becomes the spot of consolation both given and received.

This all-important grace, therefore, I will ask for you and all other missionary priests, our brothers, that we may find happiness in sacrifice, consolation in suffering, rest in toil, God in the life of death, and His Love and Mary's eternally.

OUR GREATEST GIFT TO GOD

My Dear ——:

I did receive your first letter and should have answered before now. However you know how busy I used to be, and you can surmise how busy I still am in the service of Our Dear Jesus.

I am so pleased to hear from you and from the other boys at ——, and especially to learn you are all persevering in your God-given vocations. God's second greatest gift to us is our greatest gift to Him, unless we think of the Holy Sacrifice of the Mass in which, as it were, we give God to God! God's greatest Gift to us is of course Himself, and His second greatest gift is the grace by which we give ourselves whole and without reserve to Him!

Jesus, the Divine Word Incarnate, loved us so much that He gave us all that He possessed, Himself, His Father, His Spirit, His Most Holy Mother. Our greatest proof of love is consequently the reverse, the gift of our own selves with all that we possess to Him and for His Service. "Greater love than this no man can have, than that a man lay down his life for his friends!" You, if you persevere, will lay down your life, day by day, on the altar of the missions for your Divine Friend, with your Divine Friend, and in your Divine Friend.

To do this well, not so much now with your lips but later on in your actual mission life, is something that is beyond your unaided strength. But Jesus knows this better than you do, and has provided for your need.

On the First Pentecost, His Holy Spirit brought to His first missionaries the fiery grace to accomplish their arduous and heroic apostleship. If you but pray perseveringly as did those first missionaries in union with Mary and her saints, you too will feel leaping up in your soul, inflaming your heart, illumining your mind, tempering your will, the strength and the light and the love of God. God's Holy Spirit will be with you, dwell in your very soul and in His Strength you will carry on until the final victory is yours.

How sweet that final victory will be to us, yes, sweet also to God, for His Spirit has written "blessed in the sight of God is the death of His saints," and a faithful missionary practices heroic virtue and after all virtue in a heroic degree is what makes us saints and gives to us the final victory.

EQUIPMENT

Dear Brother in Christ:

I was pleased to learn of the change in obediences that has opened for you the ancient portals of the Indies and the high road to adventurous conquest for Christ. Since we are all travelers and the paths we tread each day new, there is in each of our lives elements of adventure and, if we wish, the glint of divine romance; yet still, or so it seems to me, there is no adventure that equals that of the foreign missions, and consequently those who would fare forth upon such questing should go well-equipped. Everywhere, every hour, we need God's grace and the contacts with grace which prayer and sacrifice give us, yet the soldiers of Christ who would hold the lines in the far places of the globe must build for themselves stouter barriers of prayer and sacrifice, and deeper cisterns for the holding of His grace. It would be accounted pure folly to attempt front-line service under the conditions of modern warfare without proper equipment and training. It would be even higher madness for a missionary to neglect his equipment and more especially the spiritual elements thereof.

Of the material things you will need you are better aware than I. Undoubtedly they are numerous, yet the loyal legion of God's humble lovers scattered through the ranks of the laity and the clergy will supply them, I am sure. Your spiritual equipment, however, must be, at least in large measure, bought and paid for out of the sacrifices of your own heart and this is where I shall try to help. My contribution shall be to pray "the Giver of every good gift" that He may flood your soul with graces, that He may give you so great a faith in Him that you may never lose faith in humanity, so constant a spirit of hope that it will be always morning in your soul, so deep a love of Christ Crucified, that you will be happiest while fastened to the Cross, and that your affections may never be stranded on the burning, arid sands of creature attachments. Such a deep love, dear brother, is the most precious equipment of a missionary, for only a great love of God can fill the gaps inevitable in all lives but more especially so in yours.

Hold up, therefore, your soul to God in Christ when each morning you lift up Christ to God, and silently beg the Triune God you serve to make you daily more worthy of His embassy to souls that are dark yet beautiful and waiting for the morning. Semper per Mariam.

CHRIST'S BLACK LEGION

MY DEAR ——:

It was thoughtful of you to let me know of your reception of the habit—the black habit of the servants of Christ. To do great things for Him, you have now only to live up to what your habit stands for! If you did nothing more than live in true conformity with the uniform you now wear, you would not only be God's efficient instrument for the salvation of souls but you would as well scale the heights of spiritual perfection.

Perhaps nothing reveals more tacitly the spirit of a religious than his attitude toward the habit which he wears; for our habit symbolizes the mortification of Our Master, that death to the three-fold concupiscence of the spirit of man that we must attain to, if we do not wish our lives to be a mockery and our characters but caricatures of the life and character of Christ. Black is the symbol of death, and Mother Church clothes us in black to remind us that we have undertaken to die to self that we may live through and with and in Christ Jesus.

It is thus that our uniform constitutes us members of a "black legion," but how different from that infamous group of whose activities the citizens of our country have so lately become aware! These latter legionaries are engaged in the propaganda of Hate, we in the cause of Love; these are vowed to the killing of others, we to the death of self! The fruition of their progress is found in bullet-riddled bodies of their fellow men, ours in the grace-laden souls of the children of all races, regardless of color or class!

In what a glorious mission, therefore, my little brother, you became a sharer when you slipped around you for the first time—and let us hope, for life—the black robe of a vowed servant of Christ! With you He, the Master, now shares His own lifework; through you He wills to carry on that work of giving life, spiritual life to men. This life is the life of grace by which homes are preserved not destroyed, and the erring sons of men nursed back with patient, loving care to life more abundant rather than hurled unshriven across the great divide.

These, then, are some of the thoughts which your note brought to my mind, dear brother, and I have only to add the promise of a daily prayer that you and I, and all our brethren of Christ's Black Legion, may wear our darksome livery, ever mindful of His Passion and His Blessed Mother's Sorrows, and ever responsive to the fruits of so great sacrifices. So may God's Holy Spirit find us "black but beautiful" and worthy of Love's accolade.

SILVER MEMORIES AND GOLDEN DREAMS

My Dear Sister:

On the day when you celebrate your Silver Jubilee of consecrated service to the Lord I am to have the privilege of making my final vows as a religious of the Holy Cross. It is fitting, therefore, that we should pray for one another on this day that holds for one of us silver memories and for the other golden dreams of service. I would exchange my gold for your silver; for my gold is yet to be mined while your silver is already safely deposited within the vaults of Heaven.

I think that both of us have been very happy in the service of the Master; and I know that you will agree with me that life offers few tragedies greater than that of a servant of God who fails to find in the love of Jesus and Mary an ever-deepening satisfaction and an ever-increasing joy. Why should we not be joyful, we who have the best of Masters and the most gracious of Queens to serve?

It is one of my favorite themes to point out the essential servitude of man, to analyze the various freedoms of which men boast and find within the mantle of vaunted liberties the tyranny of passion or the servitude of pride. Man may boast of his freedom, but he was made to serve; and when he chooses to reject the reign of God he finds himself very swiftly a serf of the kingdom of darkness. Hence, dear Sister, we may be joyous in the knowledge of the wisdom of our election. We have indeed chosen God as the portion of our inheritance and our cup. It is true, of course, as we are well aware, that God on His part has in His own mysterious ways guided our choosing and inspired by His grace our choice. Paradoxical as it may seem God has chosen us but we have ourselves responded to His invitation, we have confirmed His will.

Therefore, dear Sister, as you begin the final decades of the rosary of your religious life, please whisper a prayer for me; and I promise you as I lift the chalice of my Master's crimsoned Love I shall remember you and ask for you what I most desire for myself — the grace of fidelity to all that God has asked and we have promised even unto the end.

OCTOBER

October touches the fields and woods with death and glory, but with glory first; with men, the order is reversed.

A DECADE OF THE ROSARY

DEAR CHILD OF OUR LADY:

Your note was an unexpected pleasure, for it is always a joy to find souls who are alive to the beauties of the world of faith. How many there are who live and die in the valley of faith yet never more than glimpse the glories thereof. They never lift their eyes to the mountains of truth that protect them; never rejoice in the gladsome sunshine of God's Son that warms them; never hasten with a song of gratitude to the Sacramental River that courses silently and sweetly, watering the meadows where God has privileged them to live.

But to those who have eyes to see, minds to reflect, hearts to answer the throbbing love of God, to such life is a wondrous thing, an astounding adventure, a sublime romance. To such, vocation, Mass, Communion, the Priesthood have a terrible reality. To such, vocation is Christ-claiming, the Mass Christ-dying, Communion Christ-giving, the Priesthood, Christ living again.

Dear child, the Priesthood is a terrifying exaltation—you can indeed do nothing more consoling to His Sacred Heart than to pray as you have suggested for His Priesthood, for by the institution of the Priesthood God has committed His stainless Honor, His deepest interests, to the keeping of created clay. Therefore to sustain the Priesthood by the mighty arms of prayer and sacrifice is to play the part of Aaron and Hur holding up the arms of Moses while Israel fought against Amalec. St. Theresa of Jesus knew this, and that is why she made prayer for the Priesthood the first duty of her Carmelite family. A faithful Priest is God's greatest consolation, an unfaithful priest the source of His deepest sorrow.

Surely then, it will be God's own Sweet Spirit that prompts the thoughts of your heart. Take your offerings, place them in the hands of Mother Mary; she will distribute them where they are most needed and will bless the giver with a gracious smile, a smile that is the pledge of eternal felicity.

For myself I would beg one decade of the Rosary each day, thanking Mary for my Vocation and asking that I may be each day nearer and dearer to her Heart and to her Son Divine.

OUR LADY'S SWORD

DEAR ——— :

God love you for the charity that has secured for me a Rosary so uniquely indulgenced. I shall remember you and Sister when I say my beads.

As I grow older, the Rosary means more and more to me. Like a soldier's faithful weapon, like the gleaming blade of a crusader of old, the Rosary has come to be to me—as I know it has or will to you—to be in very fact, Our Lady's sword—symbolic of prompt victory over the ever-present enemies of our souls' peace and happiness.

David's sling with its five smooth pebbles was small but efficient, so is Our Lady's Rosary when rightly used in our own or another's spiritual defense. I rather envy Religious who have the privilege of wearing their beads swordlike at their belt. But the Blessed Mother's weapon is denied to none of us—she knows so well how much we need her help—and so though we may not carry her sword at our side, we can at least carry it unsheathed in our hand, while the memory of her stainless victory lifts our souls nearer to the Heart of Heaven which once rested in her Virgin Womb. Remember me to Our Queen.

ANCHOR CHAINS

Dear ——:

You are being married in the month of the Holy Rosary. I want you and —— to place your lives and live your life within the circle of its sweet influence. How happily could I foretell the future for you did I know the Rosary was to be your daily prayer binding both your hearts the closer to the Good God who gave you to each other and has placed you as one within His Mother's loving care.

The Rosary—words can never express all it means to us! To outsiders it seems but a tiresome reiteration of words, but to us it means a glimpse of Heaven, Heaven on earth, Heaven in Heaven, as our souls follow the course of the Greatest Drama of all time, the life of God's Incarnate Son from the hidden throne of His Mother's Virgin Womb to the angel and saint rimmed throne of His Father's Home where He crowns His Mother Queen.

Who can measure the depths of solace, strength, courage, high resolve and sure love that have been sounded by souls while the beads slipped through their fingers? Souls of little angels lisping the desires of childhood, youthful souls joyously knocking at the gates of Life, mature souls at hand grips with the great problems of existence, aged souls groping feebly for the way that leads beyond, souls of saints soaring upward, souls of sinners wavering perilously—the myriad souls Christ lived and died for, all looking upward, seeking Him whom the shepherds and Magi found in the keeping of a Maiden Mother.

One of the pleasantest memories of my childhood is of our Grandma by the fire, her beads moving slowly through her fingers. To the life of Faith there is a golden sunset that bespeaks an eternal dawn. I wonder do you love your beads of silver as she did her's of thorn?

This then is my recommendation to you, dear—as you enter your new life—say your Rosary. Say it thoughtfully, choosing the mysteries to suit the temper of your spirit, joyous, suffering, triumphant. Say it unfailingly, day by day, and like the stout anchor chains that hold a tide circled ship from off the white-fanged reefs, Mary's Rosary will hold your soul and the souls you love fast to Jesus amid all the storms of life. Then the evening peace shall rest upon the waters and the harbor lights gleam out and your soul find safe anchorage with Mother Mary in the Harbor men call Heaven because it is God's Home.

THE BIGOT

DEAR ——:

I am sorry to learn that you are suffering by reason of the blind passions of your neighbor. Bigotry, always and anywhere, is an ugly thing; it is especially ugly when it lifts its head to disrupt a peaceful, friendly, little community like yours. However, let me say in the beginning, Faith offers its consolations in all the tribulations of life, and Faith now whispers to you the benediction of the Master—"Blessed are you who suffer persecution for My Name's sake, yours is the Kingdom of Heaven."

Bigotry would be quite humorous, like a loose pig, if it were not for the really serious damage which, like the loose pig, it can produce. When we hear the grotesque assertions and perversions of Catholic faith and practice, our first impulse is rather to smile than to weep. But when one knows that these assertions, crude or clever, make festering wounds in our neighbor's soul, that Mr. A —— no longer smiles on us from his heart's depths, that conversation takes a sudden pause and fresh turn when you drop in at Mr. B——'s, that little Mary C—— is no longer needed at Blank and Blanks, when, in so many words, Slander,

Mistrust, and the Hatred to which these two give birth, come to live in an American community, then indeed, it is time for tears rather than laughter.

There is no bigness either of heart or mind in Bigotry. Bigotry is the platform by which little men and women seek to lift themselves above the crowd. It can be excused in the ignorant, it must be despised in those whose training and education have given the opportunity for enlightenment. But, as Our Lord once sadly said, "there are some who prefer the darkness to the light," and they will not come to the clear light of Truth, less the Truth should reveal to them facts that they are unwilling to accept.

Dear ——, I personally believe that Bigotry will never die. The prince of lies will never abandon such a powerful weapon, and little minds will ever seek its shelter to conceal their own deficiencies. However, it is your duty as a Catholic gentleman so to order your life that all reasonable men must come at last to know that in your heart, love of God, Church and Country, love of Christ and fellow men, are all one harmonious whole, that you love your Country only the more because you recognize it as the Home God gave you, in which to practice the Faith God gave you — the Faith which tells us of the ultimate triumph of Christ, and of His Church, against which the Gates of Hell shall not prevail.

Let us pray our Blessed Mother that this fair Land, dedicated to her, may never be torn from the foundation upon which it was built — Liberty, God given, God preserved.

OUR TASK

Dear ——:

It must seem to you that your spiritual father has forgotten you, and he does not blame you for so thinking. However, he would wish you to reflect that, when one tries to serve God, the hours of the day are not long enough to accomplish all there is to be done for Him, and that it is a constant source of humiliation to see so much to be done, and one's own feeble efforts to accomplish even a wee bit of the Task. Now the Task is the coming of His Kingdom upon earth.

You, dear ——, have undertaken to assist your Creator in the salvaging of His creation! This is the meaning, or at least a part of the meaning, of your vocation. You have pledged yourself to spend your life in making the reign of Jesus Christ a reality in the lives of men. To do this, it is essential that first you establish the sovereign reign of Jesus Christ in your own soul.

In vain shall we strive to enthrone Jesus by Faith and Love in other souls unless we enthrone Him first and firmly in our own. Here is where the greatest difficulty comes. It takes more courage, it costs more of suffering, it hurts more to conquer self than to suppress others. And yet this self-conquest is most essential, and that is what Jesus meant when He told us, "Unless the seed, falling in the ground, dieth, itself remaineth alone." Yes, dear ——, unless we have died to self, our lives cannot fructify, our souls cannot become powerful for good in the Service of the King.

Set yourself, therefore, dear ——, to the Task Most Glorious which Jesus has deigned to let you share. Establish by vigilance, prayer, sacrifice and the greatest of sacrifices for human nature, i.e., obedience, the reign of Jesus Christ over your soul. Though the process will be painful, the result will be both glorious and joyous. For thus crucified, you will glorify Him Who for you was crucified, win Him the souls He seeks, and find in His Heart that Perfect Love and Lover which God most truly is.

Ask Our Lady Mother to bless FATHER PAGE.

"TRAIN-TRAVEL"

My Dear, Dear Child in Christ:

Were it God's Holy Will I would love to be present for your final Profession on the Eighteenth, despite the long purgatory of train-travel; I would be there, too, save only for my duties. I will, however, have the consolation, please God and Mary, of offering the Holy Sacrifice for you upon that morn, and as the lips of Jesus and His Heart are close to mine I will beg Him to give you whatever gift or gifts will most endear you to Himself—make you most worthy of His Most Perfect Love.

Life is like train-travel, is it not? A long purgatory which worldlings strive, like little children, to make more bearable by playing with their toys, and we by fixing our hearts and minds upon that Beauty ever ancient, ever new, the uncreated Beauty of God, which has overflown into His Creation and touched the stars and the hills and the fields—yes, and our own souls with a beauty so precious in the sight of God that He has not disdained to use for their restoration the very Heart-blood of His Divine Son! O how precious are souls, Sister, in the sight of God, seeing that He is at such pains for their sanctification.

Now the glory of your own life rests in this: that you assist your Divine Lover first in the beautifying of your own soul which means the restoring of its original beauty, that is, the beauty that was the birthright of our first parents before the Fall, and then assist Him in the beautifying of other souls whom you shall mother for the love of Him.

I think Religious, especially teaching Religious, cannot too often reflect upon the sweet parallel between their own lives and the life of the Ever Blessed Mother of God. Her glory we sum up in the Divine Praises, thus: "Blessed be the Name of Mary, Virgin and Mother!" Now every true religious will strive to be like her Blessed Mother and Queen, a Virgin Spouse, and at the same time a loving and patient Mother of the little souls committed in the classroom, and elsewhere, to her care. Blessed is that Religious who so loves God herself that her every word and action tends to brighten within other souls the image of Jesus Christ.

Aim at perfection, dear Child, but be patient with yourself in its attainment. Have great confidence in God's plan of love. He will perfect His glory within our lives if only we impose deliberately no stubborn barriers to His grace. Only one thing prevents the souls of Religious from the flights of God's heroes and heroines — lack of generosity, which reveals itself in inconstancy in prayer, affection for venial sin, acquiescence in mediocrity.

Upon all such failings, my dear daughter, I want you to turn the sword of God's Holy Spirit and the shield of a good will. With these two weapons of offense and defense you will conquer the hardest of all positions which is Self; you will sanctify your own soul and others, console the Hearts of Jesus and Mary and glorify, as it is your vocation to do, for All Eternity, the Merciful Love of God.

YOUR KINGDOM

Dear Friend in Christ:

The term, friend, has been subject to so much abuse that one hesitates to use it, yet all the abuse it may ever receive cannot rob it of the consecration it received from the lips of Christ when His Heart chose it to express His affection for His disciples, "I have not called you servants, but friends." Would not this world of ours be very close to Heaven if only our lives and the lives of all our fellow beings were dominated by the friendship of Christ, and thus partook of that spiritual unity which is of the essence thereof?

Now this is, indeed, the Will of Christ, the express prayer of His Sacred Heart on the eve of His Passion, "I pray, Father, that they all may be one." But against His Will there has been arraigned, almost from the beginning, the rebel-will of man, and the net result of man's failure to carry out by loving cooperation God's Holy Plan has been abiding discord, suffering and discontent. It cannot be otherwise, for God's Plan is the exclusive Way of Peace, and those who seek for lasting peace by any other plan are but pursuing a mirage.

In every age, by reason of our individual endowment of free will, the fulfillment of God's Plan, at least as it concerns the individual, has depended upon the cooperation of the individual. There is an old saying to the effect that "an Englishman's house is his castle," but in a much deeper and more universal sense is it true that each one of our souls is a little castle, a little kingdom unto itself, where, if there be Peace, it is a Peace that has come, through God's grace, by self-conquest and prayerful obedience to God's laws. There is Peace in the Kingdom of a soul only when Hope has taken counsel of Faith, and together have enthroned Love in the will. There is Peace because there is God, and His reign recognized by loyal and filial service.

Now then, there is, because of this sublime Truth, always this road to Peace open to the individual soul. Whatever the rest of the world may do, as long as I live, I may open my own soul to God, accept His overtures, welcome His legates and ambassadors, and thus make my soul an integral part of that mystical, yet none the less real, Kingdom of which Jesus spoke when He said, "The Kingdom of God is within you."

I know, dear friend, that Christ already reigns in your Kingdom. I pray He may never cease to do so, for He is the King of Kings. I pray His Spirit of Holy Love to direct all your affairs of state, and Christ's Mother to be Its Queen, and that thus having given a Kingdom to God you may be found worthy to receive one at His hands.

Please pray for FATHER PAGE.

CARGO

MY DEAR ——:

This is a fair day on earth — fairer in Heaven — or let us put it thus, fair everywhere, fairer on the Cape, fairest in Heaven where vacations never come to an end and the problems of life shall have all been put away behind us to gather dust on the shelves of time.

It was good of you to think of me while on vacation, and a rarer goodness — as the world goes — to think of sharing your vacation home with me. I appreciate the kindliness behind the thought even though I shall be unable to avail myself of your hospitality.

My own vacation is over. Little by little as I grow older and, I trust, a little nearer Our Journey's End, I find myself growing more satisfied in the day's work that lies at hand, and so treat vacations like friends whose comings I bless and to whose goings I give God-speed.

What are our souls but little ships making their way, some swiftly, some slowly, some with apparent ease, some with evident difficulty, across the waters of Time toward the eternal shore and our Home Port which is — at least if Our Owner's plans are carried out — God and His Heaven.

I wish you, ——, fair weather for your passage, the sure hand of Faith on the wheel, and the precious freight of God's and your dear ones' love and affection.

How foolish are those soul-ships that aim to carry lesser, cheaper cargoes! As they near their final anchorage, surely they must be prepared for sad disillusionment, for the only cargo that has value there is love — God-given, God-blessed and God-centered.

This, then, I wish you always — the love of God, the love of your wife and children, the love of your friends — among whom please count — FATHER PAGE.

LIGHT IN DARKNESS

My Dear ——:

This beautiful month, dedicated to Our Lady's Rosary, dictated to me this little note of consolation for you.

While we are young it is the joyous mysteries of Our Lord's and Our Lady's life which we choose ordinarily when we take beads in hand and seek in reverent love to hold, with Mother Mary, her Love, her Joy, her Little Son, close to our hearts. But the years slip quietly through the fingers of Time, and before we are aware of it our joyous mysteries are at an end and it is time to begin the mysteries of Our Lady's Sorrows in the Passion of her Son.

Then it is that we need courage, for then it is that the Christian soul realizes in earnest and in fuller measure that it has been called by its heavenly birthright in Christ Jesus to share not only His joys but His sorrows as well; and then it is God gives the Christian soul the grace to suffer for and with His Son through the sweet maternal intercession of His Most Holy Mother, Queen of Sorrows.

In the darkness that veiled with Nature's grief the last three hours of Our Lord's sufferings on Calvary, His dimming vision saw a light in the dark—the white, upturned face of his Most Holy Mother! My dear ——, in your own house of grief, suffering and abandonment, when, you, too, are with Jesus on the Cross, may He give you the grace to see through His eyes and in His heart that same light in the darkness, that same face of His and your Most Blessed Mother.

Meantime, please pray for me that I, who have had so little occasion to taste at least in fuller measure the Sorrows of my Crucified Master and of my Most Sorrowful Queen, may not be found wanting in generous courage and constancy when my hour shall have come.

In Their Blessed Service—ever— Father Page.

CROSSROADS

DEAR ——:

This is a very tardy response to an invitation to a wedding which is already a happy memory. However, it is never too late to assure our friends of that invisible meeting in the Heart of God that prayer makes possible and loving thought accomplishes. This is what I want you and —— to know, that I am praying for you and will continue to do so through the years-to-be, that the joy of your wedding morn may only deepen and become more sacred as you walk together that road that stretches across the hills and down into the valleys and, at last, in the hush of the evening out over the plain to the very gates of the City of God.

You are not so inexperienced in the ways of life as to be unaware that all roads humanity travels are eventually "crossroads"; at least no others have been discovered leading to "Heavenstown." Yet since this is so, and I think we would not wish it otherwise when we reflect on the Way Our Blessed Saviour and His Sorrowful Mother traversed for love of us, surely it was a gracious revelation of the love of Our Heavenly Father that He has not required His children to walk these roads alone.

Walk then, dear ——, with high-hearted and joyous courage the crossroads of the future, walk hand in hand with the partner God has given you for the journey, mindful that your partnership is as well a sacred trust in which God holds a vital interest. The cool and the freshness of the morning now give you courage for the day, and when the road grows steeper and more difficult, when you both are tired and feel the need of rest, do not forget to stop at the Wayside Inns that the Divine Love has established for us and where a Divine Host asks no recompense save that of grateful love.

Travelling thus the crossroads will be love-roads,

bringing you surely and safely through this "vale of tears" and in the twilight you will be able to see what some call stars but which are really the lights of the Heavenly Jerusalem, God's Palace and our Home.

Asking Our Lady to bless you.

ROOT-CROPS

My Dear ——— :

Your note brought me real joy, because I had begun to fear that my little sister was going to be like one of those western farms whose soil is now so easily swept away by the winds. There are souls like that, souls that give themselves readily and, as they deem, intelligently to every breath of error! How much souls need the root-crops of Faith and common sense! And now I am sure, that, by the mercy of God, my little sister has both of these precious gifts of God.

Perhaps you will be surprised to think of common sense as a gift of God, but so it is in the natural order, and in the Christian this gift is closely allied with those supernatural gifts of the Holy Spirit which elevate and perfect the intellectual faculties.

Because of this, I am going to ask you to pray especially to that Silent Partner of every soul in grace—the Holy Ghost. Beg Him reverently to make good, by His all powerful aid, your escape from that little world of naturalism wherein we too often seek to live and find our lasting satisfactions. Need I comment on the ultimate futility of such questing? Ask Him to strengthen your will in its allegiance to Good, and to inflame your heart with so great a love of the Adorable Trinity that you will be unwilling merely to play on the pleasure-dotted sands of the passing hour but will plunge instead into the ocean of God's eternal Love.

TO A LITTLE SISTER

DEAR ROSEMARY:

I must thank you for your little note, which I received as a part of Our Lady's gracious kindness to me on the Feast of her Assumption.

Perhaps mother has told you of the great privilege that was granted me on Our Lady's Feast. On that day I was permitted by Mother Church to promise Our Lady's Son that I would devote permanently all the powers of my body and soul to making God better known and loved, first by myself and then by all of God's dear children.

You sent me a sweet picture of Our Lady with the Christ Child watching her hanging His little garments to dry upon a rosemary bush. Is it not wonderful to remember that Little Jesus gives you His living rosemary bush, not alone His white garments, but His White Self hid therein, whenever you go to Communion! And how sweetly must His little Rosemary strive to perfume with love of her heart and the fragrance of her thoughts her little Visitor from Heaven!

As you grow older, little sister, you will learn how the Child Jesus grew older and though not ceasing to love His Heavenly Father and His sweet Mother, nevertheless, for love of you and me, permitted His enemies to fasten Him to a leafless tree with thorns of iron. It was thus the cross became by the love of Jesus a rosemary bush with Jesus the Rose born of Mary as its First but not its last blossom. I have written "not its last blossom" because we are all brothers and sisters of Our Blessed Saviour and if we grow, as we must, by God's grace and Mary's prayers in the love of God, then we, too, will find all our being opening like a rose and reflecting, by the beauty of our living and the sweetness of our charity, the image of the First Blossom, Mary's Son, our God and Brother.

I am sure Our Lady watches day and night over the rosebuds, of which you are the largest, and likewise over the gardeners, whom you call mother and dad; and should you, little sister, ever have need of an extra guardian angel, I will send you mine. In Her Name.

CROSSROADS OF MEMORY

DEAR FATHER:

This is a rather tardy note of thanks for the very beautiful additions you made during my absence to our seminary set-up. It was characteristic of you to do so in the way you did, and I am glad the Lady-blue of the set made you think of me.

Kindly think of me always, Father, when in the quiet of the late evening with the cars murmuring by outside, you sit in your big arm chair with the beads slipping through your fingers. And I, on my part, will think of you in prayer until I find you safely ensconced in the blue-hung living rooms of heaven.

To be remembered is a very precious thing to human nature, and indeed to God also. Was not Jesus, the Son of God, pleading for remembrance when at the last supper He instituted the Unique Reminder of the Eucharist? How wonderful, dear Father, is that Sacrifice and Sacrament which is so closely associated with our priestly existence and by means of which you and I, though separated by diverging ways and years, may yet meet every morning at the crossroads of living memories in the Heart of Our God and Love.

THE IMPATIENT SERVANT

DEAR ——:

Back last evening from —— where a wee bell in the hands of a persistent portress punctured any interior complacency I might have taken in the good measure of success. If the world continues to add to the number of contrivances for destroying solitude, the

Trappists are in danger of being afflicted with a postulant in the person of an ex-retreat director. I preach the patience of Christ, but how difficult it is to bear with that fidelity to duty that is not rimmed with the thoughtfulness for others. Anyway, it would be easier to bear being splashed with dirty water, like Thérèse, our little sister of Carmel, than to be splashed with noise when one is striving to think deeply—and help others to do the same—of the things of God.

Yet, let me anticipate your reply, and take a dose of my own medicine—"to those who love God all things work together unto good!" So behind the concentrated, almost consecrated, persistency of that bell ringer was God's design to bring home to me how far, far away I am from the patience of the Master. And surely it is a special grace to be made aware of our nothingness especially when, by God's mercy, this is accomplished without grievous offense to Him. For to be aware of our own nothingness is the first essential condition for receiving the graces of vocation. Peter had first to urge the Master's departure from a sinful fisherman before the call to follow Christ more closely fell on his wondering soul. And may my acknowledgment of impatience be a prelude to the grace that long has waited—both of us—to follow more closely His path. Nevertheless, I hope there are no bells in Heaven save the Angelus and one wee bell to announce the Passing of the Lamb. When last He passed, I did not kneel!

"THE GLORY WHICH IS YOURS"

Dear Brother in Christ:

Your letter reached me about two weeks ago. It brought me joy in the knowledge of one more faithful soldier of Jesus and Mary on the far-flung and distant frontiers, and, to be honest, a little more human happiness in the thought that a note of mine had brought a little consolation and courage to you.

Oh, Father, all a missionary needs is grace, the grace in particular to realize the glory which is his in the faithful fulfilment of his sublime vocation. After all, this is true of any of God's creatures no matter where they be, or what the work God has assigned them. In the Service of God the lowest place is honorable and love can make it glorious.

But the Missionary Vocation stands apart with a glory of its own, and, I think, if we analyze that glory it will be found to consist in this, that whereas every Christian is called upon to preach the true Faith at least by living in a truly Christ-like manner, yet the foreign missioner glorifies God by a preaching of the Faith that involves the supremest measure of oblation and sacrifice.

The foreign missionary, whether priest, Brother or Sister, gives up for the advancement of the interests of the Sacred Heart not only all that we on the home missions give up, but much more besides, as you, dear Father, very well know. But on the other hand never forget that since we have only one life to live it is certainly wise to make good use of that one brief period that is in a sense our own; and what use of life can compare with its complete oblation in the isolation of a foreign land, where strange manners and primitive minds make a cloister wherein a missioner may live and love and suffer alone with the Heart of God.

I pray, dear Brother in Christ, that the very loneliness your letter reflects may hold the grace of drawing you into an ever more intimate and more conscious companionship with Jesus, especially Jesus in the Sacrament of His Love. I envy you missioners that isolation from kindred minds and hearts that makes possible the cultivation of a more intimate friendship with the Divine Mind and Heart of Jesus Christ.

Pray for me, Father, that here where life can be quite easy, I may not forget that the true happiness of any one in God's Service is not to be found in comfort and human companionship but in hardships and a loneliness that is filled with the Presence of God.

"SEMPER FIDELIS"

MY DEAR ——:

I am glad to know you are out of the hospital and resting in the golden sunshine on the silver sands at ——. May I, as an old soldier, offer you, a very young soldier, some advice?

Rest your body, but let your soul within be always ready for the fray. "*Semper fidelis*" is, if I mistake not, the motto of our gallant Marine Corps. I offer it to you as a very fitting watchword or motto for your own spiritual advancement. If you adopt it and live up to it, what a reward will await you when you hear Our Blessed Lady of La Salette speak it of you to her Son Divine, "Son, this, our son, has been always faithful!"

Now for fidelity, watchfulness is absolutely necessary. It is the careless soldier who neglects vigilance that falls easily into the snares of the devil. That is why Our Lord's first advice after the terrible ordeal in Gethsemane, when, as we devoutly believe, He foresaw and fore-suffered for all sin, that is why His first advice to His disciples was simply: "Watch and pray that you enter not into temptation!"

In the Compline Office which we say daily, you will recall the touching prayer "that we may watch with Christ and rest in peace." If we are to rest in peace we must first learn to *watch with Christ!*

Thank God, that He does not ask us to watch alone. He, the Divine Commander, not only visits each lonely outpost, each suffering sentinel of His far-flung battle-line, nay, He abides with each of them, in order to be not alone the Goal of their heart's affections, but the Source and the Way thereunto.

Therefore, dear brother-in-arms, be vigilant in Christ, with Christ, for Christ, and when the tide shall have gone out, and the stars shall shine in the evening skies, and taps sound for you, and the Captain call you from your soldiering, then you shall find true Peace, the Peace that only the eternal possession of God can give to a human soul.

"IN THE SERVICE"

Dear Brother in Christ:

Your last letter brought me consolation in the knowledge that you are pressing forward in your Master's Service.

I have written "in your Master's Service" deliberately, because I think every seminarian should consider himself as already in Service, and thus avoid the possibility of slipping into a dangerous state of mind, that of considering God's Service as something yet to come, yet to begin, rather than as a Service we are already engaged in.

Now the danger in thus looking forward to a future service rests in this, that it is conducive to day-dreaming, to living in the future rather than in the present, to planning to-be-tomorrow, rather than being today, what God expects of His soldiers.

There is only one way for you, dear Brother, to be an ardent, faithful missionary, and that is to be such this very day and hour. After all, each day brings us into untraveled country, each hour is a flight in Egypt, each moment is a bit of the future placed for the first and last time in our hands!

Strive, therefore, ——, to be this very day a perfect soldier of the Best of Captains, and in His good time He will Himself place on your shoulders the epaulets of His Priesthood, and pin on your breast the badge of fidelity in His Service, His Most Holy Cross.

Please pray for me.

THE FINGER-TIPS OF CHRIST

My Dear ——:

It is such a long time since you have had a letter from your brother in Christ that surely this note will be a gladsome one to you. Though I do not write, yet that does not mean that you are forgotten, I mean never to forget the finger-tips of Christ!

You will ask what I mean, perhaps? Well, is not the Church the Mystical Body of Christ, and what else then can His servants in the far-away missions of the earth be than Christ's finger-tips reaching for souls! I am sure He loves them and that His Mother kisses them frequently while they are quiet in slumber.

Perhaps you will object that you are a contemplative? Well, again, the Little Thérèse has answered that for all time, a contemplative who is true to his or her vocation is in the truest of senses a missionary. True contemplatives are always active, touching distant places, and souls distant from Christ, with the fingers of prayer and sacrifice. So again, you are of the finger-tips of Jesus.

They were stained with blood, those blessed finger-tips of the Master, and whenever and wherever they rest upon souls they leave behind them their crimson stain, the bright glory of a Victory won in apparent defeat, won only in death.

Thus, too, is our victory to be won for Christ, my brother in His Blood, only in the hour of apparent defeat, and only by death of self.

When, therefore, during these days, Our Lady's beads are slipping through your fingers, remember the souls of the untold pagan host that it would seem were slipping from Christ's fingers—perchance not as yet touched by His finger-tips. Pray for them, Brother, the mighty army of souls, beloved by the Sacred Heart, redeemed by His Blood Most Precious, but not yet touched by His finger-tips!

Though, thanks to God's mercy, not a pagan, yet I need not add—let your finger-tips in prayer touch with Christ's Blood the souls of all priests and your brother's—

FOR THE KING

Dear Sisters in Christ:

I must thank you for your visit which proved a pleasure to me. I often think, when I see the white habit of St. Dominic's children, of the white hosts their souls and all souls should be in the sight of our Heavenly Father. For whether we wear exteriorly the white of His innocence or the black of His and His Mother's sorrows, or the brown, symbolic of His labors and mortifications, yet still within, by the grace of His Blood, should we not be all and always white hosts for the King!

Every morning when I uncover the chalice at Mass, a small host rests upon the white breast of the larger Mass host. It is the host for the Communion of my server, but I love to think of it as symbolic of the desire of my King that my being, both soul and body, should rest upon His Virginal Breast, One Host and One Oblation to One God. I know, of course, there is many a weary mile of sacrifice and many an arid hour of trial to be completed before the thought of my desire shall be a spiritual reality, yet surely the desire harmonizes with my Lover's will. And our Lover's will, dear Sisters, does it mean all in all to us? So should you ask me for one thought to treasure through the years that lie beyond the horizons of tomorrow, I would make it this: Be, dear Sisters, white hosts for Jesus, loving hosts, virginal hosts for the King of Kings.

To some, I know, this may seem too much a matter of sentiment and sugary emotion. Yet let those who feel thus strive for just one day to be just a host of the King, with their wills resting firmly, quietly, on the golden paten of His will and their faculties of body and soul detached host-like from creatures and elevated by the sacrificial hands of their vows to God. Let them try just for one day to be white hosts for Jesus, and they will find that the race is only to the strong and only the strong can hope to be really God's hosts.

However, Sisters, let us never forget, though we be weak, Jesus, our Love, is strength divine, and He offers all His strength to us in the white Host every morning. Semper per Mariam.

BEFORE THE DARK

My Dear Child:

This letter will reach you in the month of the Holy Rosary, and hence, I trust, will bring a double measure of Our Lady's graces to you. Since your last note presented no special problem for solution, mine will deal with that final conversion to God to which we should all attain before the coming of the night. I need not tell you what a terrible thing it would be for the servants of God to find themselves with oil-less lamps, when the shadows of the evening shall have woven a shroud of darkness over life's familiar scenes. Dear Child, do not delay. It is folly to wait one hour in the pursuit of our conversion. We are, of course, dependent upon God's hour, but it is my conviction that God's time is our time, in as much as God will respond very readily to the slightest unfolding of a humble soul to the touch of His grace. After all, it is He "Who worketh in us both to will and to accomplish," and, as He is always present, so is He by reason of the mysterious and unfathomable depths of His love, always ready to come to our assistance in a work so allied to the designs of His glory.

Sometimes, indeed, as at the end of the journey of the disciples to Emmaus, He may pretend that He will go farther, but this mysterious pretense, of which human affection gives so many sweet reflections, yields almost instantly to the sincere invitation of our souls. We have only to cry out as did the bewildered disciples of old, "Remain with us, Master, for the day is far spent," and immediately He, who has waited for the proper invitation, turns in with the eagerness of love to share our humble board.

Perhaps, Child, perhaps for you as well as for many another of His servants, the day is, indeed, far spent! Do not delay that advance in intimate living with God from which will come so many and so great consolations. Surrender once and for all, your will, your affections, your judgments, your every thought to Jesus through Mary. Cultivate the art of walking with Christ, talking with Christ, working with Christ, loving in Christ; and that you may be skillful in these blessed accomplishments fail not to take a daily lesson at your Mother's knee with the school-book of innumerable saints—her Rosary—held attentively in your hands. Always in Christ Jesus.

ROSARY TRAILS

My Dear Child:

I have much to tell you yet so little time for the telling. I will, however, do the best I can. Since I wrote you last I have had the privilege of making my final vows. Perhaps before I die—if I live long enough—I will come to some sort of comprehension of the greatness of this grace. After all when we look more deeply into our own souls we find always that it is God who has claimed us rather than we who have claimed God. Saint Paul put this—as so many things else—very succinctly when he said, "By the grace of God I am what I am." The joys of life, however, must always be associated with sorrows. It is the sunshine that makes shadows. And if it were not that I desire to be in all things conformed to God's Holy Will, I would be reluctant to enter the shadows that await. The shadows I will share with Mother Mary; of the joys of the moment, two I can share with you. *Kenedy* is publishing my Life of Father Moreau this fall and *The Magnificat Press* is bringing out a little volume of my verse. I know you will like them both.

As regards yourself, remember when Jesus is loved deeply enough one's own heart becomes a Carmel. Your union with Him is alone essential, the time and place of your activity only incidental. No one has even approached to Our Blessed Lady in the rôle of a contemplative and yet her cell was a Carpenter's home. When you find yourself too deeply concerned over secondary considerations you will oftentimes find self-will lurking just beneath the surface of your intentions. Be courageous in its elimination. This is what Our Blessed Lord meant when He declared that it would be necessary for His true disciples to hate their own souls.

Somewhere, somehow, I am going to have the privilege of doing something at least in a small way for the conversion of Israel. Christ and His Blessed Mother must cast longing eyes over the scattered flocks of Their Judean hills; and while I await the opportunity to translate Their desires into apostolic activity, I will follow with you Rosary Trails questing the lost sheep of Israel.

Asking Our Lady to bless you.

THE WISH OF A CHILD

DEAR SISTER:

The question you submitted in your letter of last month opens a very interesting and rather extensive problem. You asked me if it is right to pray that one might die on a feast day of Our Blessed Mother. My answer is yes, certainly. Desire this grace—for it certainly is a grace—and pray for it to your heart's content. And you can rest assured this prayer will be pleasing to God and Our Blessed Lady, under one condition, that you add the fundamental clause of all prayer of petition, that of ultimate conformity of your will to God's.

This advice which I give you would probably not be the counsel given by others. The Little Flower of Lisieux, for example, out of her love for humility did not wish to be distinguished by dying on a feast day. She, therefore, prayed not to die on a feast day of Our Lady, and we may be sure her prayer was most pleasing to God. But, on this point I would have you remember that in the lives of the Saints we find the emphasis first on one and then on another of the virtues, and whereas Saint Thérèse was here acting on the principle of humility she might just as well have asked this favor acting on the virtue of simplicity. Indeed if you have studied her life, you will find our little Carmelite Sister played quite steadily the rôle of a child, and what is more characteristic of childhood than asking with simplicity for the desires of the moment?

Be not afraid, therefore, to take God at His word—ask and you shall receive, and as the glorious mysteries of Our Lady's rosary glide across your mental vista, I am sure the Gentlest of Mothers will hear and be pleased with the wish of a child desiring to go home on a Day redolent with memories of her own triumphant homing.

I, too, hope to die on a Feast of Our Lord or of Our Blessed Lady for I figure there must be special graces of repentance and forgiveness awaiting souls poised for final flight on these days.

ONE MASTER

DEAR BROTHER IN CHRIST:

Your final Profession brings me much joy. It is

undoubtedly a special grace to belong to Our Blessed Lord with a finality of decision both on our own part and equally on the part of those who represent God by reason of the authority entrusted to them.

Because the world is accustomed to think of vows in terms of the imprisonment of the human entity, her children can never hope to comprehend their grandeur. In reality the vows do not bind any more than in this sense that they are intended to release us from the petty things of life. An apt comparison would be that of a balloonist or traveler by air who enters indeed a narrow compartment, adjusts a life-belt but presently by reason of this preliminary confinement finds himself lifted up above the earth and at peace among the clouds.

Some may object that the vows of religion do not always accomplish such an exaltation of the individual soul. Sadly we must admit that this is too often true; but again, upon proper analysis in these cases the fault will be found to rest not in the nature of the vows but in the character of the one who makes them. Some there are, as you must know, dear Brother, who wish for the impossible; they would have the liberty of earth as well as the freedom of heaven; they would wish to soar to God and yet retain all the creature satisfactions of earth. They are unhappy, not because they have made vows but because they have not a mind and a heart to keep them. Still is it true: no man can serve two Masters; no man can successfully give himself to God and to self. Happiness for men rests ultimately in that donation of self to God which you are about to seal.

Of course I will be with you in spirit, and though my Mass is engaged for the day, I will think of you when Our Lord is hosted in my hands and pray for you when Mother Mary is listening to the Aves of my evening rosary. May she keep our vows all fair and all-untarnished in her Heart of hearts.

NOVEMBER

November's fallen leaves — rustling beneath
our feet — whisper of the Holy Souls.

BEFORE THE DAWN

DEAR FRIEND:

Perhaps you have begun to think I had forgotten you since the shadow of the Cross fell across the doorway of your little home. This letter is to say to you that though I have little time for writing yet I do remember you each morning as I stand at the Altar of God.

It is there with God within my hands that I can do most for you and yours whom God has claimed. Behold the exquisiteness of God's love for us. The same arms of Christ that reach out to console you from the Mystic Cross of the Altar, reach out as well to bring sweet relief and consolation to your dear ones—if perchance they are waiting in Purgatory for the Dawn of the Eternal Day.

Have you ever waited for the coming of the dawn, not a dawn that meant new trials or unkind realities, but a dawn crimson with hope of life and love and happiness, a dawn like that of your wedding day? Well, so it is with the blessed souls in Purgatory; they are waiting for a Dawn whose glory shall never fade, whose promise shall never be broken, whose warmth shall never grow cold, for it ushers in an Eternal Day whose Sun shall never set. "And God shall wipe away their tears."

Be patient, therefore, and plod onward. Faith, our Faith alone, supplies a satisfactory answer to the mystery of earthly trials. Follow with Hope where Faith leads you through this valley of tears, and I promise you shall find, in the light of the Morning Star, Love Eternal and the dear ones Love Eternal created for you.

Please pray for FATHER PAGE.

THE PRESENTATION

DEAR ——:

This note should reach you about the twenty-first, the Feast of Our Blessed Lady's Presentation.

I like to receive little consolations on our Lady's Feasts, and I am hoping this will be one to you.

What a beautiful subject for our mind's eye the Blessed Mother's Presentation offers. Behold the wee maiden ascending the Temple steps with that sweet, simple dignity of childhood that is so hard to regain when once it has been lost. St. Anne and St. Joachim look on in distressed wonder, and even the aged Doctors of the Law feel a fresh warmth of devotion creep into their hearts as they gaze on this childish prodigy of innocence, wisdom and devotion. "Who is this one?" this child of grace, they must have whispered as they looked upon the future Mother of their God. The Temple of God is come to the Temple of God; the Holy of Holies, the Ark of the Covenant have now a new significance. God's Mother-to-be is a handmaid in the House of the Lord.

Not to all is given this gift of gifts, this grace of true wisdom, of belonging to God from one's youth. This is the gift of the chosen few—but, at least, if we have lost this grace God has offered us another of only less value. To us He has said, "You have not given me your youth, but there yet remains your life—will you not give Me this?" Because we have not given the one, shall we refuse the other? Nay, does not the very fact that we have not given our youth make it the more imperative that we hasten to recoup our loss?—for surely what is not given to God is lost, gone forever.

This and many another lesson we can draw from the consideration of our Blessed Mother's Presentation. Thank her, then, that she has led you too into the Temple of God—even though it be a little late.

There is an afternoon to Life's day as well as a morning, and during its long hours, which I pray God to give you, may you labor faithfully, steadily in His harvest field till the evening Angelus shall summon you to prayer and rest and peace, to a place at His table, and a home forever in His Heart and Mother Mary's.

NOVEMBER

Dear ——:

God be praised for everything and may He give us the grace to praise Him and see His fatherly guidance in all the exigencies of our lives. How sweet life must be for those who really love Him, for they do really trust Him blindly and therefore live and walk through rain or sunshine, darkness and light with the smiling eyes of Faith.

This month of November is a trying month for worldlings—all Nature is making a profound and pointed meditation on Death, and refuses to cheer the hearts that live on externals only. They may talk to her but she but whispers "Death."

So the worldling turns from the outdoor world to the comforts or distractions of the living room, library, bridge, a book or a cup of tea. A fire gleams on the hearth with its gay chatter or perhaps moody murmuring. Here at least is some consolation for body if not for soul.

But oh—what is this life to the life that is yours? The fire on their hearth shall die. The book they read be finished. The game of bridge have its score tallied up. The armchair shall at last be vacated and the lights go out forever. And you, you kneel close to the Everburning Hearth of Christ's Heart. Its radiance warms the depths of your soul, not with that repelling heat of earthly fires but with a gentle warmth that draws you imperceptibly, yet steadily, closer to God and His gleaming, loving Heart. Earthly fire destroys.

The Divine Fire of God's Pure Love destroys indeed earthly dross — but leaves the immortal soul glowing with pure affection — reflecting from its radiant depths ever more clearly the image of its Maker. And so your earthly joy is but the prelude of that which is eternal when the Master shall reveal to you the glory of His Father's Home.

As you rest at the Hearth of God, I know you will not forget those who for the love of the Master must walk the windy roads, climb the bleak hills, search the cold hearts of the multitude to light a few fires for God.

Some day we too trust we shall be called in out of the rain and the cold, be welcomed by the Master, stretch our weary limbs at His Hearth and rest our little hearts on His — through Mary's prayers.

GOD'S TAKING

Dear ——:

It is a long time as the world reckons back to those joyous days of our boyhood, and we have walked by different roads since then. But now that the fingers of sorrow have rested on your soul it is time I hastened across lots to bring you friendship's sympathy and I humbly trust God's consolation.

How blithely lives ofttimes flow on like meadow-brooks until they reach the deeper stream of humanity. Then their singing ceases or rather changes, their joyous theme becoming now deeper, more subdued, always more thoughtful, and sometimes mournful. Your life must not change its song. There is still a God of Love and a Home of Love beyond the stars. It is in love that God has taken from you the half of your heart, taken that He might preserve it from evil, keep it safe for you, and having thus lifted your heart up from earthly desires draw you and unite you to your heart in Heaven.

Please, therefore, let not your heart-stream, swollen by tears, set up a sullen murmur. What God gives, He gives in love; what God takes, He takes in love. The same Love worketh both. You know this by faith — live by faith; by faith in God's Love, all-wonderful, and let your life, like a peaceful river, flow onward till it be lost in the ocean of His eternal love — and may the souls that look down in love on you from Heaven, find, like the stars, their image mirrored in your clear unsullied depths.

I shall pray for you to Mary.

TRUE SPIRITISM

DEAR ——:

A saintly old priest, friend of mine, said to me lately, "Father, I find myself touching Providence many times a day." We all touch the hands of God's providential care many times a day, but it is only the heart of faith that recognizes the touch.

Now you write, with, it seems to me, a certain note of pride, that you have been dabbling in spiritism. My dear ——, I thought you had better sense, deeper discernment. Do you not realize that the Faith in which you were born offers you the closest possible intimacy with the world beyond! O how senseless, how childish, is all this dickering of silly women, and learned professors and professional mountebanks!

Do you honestly think the angels of God's light dwell in the darkness of private seances, and answer the gibberings of bewhiskered impostors and the desires of emotional women? Put all this folly from you. There is a world beyond this world; Faith taught you that as a child. There are spirits both good and bad. Faith taught you that also; and there is above all, and over all, a Supreme Spirit of Infinite Holiness and Beauty, to Whom you and I and all this world of ours shall pay tribute in the end, willingly or unwillingly.

My advice to you, dear ——, is this: stick to your guardian angel. He will not ring mysterious bells for you, though he may remind you of the Angelus. He will not rap tables in Western Union code, though it is quite possible he may remind you of the Ten Commandments. He will certainly help you to save your immortal soul, guide and protect you on your journey to the world beyond the vale. All this nonsense you speak of is unworthy of God and His faithful spirits and, I am sure, at times it must make even the spirits of wickedness laugh. We live in a world of spirits because, after all, we ourselves are more than mere flesh; we, too, are immortal spirits, but the glory of our immortality will not be found at fortune tellers and seances, but on our knees in the confessional and at the altar rail. This is the True Spiritism — to be in the world but not of it, to be the loving and trusting children of a Heavenly Father Who is never far from us, and the faithful servants of a Heavenly Queen.

THE CHALLENGE

Dear ——:

During this somber-hued month when the leaves idling down from the wayside trees remind us of the passing of another Summer and the coming of another Winter, and perhaps, if we be so minded, calling us to pray for those who, like the leaves, have fluttered down to rest in silence upon the Earth's soft breast — during this month let us consider not the thought of dying, but the joyous thought of living well and using well your life.

You have youth, and youth has always a challenge to be met. The nobler the heart, the nobler the challenge it will accept. The baser the heart, the baser the call it will answer. There is the challenge of Pleasure, of Fame, of Comfort, of earthly Being, and many are the hearts that accept and give themselves to the winning of these Things.

Now, naturally, you know well it is not such challenges as these that I am writing of to you. These are challenges that reach one at all times, that confront one on all sides, at least when one is eighteen years of age. No, the challenge of which I write is the Supreme challenge, given by God Himself from out the silence that marks His Presence in His Eucharistic Home.

Jesus in the Blessed Sacrament is the Sublimest of Challenges to the man or woman of true faith and generosity of soul. The momentous words spoken first by God's Own Son and echoing down through the centuries by the lips of His priests constitute a perpetual challenge to generosity on the part of God's creatures because they tell us of the absolute generosity of God Himself.

In the Blessed Sacrament, God's Son has been so generous unto us that many find it impossible to bow to the words of Him Who is Eternal Truth. How little they know of the depth and the breadth and heights of Divine Love. God could do no more, it is true, than give us Himself; and God, being God, would do no less.

During the coming months when your mind will be so constantly busy with lectures and books and the findings of earthly professors, I hope you will find time to kneel daily for a few moments before the open book of the Eucharistic Heart of Jesus and read therein the greatness of God's love for you, and come to find in the knowledge of that love, strength to bear all the trials and disappointments that await you as they await all others along the road of time, grace for the cheerful fulfilling of Life's duty, and perchance, if Jesus so wills, the inspiration to answer the challenge of His Sacrifice with a sacrifice of your own, that you may be for Jesus as Jesus is always for you, a little white Host, living apart from any one home in order to serve many, and bring all hearts to one Home and that Home, His Father's.

Asking Our Lady to Bless you.

"HOLY SOULS"

Dear Father ——:

This note is to offer to you my sincere sympathy in the death of your good father. After God Himself, what greater gift can God give to us than noble-souled parents, and I think I can say of your father, that he was truly a father after God's Own Heart, one of Christ's Holy Souls. Therefore, it seems to me that when we consider your father's character and the long years God spared him to you, your very sorrow should be deeply tinged with gratitude, with humble gratitude, for the older we grow, the more I think will the thoughtful man realize the debt he owes under God to his parents for the natural virtues that he finds enshrined within his soul.

Today, with new notions and new ideals that are indeed hardly worthy of the title ideals, becoming more prevalent, and the true glory of parenthood becoming more and more obscured behind the verbiage in which modern selfishness seeks to veil its hedonistic purposes, today more than ever, we need to teach our people the true glory of fatherhood, Christian fatherhood, that our homes may continue to be what under God's grace and planning they have been in the past, shrines of God's Love, temples dedicated to the Honor of the Eternal Father.

God gave you, dear Father ——, a wonderful father, and you have, I know, given to your father the greatest of consolations by your own life of spiritual fatherhood, consecrated to the unselfish service of souls that Jesus Christ might find himself at home in all homes, especially those of the household of the Faith. I am sure that looking down from Heaven, your father will continue to find consolation, perfect consolation now, because of the fuller appreciation in the light that streams from the face of God's Eternal Son, of what the Priesthood really is, of its glorious prerogatives, its sacred duties, its abiding obligations, its eternal rewards, and you, looking up to your Heavenly Father, will find consolation in this thought, that there are now two Fathers looking down together upon two Sons looking up together, two Sons who are but One, for this is the deepest meaning of our vocation, dear Father, that Jesus Christ should live in us, and we in Jesus Christ. Semper per Mariam.

THE OCEAN OF GOD'S LOVE

Dear Sister:

I received your little note safely, telling me of your mother's going home. I said Mass for her this morning and I will remember her in my prayers all during this beautiful month of the Sorrowful Mother.

However, as I probably have told you before, I have the greatest confidence in the salvation of the parents of faithful priests and religious, and the basis of my confidence is this: Our God is a God of love. A God Whose Infinite Wisdom has been used to find means of accomplishing the plans of His Infinite Love despite the disobedience, at times malicious, of so many of His creatures. God loves every soul He has created and He delights to find an excuse for extending His mercy to yet greater extent. Now a faithful priest or religious furnishes the Sacred Heart with a very valid and potent reason for extending His Merciful Love to overwhelm, when needful, the soul of a mother or father.

Of course, in the spiritual life, as we realize as we grow older, all things go back to that Ocean of God's Love from whence all the streams of love that water the plains of life have had their origin and source. As the sun lifts the waters of an ocean in order to bear them inland to water the hills and vales whence they return by the rivers to sea, so God lifts the dew of His grace from the ocean of His infinite love and bears it to the cities and towns of men from whence it returns in souls saved and sanctified, and thus the circle is completed. Out of God comes all life and love, and God's beautiful plan calls for the return of all life and love into the Ocean of His Love, into the Eternal Sea. Therefore, Sister, let your tears in their falling be as pearls of grateful love to a God Who loved your mother long before you were born, Who will love her long after you have ceased to be here on earth, and Whose love gave both of you life, and will some day reunite you in that place we call Heaven, where reunions shall never come to an ending nor evening tide bring the sadness of parting. At the Golden Gates I know you will find your mother with Our Mother, and there I hope you will pray for a wayfarer left behind on the dusty road.

THE ONLY ROAD

Dear Sister in Christ:

I have been hoping that it would be possible for me to attend your Profession, but despite the fact that I am on vacation I cannot, without deserting other duties, get away at the present moment. However, I promise you now that, God willing, I will attend your final Profession which will bind you to Jesus—Gentlest of Lovers and Best of Shepherds forever.

The spirit of profession may be summed up, it seems to me, in the one word—"forward!" All life is a journey; all life marks progress onward; but not always progress upward as well. Therefore, the profession-spirit of a true religious should be that of renewed consecration to the attainment of that spiritual Calvary that becomes for such as gain its summit an eternal Tabor where they shall see the unveiled Glory of their Divine Lover and dwell forever within the bright rays of the benediction of His smile.

Forward, therefore, dear Sister, along the only road that leads to Jesus Crucified. He is ever, at least for us who tread this earth, to be found upon His mystical Calvary, and the only road thereto is called the Way of the Holy Cross.

You will not journey that way alone; you are one of a mighty throng that, streaming across the centuries, have followed the Saviour up that tortuous pathway to the heights. Blessed Mother Mary will be with you, and like Simon of Cyrene seeking to aid the Master, in very truth, it will be the Master Who will be aiding you, still carrying your Cross which His Divine Love has already made His very own.

Forward, therefore, dear Sister; let nothing disturb you, nothing dismay you. God is with you, God be with you, Mary guide you, homeward bound to God.

HOLY PRISONERS

My Dear ——:

I can never thank you enough for having directed my attention and consequently my devotion to God's holy prisoners, the holy souls. If I tell you now that my devotion to the souls in Purgatory is still increasing it is only that you may be the happier in the knowledge of another friend made for these dear friends of yours.

There was a time when the needs of the living—of the Church Militant—so engrossed my thoughts that like an officer on front line duty I gave comparatively little thought to the wounded who were carried to the rear, destined to suffer but not to die. But now I see more clearly the claims of these sufferers of the Lord and feel more deeply their silent yet eloquent plea for succor. A real Catholic, a true Christian, must be Catholic in the extension of his charity; like Christ, his heart must go out to all, not only to those who walk in the full Light of Faith, but as well to those who live in the half-lights and to those who sit in the darkness of paganism, yea, and beyond the gates of Death his love and his prayers must follow to succor and to cheer those who wait our aid in hopeful suffering, prisoners of God's merciful justice, this side of Heaven's gates!

So, dear ——, rest assured I shall not forget these good friends of yours during this month Mother Church dedicates in a special manner to their needs, and when in God's chosen time you, too, shall be en route to Heaven, should perchance there be for you a stop-over with your friends, faithfully I promise you, in Christ Jesus, I will visit you; I will come to bring you light in the darkness, for you I shall lift above my head—God's Divine Lantern—Jesus Hostia, Light of the World!

THANKSGIVING IN SORROW

My Dear Father ——:

I arrived here Wednesday evening only to learn of the sudden sorrow that had come to you in the death of your dear sister. How unexpectedly these final realities break in upon us, and leave us thoughtful, like tourists at the rim of the Grand Canyon, or as pilgrims in a great cathedral, or again as children beside the fringes of the sea. Then it is that a sense of our finiteness sweeps over us, and, at times, only God's grace saves us from despair.

Only God's grace, but thanks be to God, His grace is never lacking to souls of good will, and His Hand is never more surely that of a Father than when He leads us close by Calvary.

Thank Him, therefore, dear Father, even in your sorrow, for all His gifts. Thank Him for the faith that makes it possible for you to gaze with steady eyes across that Valley whence travelers do not return. Thank Him for the visions faith has furnished you of this universe as one vast cathedral of His Glory, and of time as a sea with another and happier shore. Thank Him for the comradeship of Hope that has cheered you through the lengthening years, sharing your dreariest hours and whispering of blessed reunions in the port of missing friends. Thank Him for the graciousness of His planning that makes of your little sacrifices helping hands of prayer for your departed and His Great Sacrifice your very own by reason of the White Host morn by morn.

Thank Him, above all, for Himself, and for His love which runs like a golden thread through the tangled skein of our lives, which breaks upon our wills more impetuously than the surf of the stormiest sea, which shines as the sun by day and as the moon by night through the rose windows His grace has fashioned for our souls, bathing our minds and hearts in light and warmth and inspiration. Thank Him for His love which gave you your sister, and trust Him to keep His gift till Life's swift evening fall.

Then, dear Father ——, having hymned His Glory in sorrow, and learned to thank Him for the sheltering shadows of His Cross, from beyond the Valley will come His voice calling you Home, calling you to thanksgiving in joy, calling you to Himself, and to your sister whom I know you will find close—

To Our Lady's Heart.

GOD'S MARINES

Dear Father —— :

I have been busy working on the life of Father Moreau, our Founder, which, please God and Our Lady, I shall have finished this month, but I pause now to fulfill my promise of a letter to you.

As you know, my favorite fantasy when thinking of the various religious Orders and Communities of Holy Mother Church is that of the varied branches of the service within a nation's military forces. Since there can be no doubt of the reality of our warfare, both with the powers of darkness and the weaknesses of our common humanity, surely it is not far-fetched to think of the various groups within the Church Militant as so many distinct regiments each with its specialized service to be rendered and each with its own proud record of campaigns now past; and as I once told you, I like to think of the Company of Jesus as the Marines of God.

Soldiers of the sea — that is what marines are — and the Company Ignatius founded has been from the beginning Soldiers of the Holy See, traversing the seven seas at the bidding of Christ's Most Holy Vicar. Our country's Marine Corps has the proud slogan, "First to Fight," and, from the day your Captain received a shattered leg and a unique vocation at Pampluna, it seems to me the Sons of Ignatius have managed to bear a hand in almost every battle waged for Christ's sacred interests throughout the drifting years.

More precious, however, than the Marine slogan of "First to Fight" is their inspiring motto, "semper fidelis"; and I wish, dear Father ——, to you and to all your comrades-in-arms, the grace of being ever faithful to the purpose of your Company, the glory ever greater of Almighty God and the consolation ever deeper of His Son's Most Sacred Heart.

A true Jesuit is indeed a valiant and efficient promoter of God's greater glory and a deep and abiding consolation to Our Saviour's Heart. And thus, some day, when taps shall have been sounded for a last time above the battlefields of earth, I humbly hope to stand at attention while God's Marines march by in triumphant review before their Commander-in-Chief and His Most Blessed Mother.

My Dear Dad:

I want this note to be a birthday note for you, not my real birthday note, for that, please God, I shall send you from the altar in the silence of early morning on the 22nd, but just a little note of felicitation on the laying of another stone in the arch — now nearing completion — of your life. I think our Heavenly Father is pleased to have us thus honor those who on earth have the high vocation of walking in His image.

Daily I thank God for you, dear dad, for the precious gift of life He gave me through you and for that mysterious inheritance of faith in Him and love for His creatures which constitutes an inherent part of my heritage. It is true you will leave your sons no earthly wealth to wedge their hearts apart. You will leave us instead, by the grace of God, a spiritual inheritance far more precious than any and all material possessions. You will leave us the memory of your abiding honesty, unwavering generosity and faith no less virile because unostentatious.

Because we are your sons, we ask, we want nothing more. Time will sweep away the material wealth of individuals as well as of nations. Time cannot efface or destroy the dowery of humble righteousness which is your gift to us. Time can furnish naught else than lengthening and deepening memories of your whole-hearted devotion to the interests not only of your own children but of all those children of the Heavenly Father whom His Providence placed within the reach of your care.

One fault perhaps, dear dad, I may be forgiven for mentioning, first because it is a fault in which we share, and secondly because it seems at times almost a reflection of divinity. You have been proud of your sons and your sons have been proud of you. But the Heavenly Father Who eulogized His Divine Son at the Jordan and on Tabor will forgive you surely on this point. After all, your paternity is but the reflection and earthly extension of His very own. Nor will Jesus forget when I whisper your name to Him each morning, how much easier your example and unselfish love has made it for me to learn to love and serve that other and Heavenly Father Who fashioned your life in His image.

Always asking Him to bless you.

WHEN EVENING COMES

My Dear ——:

Yours is a problem of unusual intensity but the issues are nevertheless unusually clear. Music is certainly one of God's great gifts to men, a revelation through sound of the harmony that pervades all things that God has made and that are not subject to the intervention of His creatures. But, great as is the gift of music, precious as is the talent of your musical attainments, what is a lifetime of musical triumphs compared with the privilege of offering just a single low Mass! As a great musician, and I believe you can become such if you so choose, you will play upon the heartstrings of humanity; as a priest you will touch daily the heartstrings of God! As a master musician you will move vast audiences to tears, as a great priest—and you must be no less—you will wipe away the tears from countless eyes, you will mend shattered soul instruments, you will sing and God's angels will listen, you will absolve and God will ratify, you will speak and God Himself will obey.

As for your dear ones—and here is the real test—be mindful of Him who left the dearest of Mothers for you, and went forth to restore at the price of His life-blood the broken harmony that once made God's visible universe but one vast cathedral and His creatures but one chorus with man directing. More profoundly — the proper answer to your question is one of great simplicity — go forward to the altar only when in the depths of your being you have concluded you would rather whisper "Jesus" in the silence of a lonely chapel than bow amid the reverberating echoes of music-waves of your creation mingled with the applause of men.

By the way, when evening comes, as it will presently, which do you suppose will bring the deeper consolation, to have climbed the peak of musical fame or to have sounded the depths of Divine Love?

May Our Lady whisper you the answer.

BEHIND THE LINES

Dear Mother in Christ:

You know how frequently people in the world, even educated Catholics, fail to realize the power of prayer in the extension of the Kingdom of Christ. It is a truth which only Faith teaches us and yet if we have Faith, how well the lesson will be learned. The life of the Little Flower, the striking efficacy of her intercession which has won for her equal rank with St. Francis Xavier as the patron of the missions and the gratitude of practically every soldier of Christ engaged on His far-flung battle lines, her life alone should be proof enough of the value of prayer as a potential factor in the winning of the world to the Sacred Heart of the world's Redeemer. You and your children, Mother, though far behind the lines, are yet very close to God if you are fulfilling, as I know you are, your God-given vocation; and the heart-throbs of God are ever the same, they beat always for the salvation of all souls everywhere.

It has struck me forcefully, more than once, that our Divine Redeemer when He pointed out the harvest-fields, white with the harvest, to His apostles, it has struck me forcefully that He did not say "go ye into the harvest" but rather "pray ye that the Lord send laborers into the harvest." Always our dear Divine Lord emphasized the necessity of prayer, both by word and by example, and you, dear Mother, must do the same. You and your Sisters by praying for Our Lord's lonely missionaries can be missionaries, share their labors and their trials, strengthen them in temptation, console them in their sorrows, taste of their joys here, and merit to share their Eternal Reward. The cloistered Sister whose heart is one with Christ's, can go with Christ, as indeed Christ goeth, the Commander-in-Chief, in the silence of the night visiting the front-line trenches, whispering words of cheer to the tired sentinels, bandaging the wounds of the fallen, feeding the hungry with the Bread of Life, and thus though behind the lines, in Christ and with Christ and for Christ you will be always in the front-line trenches.

May Our Lady, Queen of Apostles, bless your prayers.

"THE FIRST VICTORY"

My Dear ——:

I was very much pleased by the spirit your note revealed. Yes, it is a long road to God's Holy Priesthood, but I am sure you will be so happy you persevered, on that morning when God shall rest for the first time in your freshly anointed hands and then pass from your trembling hands to the lips and hearts of your dear ones. One day in God's Priesthood is worth a life-time of preparation.

Let me urge you, ——, from the beginning to motivate your studies and exercises with the high aim of becoming a perfect soldier of Jesus Christ. When you get out into the battlefield of the world, then it will be too late, at least from the point of good soldiering, to begin to be a soldier. You must begin now. If we fight valiantly today's battles, tomorrow's will take care of themselves. The student who conquers himself today, is the priest who tomorrow will conquer souls for Christ. Self-conquest is the first and most essential victory to be won.

Therefore, ——, set yourself cheerfully to the great task before you. Do your part manfully, but at the same time remember that you cannot do it alone. God must give you the morning dews of His graces and the sunshine of His benediction. Mother Mary must intercede for you. Do you pray daily, therefore, that the swift-winged years may find you ever better fitted for God's soldiering, ever more worthy of a commission from the Divine Captain, ever better prepared to carry Our Lady's Colors and the knowledge and Love of Her Son to the farthest parts of the earth.

THOSE WHO REMAIN

My Dear ——:

I want to thank you for the thoughtful invitation to attend the Reception and Profession on the eighth. You know that I would like to be present, and that I will be in spirit and in prayer.

What mingled sentiments of joy and sorrow must flood your heart as year by year you see your little ones grown fair under God's grace—of which you have been in so many ways the channel and guardian—preparing to leave for the mission front.

I, myself, have seen the eyes of a saintly Master of Novices fill with tears at the mention of his spiritual sons' approaching departure, and if a man's heart can know such holy tenderness what depths may not a spiritual mother sound!

However, such is life—a net in which the living strands weave in and out! Did not Our Divine Master say "the Kingdom of God is like to a net cast into the sea?"

Well, your part, dear Sister in Christ, is to share that of the Blessed Mother who had played such a part in fashioning the Human Strands of the Divine Net which God had cast into the ocean of Time! You with Mother Mary must stand in spirit in the doorway of the little home at Nazareth and watch the white-clad figure of the Christ depart upon His mission. After all, even your little daughters are in a very true sense other Christs! Does He not live in them? You know well that He does! Are they not entirely His? Is not their mission His mission, and their every heart-beat one with His Heart-beats for the extension of His Father's Kingdom!

Place, therefore, dear Sister, your hand in Mother Mary's as you place your daughters' hands in Christ's. Someday your little ones will come Home to you, and that will mean Heaven, will it not!

GOD'S GLEANERS

Dear Sister in Christ:

This is a time of year when we have special need of our innate Christian optimism. Whether we are ready to admit it or not, the moods and fashions of Nature rest strong fingers upon the pliant keys of our senses, and our souls, organ-like, reverberate in facile harmony. Every season, indeed each month, possesses its own theme song and its own motif. Winter sings of fortitude; Spring of hope, new-born; Summer of love's fulfillment, while Autumn chants a requiem over her fading beauty. That is why in the fall of the year, it seems to me, we have need in a special degree of that warmth and light that Faith, and Faith alone, can bring to the deeper chambers of our souls.

The crickets, wee troubadours of cheer, have been busy seeking shelter from the chill which now walks nightly through the fields. Amid the stubble, where but yesterday the grasshoppers were playing leap frog, now silence reigns. God's little gleaners have finished their appointed tasks. We, too, dear Sister, are God's gleaners; I wonder when shall we finish our work!

Others spend themselves for Jesus amid the yellow harvests of the East where souls, like parched rice fields, await the saving waters of sacramental life. Ours is a humbler adventure, a more hidden romance. Like the wee creatures of the fields, we are only gleaners, gathering up the fragments lest they be lost.

Yet how wonderful is the alchemy of Divine Love! Our petty sacrifices, our feeble prayers have, in God, the power of strengthening the arms and confirming the hearts of these more distant and more valiant reapers of the Lord! Surely in this thought which little Thérèse of Carmel so well illustrated in her life, we can find inspiration for saving even the pennies of our spiritual transactions; and meanwhile, here at home, there are always waiting for our charity to find and our zeal to gather the stray blades of God's wheat —immortal souls neglected and at times forgotten by all save Jesus and His Most Holy Mother.

As you pass, therefore, dear Sister, up and down the pain bordered corridors of St. ——'s, as you walk between the white flower-beds where human dust holds the precious seeds of immortality, remember your vocation. Here before you rests a pain-winnowed harvest, and you, like Ruth of old, must glean after the reapers, close to the tent and beneath the eyes of your Divine Bridegroom, till

His Mother calls for you.

THE HIDDEN SERVANTS

My Dear Child:

If it was a pleasure to meet two more of Christ's hidden servants, it is now a pleasure to encourage you and ——, in work which is so helpful to His missionaries in many lands. From time to time we hear stories of the secret service of our own or of some foreign power, and, as is but natural, our imagination takes fire at the thought of these vast webs whose living strands are men and women pledged to the advancement and defense of national interests.

Well, dear Child, God, too, has His secret service—a service with no more sinister a purpose than that of working humbly, and thus more efficiently, for the salvation of souls. His hidden servants are to be found in every quarter of the globe, in every province of His Kingdom, and I would wish to think of you and ——, as fulfilling humbly and joyfully in Christ Jesus, this part in the advancement of His Sacred Cause.

"Thy Kingdom come." How often this petition is found on the lips of Catholics! How often, too, it would seem the words on our lips awaken no corresponding activity within our minds and hearts! If it were otherwise, would not the whole world be subject to its Redeemer? The entire earth a happy Kingdom wherein love alone held sway!

However, the silver lining to the cloud of human unresponsiveness to the generosity of God is, it seems to me, the privilege thus furnished to us of joining that little group of faithful ones once gathered at the foot of His Cross and ever since reproduced in the Passion Play of centuries. If all men were on Christ's side, wherein would be the special merit of being with the crowd? But all the world, all mankind, is very far from being on Christ's side, and hence the very coldness of the world to Christ offers us the grace of being in a special manner and degree the friends of His Sacred Heart.

"Will you also go away?" Jesus once asked of the little band clustered about Him, and His words, dear Child, are still echoing adown the centuries. Sooner or later you will hear them in the silence of your own soul, and, in the meantime your daily preoccupation with His Sacred interests bears witness to the validity of that declaration of faith and love which the Master will someday claim from your lips.

TENDRILS OF GOD'S MAKING

DEAR ——— :

I want you to know that I remembered you on your birthday, despite the fact that God's service has carried us many leagues apart. After all, we are never nearer to our dear ones than when God's interests have drawn us from their corporeal presence. Paradoxical it may seem, yet I hold it to be true that the farther we are from home for God, the nearer we are to home in God. God can never be outdone in generosity, and the more we unite our wills and hearts to His Will and His Heart, so much the more are we united in Christ Jesus to our dear ones. Besides, I am confident that in heaven there will be some special sweetness attached to the relationships of those dear mothers and fathers, brothers and sisters and friends, who have sacrificed human consolations in time for the sake of eternal interests. No one can repay as God repays, for no one loves as He loves.

What a mistaken notion some people have of the character of missionaries, as if flesh and blood ceased to be flesh and blood because of the triumph of grace. I am sure you will agree with me that we are never so conscious of our affection for our dear ones as when we have left them in order to advance Christ's interests.

Human affections are in God's beauteous plan the holy tendrils by which the soul ascends, vine-like, the rough, cold wall that separates man from Paradise. That the tendrils are sometimes misguided, are capable of being abused, crushed or misplaced, does not, cannot alter the fundamental holiness of God's plan.

And that is why, dear ——, I am remembering you in a very special manner today and shall, please God, always do so; for the more I advance in the knowledge of God's ways with men, the more I realize how gracious God was to me when he gave me such a friend as you.

Asking Our Lady to bless you.

IN GOD'S SERVICE

Dear ——:

I wrote "Jesus, Mary, Joseph," as the first words with my new pen, your gift, and now I am writing you.

What wonderful things I must strive by God's Spirit's strength and enlightening to do with my beautiful new silvery blue sword! I resolve now it shall be used exclusively to promote His interests in the salvation and sanctification of souls. May its point never pierce except to wound with divine love. May it flash, but not for human glory. May it defend all worthy causes, never be surrendered to Falsehood, nor know the rust of idleness. May it be kindly yet courageous in action, and be found worthy with its wielder to rest beside the beloved Captain whose only sword is Love.

With His Sword may He pierce your heart, dear ——, and leave you with a wound of joy that shall never heal.

Asking Our Lady to bless you.

DECEMBER

In December, the hearts of men
open to a Child's hand.

THE FIRST SNOWFALL

DEAR BROTHER:

I wish you that peace which a Little Child brought on earth.

We are all looking forward to the Christmastide here, and now that we have had our first snowfall, why it seems so much the nearer.

The first snow — I wonder if others love its coming as I do. Softly, silently out of the dull gray skies it comes to hide the deathlike sleep of Nature beneath a glistening pall. How I love it, the gentle, hardly perceptible rustle as the flakes settle down on the leaves, the distances blotted out amid the eddying whirls, the softened outlines of familiar roofs and walls, and then the sun coming through upon a world transformed into a fairyland for those who are young and innocent of heart.

See, brother, if these mysteries of Nature may not lift our hearts to God. I never see the white, unsullied snow but I think of Mary Immaculate, the Blessed Mother of God. Have you ever noticed how often we have fresh snow for her Winter feast days? I love to see in this — as did the Little Flower — the exquisite planning of God.

But if the first snowfall makes this old world fair, yet here amid the city trafficking all too quickly does the earth reclaim its kingdom and the snow despoiled of its fresh beauty is carried to a weeping grave. So, too, over and over again, upon the barren soil of our souls God has laid the snowfall of His blessed grace. Over and over again we have turned the gardens of our souls into city streets open to the traffic of the world, and God's grace has vanished like the first snow. O let us resolve that for the future our souls shall be as the Blessed Mother's — a sealed garden —

where none but angels may walk and the snow of God's grace melt unsullied to prepare the earth beneath for the coming of the Spring.

Please God, I shall see you Christmas day.

Ever in Christ, your brother.

THE DAY OF DAYS

DEAR BROTHER IN CHRIST:

It seems rather strange to be writing a Christmas letter in October, but I must needs do so if you are to have my greetings for that Day of days. And surely for both of us and for all upon whom God has lavished the gifts of Faith and Hope and Love, Christmas must always be the Day of days.

Easter is glorious, yes, but we knew He would rise again—*sicut dixit*. Birthdays bring joy, yet it is His Birthday that gives them their deepest significance. The day of our First Mass is a day apart, but what was our First Mass but Bethlehem with the little white Christ, the angel choirs, the adoring shepherds and ourselves sharing in Mary's inexpressible bliss in the wonder of it all.

Christmas then is our Day of days, warming our world-chilled hearts, lighting up the recesses of our poor-cave souls, lifting us up above the compromise which constitutes our daily lives, and sending us back to our flocks rejoicing in the abiding memory of a Baby's smile.

Yes, my brother in Christ and of Christ, you at least may rest assured of the Christ-Child's smile on Christmas morn. He left His Father's Home to seek love, the love of His creatures, the affection of our hearts. You for love of Him have left your father's home to help Him in His unending quest. O how I envy you, with I trust a holy envy, the smile He has reserved for such as you. Pray for me that before I die, I too may some Christmas morning kneel in a strange land, among a strange people, but with the Living Christ-Child in my hands. Then shall I intone for my Christmas carol — the *Nunc dimittis* of the aged Simeon, then shall I know the fullest joy of Bethlehem — that ever deepening love of Mary's Heart. Amen.

A CHRISTMAS CREDO

Dear Little Christ Child:

I believe in Thee, I believe in the might of Thy Baby arms that they will always sustain me, in the light of Thy baby smile that it shall always guide me, in the fidelity of Thy Little Great Heart that Its Love shall never fail me but be my Star guiding me to Thy blessed feet in the Bethlehem of Heaven. I believe, dear Little Christ Child, not only that Thou once were, but that Thou art even now a Babe for love of me beneath the swaddling cloth of the Eucharistic Species. I believe in that Poverty which holds Thee as Its Only Treasure, in that Obedience which submits to creatures in imitation of, and for the sake of, Thee, in that Chastity which seeks its consolations where the Virgin Mother found them — in Thy Loving Heart alone.

I believe in honoring that Mother whom Thou didst honor far above any honor human beings can bestow. I believe in honoring as well that other Mother in whose arms I have found Thee, the Holy Roman Catholic Church. Finally, I believe in Thy love for all mankind, past, present, and to be, and on the behalf of all men of good will even such as know Thee not and therefore love Thee not this Blessed Morning, I offer Thee the Faith, the Hope, the Love, that filled Thy Blessed Mother's Heart on the First Christmas Morn, together with all the Faith that has been planted, the Hope that has sprung up, the Love that has burned for Thee in all the hearts of mankind in all the ages of the world. Yes, Little Christ Child, Babe of

Bethlehem, I believe in Thee, and love Thee; be Thou enthroned forever within my heart as in Thy Blessed Mother's arms. Amen.

THE QUEST

DEAR ——:

Your life, indeed every life, is a quest. All seek, perhaps blindly and dumbly, yet all seek nevertheless. Now it is the special grace of God which has made Him the Object of your quest. God is, of course, the Ultimate Object and Goal of all His rational creatures, but most souls, it would seem, reach their Goal only by the low road of home life. But there are other souls, and I deem yours of such, whom God will not permit to take the low road to His Heart. Into their souls He pours a divine unrest, a yearning for spiritual achievement, a thirst for Himself. He has a thousand ways of doing this; one of these you have experienced — the refusing of all desires save only His Love and His Cross. Always such souls standing on the thresholds of their earthly homes, lift their eyes and see afar off a snow-clad mountain top that seems to challenge that which is noblest in man because most divine, the spirit of sacrifice.

Many glimpse that mountain peak, admire and remark its grandeur, but that is all. They turn from the doorway to the warmth and comfort and consolations of the fireside of men. Others, on whom the vision falls, stir uneasily, perhaps even dream of making the ascent some day, but that day never dawns. Youth climbs more readily than age the rugged heights that lead to God. But other some there are in whose souls the memory of that serene height will not die. It costs much, how much they alone and God can know, but they tear themselves from the warmth of home and friends and all things and set their faces to the road, to the High Road, the King's High Road that led Him and His truest Mother and His true friends of every age, and climb up, up, up to a lonely hilltop, where even God seems at times absent—"Father, Father, why has Thou forsaken Me!"

Dear Child, it is certain Jesus has numbered you among these souls. That is why He will not give you things. He wants you to see how small are the windows of human dwellings, how flicking and feeble the fires of human hearts. He wants you to forget the toys of childhood, even as did Little Thérèse, and take for your one gift the Holy Cross. This gift alone will He give you, for His love prompts Him to give you His best.

Like Blessed Mary in Bethlehem and on Calvary, you shall have only Jesus, but Jesus you know is God, and God, child, is a great Sufficiency, is He not?

When you kneel with Mother Mary at the Manger side, I know you will ask that I may be there too in Heaven.

THE SECRET OF CONTENTMENT

Dear Child:

This is a Christmas letter, and I trust you will read it on Christmas Day, and that it will do its part to keep in your heart throughout all the years to be some of the joy and peace of the first Christmas Morn.

Years ago, when you were just entering upon your life work, I gave you what I then and still consider to be the secret of contentment, not only in the religious life, but in all life, at least all Christian life. That secret may be briefly put thus—*remember Jesus.* Jesus Christ is the Source of all our happiness, nay of our very existence, for the little Babe of the manger is the Eternal Word begotten from all eternity, without Whom was made nothing that was made. Life teaches many lessons, but it has no lesson that we need to learn so much as this—that there is no lasting happiness in a life in which Jesus Christ is not a partner, in which Jesus Christ is not remembered.

Christmas will always have an element of wonder about it for thoughtful men and women as well as for little children. The little ones wonder what their gifts will be; the grown-ups wonder not what the Gift is, but why they should receive such a Gift—God's Son for their salvation—and gazing at the little plaster image amid the imitation rocks and straw and snow of the Christmas Crib in ten thousand churches, they think of that supreme wondrous Fact that makes Christmas a reality, the Fact that once there was a real manger containing a real Child, and that Child was really God!

Now to return to my first thought. To be happy, all any Christian needs is just to remember that He, Who once came to share our burden and heal our wounds and wash our soiled souls in His Life Blood, is still on earth, still busy about His Father's business, still a willing Partner in every noble Christian life, still soothing the sick, counseling the doubtful, strengthening the weak, forgiving the repentant, still toiling with the honest hearted father, praying with the sorrowful mother, suffering with the suffering, living with and in us all, we who by His grace and in His grace are seeking to follow in His footsteps that we may some day be found worthy to see the beauty of His face unveiled.

Now then, in all the hard places of Life's way, amid the mists of misunderstandings, the shadows of doubts, the chill of ingratitude, the glare of appreciation, the silence of selfishness, always and everywhere, remember, dear child, Jesus, make Him a Third Party to all your dealings with creatures, the Second Party of your life, the First Party of your heart; then only will you come to find a contentment like that of Mother Mary in Bethlehem, then only will you have found the secret of contentment in Life.

"THE CHRIST-CHILD"

My Dear Friends:

Despite the shortness of time between Masses this blessed morning, I do not wish to let Christmas morning pass without a word on the true Christmas spirit.

We are here this morning because more than nineteen hundred years ago in the humblest of surroundings, a hillside cave, a little Child was born; a little Child, Who as God's Eternal Son had existed from all Eternity, but Who for love of us became Mary's Son as well, that thus He might make us all God's happy and blessed children.

Worldlings may seek in Christmas other things, but the real Christian seeks in Christmas One Thing above all else; as the shepherds of old hastened over the hills to find their Little Saviour and new born King amid the golden straw of a manger, so we have hastened this morning under the paling stars to find the selfsame Christ-Child in the humble surroundings of our little parish Church. The same love, the same Eternal love that brought Him to the cave of Bethlehem has brought Him to our humble wooden altar this morning, the same love that filled the Shepherds' hearts as a little Child smiled upon them floods our souls as we kneel here in His smiling presence. By Bethlehem God has revealed to us that He cares nothing for human pomp or earthly grandeur, He cares only for love, your love and mine. If we love the little Christ-Child, then we possess the only wealth that has Eternal Value, the only jewel that the hands of death will not snatch from us. As the little Christ-Child comes to your lips and your hearts this morning, hold him tightly and ask Him as He gave of old, warmth and brightness to a cave, so now, He may bring to our poor cold hearts fresh warmth of Faith, and Hope and Love. The Christ-Child is still God's greatest Gift to mankind, and the greatest gift we can give to the

Christ-Child is the love He came to claim through His Mother and His Church.

"TOYS"

BELOVED BRETHREN:

Once more the passing of the months has brought us to the commemoration of that most blessed of all events, the Birth of our Blessed Saviour. Kneeling in spirit before the manger of Bethlehem, which Divine Love has made an ever-present reality by reason of His Presence upon our altars, every good man and every good woman will renew their faith and hope and love in the God Who made them and redeemed them.

Here before the altar on Christmas morn, we ought all of us to renew our childhood; here we should imitate God and become each of us once again a little child and learn from the Wisest of children the Supreme lesson He came to teach, the lesson of putting a proper value on all things. He taught the utter nothingness of earthly wealth by being born in poverty, and then He emphasized His teaching by living without wealth and confirmed His teaching forever by dying absolutely poor. And we, how shall we call ourselves real Christians, real followers of Christ, unless we learn the lesson that He so clearly taught, unless we come to look upon the things which the world holds as precious, riches and power and pomp, as so many toys to be left on the nursery floor while we give our immortal souls to the Eternal God?

Beloved Brethren, it is a strange thing to speak of dying on this day when we commemorate the Birth of Life, yet if the Birth of Jesus Christ is to have real value in our lives, then it must be by teaching us to disdain the things of earthly childhood and cling to those that have Eternal value, our moral integrity, our faith and our God. It must teach us to die to self by sharing voluntarily, at least in spirit, in these deprivations which the Babe of Bethlehem embraced for love of us.

I will ask our Blessed Lady to whisper to her Little Son when He shall have been born within my hands this morning a prayer for all of us, that like unto her we shall so love her Son that He shall be each day of our life our Chiefest Wealth and Love, and that for love of Him we shall look upon all earthly possessions as the toys of a forgotten childhood. Blessed are they who putting aside their toys shall hasten to listen to the Wisdom of Wisdom Incarnate. "Blessed are the poor in spirit for theirs is the Kingdom of Heaven!"

THE FEAST UNCHANGING

Beloved Brethren:

From the depths of my heart I wish you, as indeed I know you wish me, a most blessed Christmas Day.

There are many thoughts that, gleaming like the candles on a Christmas tree, bring joy to those who think deeply at Christmastide. Thoughts that, unlike the candles, need never burn away but rather grow brighter and brighter and shed as Time passes onward, clearer and clearer light upon our pathway. One of these thoughts I wish to set before you this morning.

For some time I have found one of the most fascinating reflections about Christmas is this—Christmas is really the Feast Unchanging.

We are here this morning because Christ is here this morning—newly born, wrapped in the swaddling clothes of the Eucharistic Species and soon to be laid amid the golden straw of our affections in the lowly mangers of our hearts! What I mean is this, the Mass is a perpetual Bethlehem with, not infrequently, the very details reproduced.

It is true there are costly and mighty Churches where Jesus will be born today, but what are their number compared to the number of smaller, poorer

Churches where His Birth will be sung. Jesus has, indeed, many altars of marble but more altars of wood, adorers from among the rich and mighty but more followers from among the poor who, like the shepherds of old, come over the hills to find Him and acknowledge Him as God and King despite the paradox of His surroundings—the contrast of His external trappings with His eternal claim.

My Brethren, Christmas is a Feast Unchanging because the Love of God that made the First Christmas is an Unchanging and Unchangeable Reality—the Greatest and Most Consoling Reality mankind shall ever know. As you bow this morning with Mary and Joseph and the angels and shepherds over the Little Christ Child mangered in your heart, adore Him and thank Him for His unspeakable, mysterious love which has given us birth to Him and given Him birth to us—that love which is the golden key to all His mysteries, the road to the Bethlehem of Heaven and, indeed, Heaven itself.

THROUGH THE EYES OF A CHILD

Along the road men call Time many a pageant and many a pilgrim have passed since that star-lit night of long ago when the Virgin Mother wrapt her little Son in swaddling clothes and cradled Him in the yellow straw of a manger. Yet every passing pageant has its purpose and every plodding pilgrim his goal, and both pageant and pilgrim shall be measured ultimately in the light of Bethlehem and through the eyes of Mary's Child.

By the supernal gift of our Faith we are aware that the love of Mary's Child has not faded like a winter sunset from the earth's horizon; always, all days, the sun of His Love rests in benediction upon us. Having loved His own who were in the world, Christ will continue to love them, and their children and their children's children, even to eternity. Only one condition He requires in return : that we listen to His authentic Voice and obey His authentic Laws. For souls who have not listened and even for those who have heard but have not obeyed, the arms of the Christ Child are extended; still does His gaze rest upon them with tenderest yearning, His Heart waiting to welcome them home.

Man has been created with a nostalgia for Heaven, and that is why in every century—and in none more so than our own—men find themselves unhappy, discontented. To be sure, a great number, perhaps the greater number of them, do not stop to analyze this homesickness aright. Like sick children, they cry out for remedies, and the wise of this world have a thousand to prescribe. Physical health, greater personal liberty, wealth, knowledge, power, pleasure, honor, these and a host of variant formulas are compounded for the yearning soul. Yet history teaches no more certain truth than that all these things have failed to bring lasting contentment and abiding peace to mankind. Men will never realize what they truly need till they have learned to look upon themselves and their fellows not through their own eyes but through those of the Divine Physician Who was once the Child of Bethlehem.

My dear ones, we can hardly hope to induce all men to look on life through the eyes of Incarnate Wisdom, but one thing we both can and must do : we, ourselves, must learn to see things as God sees them, and look on man through God and in Christ Jesus. Then, for us at least, life will hold no bitter disillusionments, no false aims, and hence no cruel disappointments. Knowing man as he is, we will respect him for what God made him to be. We will serve men but not for any wage men can pay. We will love them and, if needs be, die for them, but only as a proof of our love for God.

Wars between nations and the personal rebellion of sin will still continue undoubtedly to be commonplaces of life, but despite the carnage of man's making, whether personal or national, we shall be enabled to live in peace. With our vision focused through the eyes of a Child, all men will be our brothers to be aided, and God, our Father, to be loved.

God bless you, dear ones, whom I may not hope to greet in person this blessed Christmastide. God bless you and Mary accompany you on the lengthening miles of your pilgrimages. God bless you and His Spirit guide you past the crowded inns into the silence of a cave where you shall find Life in the arms of death.

THE CREDO OF A CHILD

Dear God:

I believe that You were great enough to become small, strong enough to become weak, wise enough to become a child, and thus find a way to my heart. I believe that I ought to believe in You, despite all Your critics have said about You; and I cannot help feeling that when Death shall have silenced their chatter You will not cease to be the God of Life.

I believe, further, dear little Christ-Child, that You are what this great world of ours most needs to make its business run smoothly, its inter-relations more harmonious, its people more prosperous and its rulers more successful in the fulfillment of national destinies. Moreover, I disbelieve in the power of machines, commerce, industry, economics, legislation and science, apart from Your Guidance, little Christ-Child, to make this world truly better. Besides, I am so hopelessly behind the times as still to believe in such things as the beauty of virtue, the rights of children to be born, of marriage vows to be held sacred, and of treaties to be observed.

I believe, likewise, in the futility of war as a weapon of peace, and of that patriotism which is heedless of the rights of others. I have, equally, no faith in any form or scheme of government which fails to recognize the sovereign rights of God. I believe in Catholicism not Communism, the uniting of the world in a common brotherhood of Christian faith and love under the vicarship of a White Father rather than under the heel of a red dictator.

I believe, to sum up, dear little Christ-Child, that the world still needs You, and needs You badly, for its security and peace; and to this end I propose with all the might of prayer and example to propagate upon earth the Kingdom of Your Peace and Love.

Little Jesus, may I wish You a happy birthday?

STARLIGHT OF BETHLEHEM

My Dear Child:

This note will pay the visit I would wish to make to you on Saint Luke's day. I am sure the dear physician—Saint Luke was a physician, you know—will prescribe for your spiritual as well as your physical needs. I have him as the secondary Patron of my writing—Our Lady, of course, coming first.

I sense you are afraid I will take away your toys. No, child, I will not do that; I promise not to do that, but I will not promise not to try to have you yourself grow tired of them in recognition of their limitations. Plays and books as well as everything else are creations of God, Our Heavenly Father, and as such have their proper place in our lives. But I cannot bring myself to acquiesce in a program for one I love that substitutes sideshows and the glamour of animated dust for Heaven and the Eternal Beauty of God.

I would not mind, therefore, having you, dear child, seek needed relaxation in the sources which Divine Providence provides, but I do not want you to find a child's absorption in these things. Hence I must always insist, although I trust with gentleness, that there is a greater horizon rimming your soul by reason of the starlight of Bethlehem. The pleasures of earth have ever a last chapter, a final curtain, a concluding course, while the drama of Divine Love has neither last chapter nor final curtain, for the final act on the stage of earth but sees the curtain lifting upon the Eternal Banquet God has prepared for those who wait His coming. Knowing these things to be so, how could I approve for my spiritual child a course of activity that would lead inevitably to the disillusionment of trivialities?

God made your heart, child, for Himself and you will never know what happiness is, till you find courage to take off the mask of pleasure and play in reality your God-given role as lover of Christ's Heart.

AND A LITTLE CHILD SHALL LEAD THEM

Dear Brethren:

Long ago St. John, the Beloved Disciple, summed up the underlying theme of our Christmas joy when he wrote: "God so loved the world as to send His Only-begotten Son!" The message of Christmas is fundamentally the revelation of God's love for us, His rational creatures, and the Cave of Bethlehem no less than the Cross of Calvary—or so it seems to me—preaches the love of the Infinite for the finite; the mysterious desire of God not only to love, but to be loved. On Calvary the God-Man reached for our sins; at Bethlehem He reached for our hearts.

In human nature at its best, what is so strong as the appeal of childhood? Nay, human nature at its worst oft-times falters before the innate sanctity of a child. Despite the callousness of modern ways of living and modern trends of thought, there is still, in the natural order, no mightier force for good in the world than the love of children, and as long as, and just as long as, our people maintain their love for children, just so long may we be hopeful of the ultimate triumph of God in our land by His merciful love.

Every house is but a house until a child has lived therein; every heart is but a cave until the Christ Child has made it another Bethlehem. It is the Divine Presence that lends dignity to our existence as creatures, it is the Christ Child who gives meaning to all our living, direction to all our journeyings, consummation to all our desires. Have we abiding happiness and peace? It is the Christ Child who has brought it to us. Are we on the high road to a happy eternity? It is the Christ Child who leads us. Bethlehem's cave of yesterday is a million times multiplied this day, and we of the Faith that was ancient before the nations of today were born, must measure our true wealth in the star-light of Bethlehem. We must learn to find our gold in the smile of Mary's Little One if we have hopes still to be wealthy when this dust shall be once more united to its kin.

The love of children constitutes a major characteristic of Christianity; its absence is one of the surest indications of the return to pagan concepts of life. Assuredly, we must not confuse with love of children that desire for national numerical increase whose source rests ultimately in the will for power. No one will justly accuse us of America of the will for power, but what we do need—as a nation—is the will to render to God less grudgingly the first requisite of all true love, the fundamental surrender of self by obedience to His holy laws. At Bethlehem, Divine Love surrendered to us; in every Holy Communion that surrender is renewed. A few brief moments now and the star of our Faith will reveal the Christ-Babe once more with us in the lowliness of the Eucharistic swaddling clothes. To that Babe, as Creator and Redeemer, as God and man, we owe all that we have or are, all that we hope to be. Well may we ask ourselves, therefore, this comprehensive, and for us, all important question: Does the Christ Child, God's Son and our Redeemer, truly reign in our hearts? If this be so, truly our souls are other Bethlehems and a Little Child shall lead us in the ways of peace.

I ask His Mother to bless us in His Name.

TOMORROW'S SOLDIERS

My Dear Little Brother in Christ:

You have waited a long, long time for this letter, but that, I hope, will only serve to make it more welcome now.

In the first place I want to congratulate you on your perseverance. Of course you have persevered by the grace of God, but the grace of God is offered to all of us, to every student, every soldier of God's great army, but not every one corresponds with God's grace. You, I feel, have been trying faithfully to do so, and therefore, I congratulate you sincerely.

Little brother, now is the time for you to build for the future. You have chosen for love of Jesus and Mary and, as I trust, under the guidance of God's Most Holy Spirit, probably the hardest position in all the far-flung battle lines of Christ. You are in training for the foreign missions, that means "overseas service," and that means separation at least here on earth from mother and father, brothers and sisters, the home and the land that you love. To be successful in the foreign service of the Master, one thing above all others you must do, you must build up in your heart a mighty love of Jesus, you must come to love Him before and above all else. He must become the all-absorbing interest of your days, yes, of your hours and your moments. He must be the very stuff of your thoughts, the very beat of your little heart!

Perhaps you will say, "Father, how can this be done? How can I grow to so great a love of Jesus, though He be my God and love?"

The answer is simple enough to write but not so simple in execution. "Ask and you shall receive!" Kneel, little brother, day by day silently before the Tabernacle where He dwells for love of you, and beg Him to pour His love into your heart and soul. Ask it of Him in the morning when you wake, ask it of Him in the evening the last thing before you sleep, ask it of Him especially when He comes to press your little heart against His Own Big Heart in Holy Communion.

If you pray thus, perseveringly, God's love will indeed grow bright and strong within your soul. Then will come the fire of zeal, the thirst for sacrifice, the burning desire to be off about your "Brother's Business."

You, little brother, will be tomorrow's soldier of Jesus, so you must be, today and always, Mary's page.

OUR LITTLE KING

Dear Sister in Christ:

Long before the First Christmas dawned in newly found roseate glory upon a waiting world, the inspired Prophet had declared the future reign of a Little Child.

We, Sister, live in the beautiful kingdom of that Little One; we are His subjects whom He governs by love and who in turn should govern by and in love all the activity of our souls.

Poor we may be, indeed, we are in the things of this world, but in the things of the spirit our Little King has made us very wealthy, has He not! We have Him, we have His love, and in Him we possess more than all the world and the grandeur thereof — for what is all the glory of this world in comparison with the immortal glory of the eternal God of truth and beauty? And all God's glory shineth upon us from out the eyes of Jesus, and all God's love encompasses us in the arms of Mary and the Heart of Jesus Christ.

Rejoice, therefore, dear Sister, on this Christmas which may indeed be the last of our lives. Whether it be the last we know not, but let us resolve at least that it shall find us following the leadings of our Little King, acknowledging His reign and seeking to extend His kingdom by the practice of His precepts, especially that of fraternal charity to all.

May our Little Lord bless you, Sister, this Christmas and always, and may you be always true to Him as He is to you and to all mankind. May His ever blessed Mother invite you to come close to the manger side and there may you abide forever.

HOME FOR CHRISTMAS

My Dear Brother in Christ:

This letter, though written of necessity early, is really a Christmas letter for you.

I think Christmas must always be for us who can remember our youth, the loveliest season of all the year. Perhaps this is because at Christmas it is so easy to push aside the years and be young again, because of the sweet memories of home and dear ones that cluster 'round this Festival, yet more especially because all these earthly precious things have been imbued with eternal meaning by the Birth of a Little Child. Therefore at Christmastime, even material enjoyments have deeper justification than at other periods.

For you, however, who will be at Christmas separated from home and dear ones, the Day will have a little undercurrent of poignancy. You will not be Home for Christmas! and yet in a truer sense you will be.

For, my Brother, when you are close to Jesus, the White Babe of the Eucharist, when you shall hold Him wrapped in His whitesome swaddling clothes, when you shall bid Him welcome to the poor cave of your heart and warm Him there by your love, remember in that hour this consoling truth.

Never are we so close to our homes and dear ones as when we are close to God. I wrote once, for a dear friend and benefactor of mine, these lines which haunt my memory—

What matter though we do not meet
Upon this Christmas day,
Within the Heart of Christ we greet,
And walk the selfsame way.

The way of a missionary is par excellence that of the Holy Cross, but the way of the Cross is the surest, straightest Road to Our Heavenly Home, to the arms of Christ, His Mother and Ours, His dear ones and our dear ones. So let us plod ahead—cheerful in the love of a Little Child, and presently we shall all be Home for Christmas, with Mary.

MYSTIC CROWN

My Dear Child:

I have learned with pleasure of your engagement and approaching wedding. It would give me real pleasure to be present for "your Day," but instead God's Holy Will gives me the greater pleasure of this little sacrifice, and in return I shall ask our dear Master at the Mass I shall say for you on the —th, to give me the happiness of being present at some future date when you will be celebrating the golden benediction of God upon a truly Christian marriage—the ordination day of a son of yours!

God's Holy Will provides for all times and all things. God must have soldiers for the battles of tomorrow as well as volunteers for the wars of today. And where, dear child, would our sweet Jesus find tomorrow's soldiers if not in the bosom of the Christian homes which His love and His benediction have consecrated today! Go forward, therefore, to your new life with quiet confidence and peace of heart in the recognition of God's ever-loving Providence and direction.

Everything would indicate God has given you a true-hearted and faith-worthy partner for the road that lies before you, veiled in the mists that only time shall lift. In the natural order of things what gift could be greater? And by the help of God's grace this great gift of God—a faithful life partner—opens for you both a Road to Happiness that need never end. I speak not of those shallow, passing pleasures so sought for by the worldly souls, but of that deeper joy that hearts founded in grace and consecrated to God's humble service find even within the shadows of the Cross. A God-blessed partnership, a God-kept partnership, a God-crowned partnership, this is what I wish you, dear child, and may that crown be nothing less than a mystic crown of golden thorns—a soldier-son, a priestly son for tomorrow's far-flung battle-lines in whose Sacrifice your proffered sacrifice shall be accepted.

HE COMES UNTO HIS OWN

Dear Brother in Christ:

It seems a long time since you slipped away from this quarter of the earth, though even as men reckon, it is not so long. And now while we are waiting for the ermine mantle of Winter to enfold us, you are kneeling before a silent White Host in far-off Australia and I am sure the snow-flakes of God's grace are falling softly upon your soul. May they melt only for your spiritual fructification, only to make you dearer and nearer to Our Blessed Lord.

I think I shall ask for you this Christmastide the same grace I am asking for myself, that of spiritual childhood. In this most blessed season should it not be easy for us to become what Eternal Wisdom became for love of us? Holy memories of the past troop 'round us and with child-like insistence seek to lead us back into the dear living-rooms of other days. A hundred reminders of happy hours present themselves to our minds. Now it is the scraping of a snow shovel on the walk, now the muffled voice of nature or a bit of Christmas green, a red paper bell in a shop window or the wee silver voice that tells in the crypt of a modern city church of the untiring perpetuation of the Reality of the first Christmas. At Christmas our lost childhood comes stealing back into our hearts and all the world seems to draw at least momentarily nearer to its Maker.

Yet amidst the joyous tumult, as on the first Christmas so now there persists a note of sadness and, for the thoughtful souls at least, in union with the Blessed Mother, a sense of profound regret. St. John in the first chapter of his Gospel has expressed with divinely inspired accuracy the source of this poignancy. Jesus, the Incarnate Son of God, has come unto His own and they receive Him not. Jesus, the Babe of Bethlehem, we may add, is still in the world and yet so many know it not, or, if they know, heed not the invitation His presence extends.

Thus missionaries especially, and indeed all Christians, should remember at Christmas those other missioners, those other Christians to whom under God we owe the supernal gift of Faith. Then at the Eucharistic crib let us as little children listen to the voice of the Divine Child, listen to His heart throbbing with love for the millions who still know not of His Birth; listen we must, and then resolve to give Jesus first our own and then all other hearts.

Blessed Christmas with Mary!

THE SILVER LINING

DEAR SISTER:

I wish this little note to add an extra beat of happiness to the singing harmonies of your Christmastide. Cradled in poverty, I know you and your fellow-Sisters are, with the resultant cares and distractions which weave, at least for superiors, an invisible yet none-the-less real crown of thorns. I only wish I were wealthy for a day that at nightfall I might be wealthier in the knowledge of good accomplished and actual poverty achieved.

It is this last item that constitutes the silver lining to the dark cloud of financial limitations, the golden inner-surface of that leaden chalice of your sacrifice. After all why should the vow of poverty relieve us of all material cares? If this were invariably true would not many thus seek the solution to one of life's most pertinent and persistent problems? If we, God's Religious, do not share the life of Christ Crucified upon what title shall we have part in His Glory?

Therefore, dear Sister, I bid you rejoice in those circumstances of fortune which make it necessary for you and your companions to share the poverty of Bethlehem.

Perhaps, I am wrong, but I cannot help thinking that Jesus, having shared the restrictions of actual poverty, having taken care to be born in circumstances of lowliness seldom equaled among the children of men, has a special place in His Heart for all those who for His sake are not only poor in spirit but actually poor as well. And this, then, is, as I conceive it, the silver lining to the dark cloud of your present financial situation. Jesus sets such a store by actual poverty that He fails not in every generation to lead souls that love Him along its lowly way.

Kneeling, therefore, on Christmas morn before the little Jesus, housed in your convent chapel, itself so suggestive of Bethlehem, fail not to thank Jesus, for having so loved you, as to invite you, as He did those whom He loved best, Mary and Joseph, to share with Him and for Him the pathway of the poor. Nor think that herein lies an excuse for those who fail in support of our Catholic Missions, for Jesus is still so poor among His missionaries as to accept with gratitude the smallest offerings of shepherds and of kings.

LIGHT IN THE WIND

DEAR BROTHER IN CHRIST:

I trust this note to bring you a little extra measure of Christmas joy. It is a joy, is it not, to know we are not forgotten even though weary leagues of land and sea stretch between us and our dear ones? I am sure that you, even as I, have found that God is ever most gracious when we try to be generous with Him. He has made us the light of the world and we are exposed to the winds of the world, yet the Hand of the Master holds us tightly and His Spirit shields our flame. As for me, I am contented so long as I can feel His Hand by the pressure of faith, and even though I should lose this source of contentment, nevertheless I am resolved that even in darkness my light shall burn steadily, my lantern hold its flame.

If there were no winds to contend with, no darkness to shroud our vision, no journeying in the dark, where would be the merit of our passage? Is it not because of these difficulties that the Master will have something for which to reward us? And yet how we shrink from the boisterous winds of adversity, how keenly we feel the cold of ingratitude, how cowardly we sometimes feel in the dark! We are the light of the world but Christ is the Light of the Light; rather we are the lanterns, Christ the Light therein. And so, dear Brother, let us cherish with care the Light of Christ within our souls. He is not only our Light but our Strength and our Warmth as well. Without Him we shall find no comfort, without Him our light will be but darkness, without Him we shall have the cave but not the Child.

Asking Our Lady to bless you.

POSTSCRIPT

How little I know!
Is my candle low,
Or yet has it years to burn?
Will it dim ere it dies;
Will there be friendly eyes
To watch the flame dulling in mine?

Will there be wind and rain
at the windowpane;
Or the sound of larks
on the wing?

What matter the weather, the hour, the place,
So long as God grant me this grace:
To find that my candle
Has lighted the way
For one other soul
—through the night
into Day!

A. Page, C.S.C.

INDEX TO SUBJECTS